Best ~~~~

Rufe McComb

4-16-98

# Benched

## The Memoirs of
## Judge Rufe McCombs

4 - 16 - 98

To Albene;

Friends are most valeable
asset and I am so
glad to add your name
to my list of friends
Best wishe

Rufe McCombs

SuperiorCourt Judge Rufe Dorsey Edwards McCombs. (Courtesy of Garrett's Home of Photography, Columbus, Georgia.) This framed photograph can be viewed in Columbus' Government Center.

# Benched

## The Memoirs of
## Judge Rufe McCombs

Rufe McCombs
with
Karen Spears Zacharias

Mercer University Press
Macon, Georgia
1997

Mercer University Press
6316 Peake Road
Macon, Georgia 31210

First edition.


∞The paper used in this publication exceeds the
minimum requirements of the American National
Standard for Information Sciences—Permanence of Paper
for Printed Library Materials, ANSI Z39.48-1984.


*Library of Congress Cataloging-in-Publication Data*

McCombs, Rufe. Benched: the memoirs of Judge Rufe McCombs /
Rufe McCombs and Karen Spears Zacharias
p. cm.
ISBN 0-86554-570-7
McCombs, Rufe. Judges—Georgia—Biography
Other authors: Zacharias, Karen Spears.
KG373.M395 A3 1997
347.758/03534 B 21
97038821

# CONTENTS

Daddy Mac

The ability to nurture is not gender based.
Your life proved that.
We were all glad you were there to change the tires
and bake the cakes.


&


Shelby Mayes Spears

Sometimes our dreams become intertwined with
our worst nightmares.
You taught me that courage is not the lack of fear,
but the commitment to press on in the face of it.

# Acknowledgments

A sincere thank you is like Granny's gravy biscuits—it warms and comforts you on the coldest of days. I miss Granny and her gravy, but I try never to miss an opportunity to say thank you.

Haven't we all experienced that frustration of trying to put part of ourselves into words? A note of condolence. A note of congratulations. We wonder, can mere ink and paper embrace the grieving, or the joyful, so strongly that one's heartbeat can feel the rhythm of another? If you've ever kept a letter to reread, or revisited the passages of a favorite book, then you know what every writer knows—ink and paper can embrace and bind us.

How is it, people ask, that a woman living in Oregon ends up writing the story of a woman in Georgia? Like all good stories, this one has a compelling beginning.

I didn't always live in Oregon; Columbus, Georgia is my home. There was a time as a wounded teenager I visited Judge McCombs at Columbus' Legal Aid office, but that is another story. In truth, Billy Winn of The Columbus-Ledger is vaguely responsible for this project; although, I'm quite sure he'll deny any responsibility, particularly should a libel suit ensue!

While a graduate student at Eastern Oregon State College in LaGrande, Oregon, I signed up for a laborious writing class. One particular assignment called for the creation of a humor piece. The one I wrote—*Marriage, Motherhood, & Money*—Billy Winn printed in the Ledger, where Judge McCombs read it. "This woman writes like the Erma Bombeck from hell," someone suggested. At least they got my origin down, if not my identity. The intellectual engineer of that laborious class, Professor George Venn, although not to blame for my maniacal tendencies, did most certainly encourage my self-delusionary proclivities. When I told him I didn't have the slightest idea about how to write a book, George replied, "You can do this, Karen. Don't worry; I'll help." And he has, immensely. George Venn guided this project from start to finish. Any failure is not a reflection upon his skills as an editor, but mine as a writer. Any success is the fruit of what George has helped cultivate within me. In September of 1993, I traveled to Atlanta by train to begin the process of revelation—interviewing, drafting, reading, and rewriting the Judge's story. That trip allowed me to meet many of the individuals that have played roles in the drama of Judge's life. I watched them at work in the courtroom and at play during Judge's retirement party. After spending time with them, I understood why Judge was reluctant to retire. Her role was changing, as were the players. Moving beyond the familiar is hard for all of us. The other thing that train trip in 1993 did was cure my paranoid fear of flying. In 1994, I returned to the land of towering pines, this time by plane, and again for an extended time period in 1996. This criss-crossing kitty-corner across our nation would not have been possible without the hospitality of the Franke family of Pendleton, Oregon, Phillip Clark, the families of Hunter Mendenhall, Darrel Harris, and Ken Callaway, all of Columbus, Georgia. These families provided comfortable beds, fine food, and warm embraces for the homeless. Thank you.

Any work in progress suffers without constructive feedback. While George Venn provided the specific guidance I needed, Eastern Oregon State College's Oregon Writer participants laughed in all the right places. Donald Wolff, who understands the power of prayer, has deemed me OWP's oracle. Beth McCombs Kissel, thank you for all those hours spent at the Georgia Archives. You should have been a detective. Oh, yeah, I forgot, you married one. I hope your momma remembers this was your idea. Tony Privett. Did you think I was stalking you? I owe you more than just a thank you and a pair of underwear. "Wisdom is priceless," you wrote, "you on the other hand want advice." Tony, you gave that advice freely didn't you? Okay, well, I'm sure Rufe intends to send you a check. Thank you. Bob Steed, I think our souls mated. If you will return the nude photos of Bob Packwood, I'll let you keep the underwear. Hal Mcure, I am proud to have you as my editor, and as my friend. Elena Amos, you could teach charm to Mable Bailey. Your father said it best—*"The Lord puts nothing into man's mind that he cannot realize if he will just commit himself to the struggle."* Just like Judge McCombs, your life proves that dreams can become a reality. Thank you for making sure others have the opportunity to pursue their visions. Call when you're ready to reveal your conspiracies. Shelby, Ashley, Konnie remember to never be ashamed of being disciplined and wanting to learn. Stephan, my protégé, continue in your commitment. God has plans. Kirby Dorothy, your name creates as much confusion as Rufe's. Thanks also to Linda Barnes. I hope my girls are as good a sister to each other as you have been to me. Karen Mendenhall Clark and Lynn Wilkes, my friends, you share the triumphs and hardships with me.

Tim, you have made our home a haven for dreamers. When reality insisted that I leave our home to act upon my dream, you faced your own nightmare and let me go. You comfort me in ways that Granny's gravy never could.

Lastly, thanks to Mercer University Press, Cecil P. Staton, Jr., Marc Jolley, and Jon Peede. As B.B. Williams Sr. encouraged young Rufe's vision, you fellows encouraged mine. Without you everything would have just stayed just that—a vision. With you I am now seeing the fulfillment of my own dream, which is such a relief after having spent so much of my early life trying to wake up from a nightmare. Do you all own white horses and suits of armor?

Readers, my hope is that the words I have chosen will embrace and bind you, thus, enabling you to feel the heartbeat of the Honorable Judge Rufe D.E. McCombs.

# Introduction

Spanning over 50 years, Judge Rufe McCombs' career in law has been one of singular dedication to her fellow Georgians. Rufe McCombs has long been a voice for reason and has always served our great state with honor and distinction.

Judge McCombs was born in my hometown of Decatur, Georgia. She attended Duke University and received her justice doctorate degree from the University of Georgia. McCombs left a lasting impression on Muscogee County as founder and managing attorney for the Columbus Legal Services Program. Her long-time advocacy of women's rights, which began when she was the only female member of her UGA law school class, culminated with her becoming the first woman elected judge in Muscogee County. Since then, the people of her county have benefited by Judge McCombs' service to the principles of justice.

Interestingly enough, the heritage and history behind Judge Rufe McCombs' interest in law dates back to a childhood experience that not only touched her life, but touched mine as well. For it seems that an upstart lawyer with passion for the law and a flare for the dramatics named Schley Howard, my grandfather, impressed the then five-year old Rufe McCombs so greatly she decided her career would be law. Rufe McCombs tells me that she has never forgotten the day in DeKalb County Courtroom in 1924 when she witnessed Schley's closing argument in a criminal defense case.

Rufe McCombs' life has been one of service to the people, and as Schley Howard inspired her to pursue a law career, so has McCombs' tireless dedication to helping people encouraged many others to pursue their own dreams.

I am honored Judge McCombs felt so strongly about my grandfather and that he was able to play a small part in inspiring her life's work. She is a jurist of rare quality and I proudly suggest her story for your reading and inspiration.

*Georgia Lt. Governor Pierre Howard*

# Foreword

In Sophocles' play *Antigone*, King Creon counsels his son Haemon not to grieve the derailing of Haemon's marriage to Antigone. She is sentenced to death for disobeying King Creon's command not to bury her brother, who opposed the king in battle and whose body was to be left lying on the battlefield. Creon says vehemently: "Never be rated inferior to a woman, never." The unfolding of Judge Rufe Edwards Mccombs' life speaks back defiantly some 2500 years later: "Never be rated inferior to a man, never." She has strived always for the best from herself and has never permitted the fact that she is a woman to stand in the way; instead, she uses it to her advantage, heeding for herself the ancient Roman adage: "Every man is the architect of his own future."

Since her girlhood, the judge has been passionately devoted to serving justice through the rule of law. She repects its greater purpose, aware that is not just a collection of laws by which society's behavior and relationships is governed but it is far more. It is a constantly present call to treat people fairly, to protect the weak from the insensitivities of the strong, to shield the minority from the excesses of the majority, and to provide orderly due process. Her willingness to share her stories provides a many-dimensioned cameo history of the time through which she has lived, a unique person who understands the golden offer meant by the word "opportunity".

Judge McCombs' dedication to the law and to the service of those around her, whether in private life or on the public stage, continues in her capacity as Senior Judge. She, thus, continues the quest for legal knowledge and understanding which is illustrated by her scholarly writings as a law student in the *Journal of the Georgia Bar Association*. There her analytical skills are displayed, as well as her well-reasoned and thoughtful suggestions for improvement in the law. In three case commentaries, she wrote about principal and agent, the delegation of power, and libel. Her broad interest in the ranges of the law suit her well for the role of a judge, who as a generalist must have an appreciation of the larger picture. Hers are the contributions of one who leaps boundaries, as she reaches from her birth in 1918 to the advent of a new century.

*Dorothy Toth Beasley*
*Chief Judge/Court of Appeals of Georgia*

# 1

# RESTORED VISION

## Loss of Innocence

Murder led me into my first courtroom. I was five and Frannie, my potential victim, was fourteen. In truth, we both wanted to kill each other.

"Momma, Momma, Mrs. Kirby's here," I shouted from our front porch as Mrs. Kirby turned her Studebaker right onto Feld Avenue. The new 1923 Studebaker was black, like the patent leathers I wore that day. It had a canvas top, "California" style, with curtains instead of windows. Leaning over the porch railing, I waved both arms at her. Mother grabbed me from behind, turned me around, and wiped dirt from the front of my blue dress.

"Rufe," she said. " 'Mother' is the proper way to address me. Just look at you. You're a mess already!" Her periwinkle eyes looked straight into my slate ones. Mother was not the kind of woman who approved of murder. I looked over her shoulder, past her upswept black hair, searched through the screen door and hoped Daddy would be there in the shadows of the screen. A fly with threadlike feet was clutching the screen's mesh. Was it afraid of falling into the evenly spaced holes?

"I don't want to wear this, Mother. It's too fancy."

"Don't sass me Rufe, and don't lean over the railing anymore. The judge's liable to send you to a new home if you go in there lookin' like some filthy orphan."

"How come I got to wear a dress just to talk to somebody? I'm not going to church," I protested, bending over to scratch at the lace around my ankles.

"Are y'all about ready, Claudia?" Mrs. Kirby inquired as she came up the brick walkway at the bottom of the porch.

"Yes, yes, we are," Mother replied. "Let me get Charlie. Rufe, you go on with Mrs. Kirby; I'll be with you directly."

Before Mother could open the screen door, I had jumped the stairs, completely missing the first one and ran right past Mrs. Kirby. I shot through the driver's door she had left open, climbed onto the back seat, and tucked my feet underneath my bottom. As we drove I looked at the treelined, wide avenues of Decatur, Georgia. Our destination the DeKalb County Courthouse.

I could see dogwood blossoms squinting at the intense afternoon light; the petals seemed afraid to expose themselves fully to a Georgia sun. Shielding my own eyes, I searched the hollows of roadside brush for nests hiding newborn thrashers. My stomach was churning the milk I had at lunch into butter. Sitting beside me in the back seat, Mother stroked my angel fine blonde hair away from my face.

"Sit still, Rufe," Mother instructed. "You're popping up 'n down like a hen on a bad egg."

I ignored Mother. I couldn't sit still. Thinking about Frannie made me tense and twisted—the way Frannie would be if I could just reach her neck.

It was the spring of 1924. I was five, "almost six." I recall that day as clearly as most do their loss of innocence and their moment of salvation. I think, probably, because that day I experienced both of these. That day baptized me into a life that would become my second nature for the next seventy some years.

Some people seem to live their whole lives apparently unaware that they have choices. They see themselves as victims. Not me. Determination has always kept me from self-induced victimization. Revenge empowered me that day. I was seeking a vision of justice. "An eye for an eye, a tooth for a tooth...." That vision of justice I never lost.

## Girl, look here

During the late fall of 1923, I had been playing on our porch when Frannie, a neighboring girl, called to me from our front yard.

"Hey girl. Come on out here and play with me."

"No, Momma won't let me," I responded, walking around the porch's protective walls, then sitting down on the top step. I did not know about Frannie's propensity for violence. Or my own. Otherwise, I would have stayed on that porch.

"Sure she will. Come on," she insisted.

"No!" I replied, boldly staring at her.

It was the last time I ever stared boldly at anyone. As I cradled my chin between my knees, squishing a pepper-colored ant with my biggest toe, Frannie picked up a rock. Curling my hands into fists, I placed them under my chin and watched her.

Frannie was tossing the red rock between her left palm and her right one. It seemed the rock followed the same arching path with each toss. Frannie's hands looked like overblown water-filled rubber gloves. When she closed them around the rock her fingers did not touch. Calling to me again, she pushed her copper bangs away from her eyes. Red grime from her left palm streaked her freckled forehead.

"Girl, look here," Frannie demanded as she pulled her right arm back and then stepped forward with her left foot. Her right arm moved high over her head as her right foot moved in front of her left one. Frannie released the rock from her bulging fingers just moments before her right arm reached its fullest extended chest level length.

Hurled in my direction, the rock gained size as quickly as it did speed, from a medium sized tomato to a watermelon. I knew I couldn't duck anything that large traveling that fast. Mesmerized by the rolling transformation this rock was undergoing, I just sat there waiting for it to hit its mark. Which was me.

Splat! Like a plunger releasing pressure and water, my own nose released its cartilage to the outside force. My head snapped back toward my spine. Astringent water burned through my cut right eye. At the edges of my mouth streams of tears mingled with warm blood. Salt-water, iron, and mucous flowed over my tongue as I screamed.

"Mommma, Mooothhher! Ahhhhh! Blood, Mommma!"

I believe Frannie took off running as soon as she let go of the rock; I know she could hear my cries as she ran. Mother qualified for the Olympic trials in her dash to rescue me. Minnie, our nanny, and Elizabeth, my sister, tied for second place. Scooping me into the cradle of her arms, Mother instructed Minnie, "Get some ice." To Elizabeth she said, "Get me a rag." Carrying me up the steps, into the house, Mother reassured me, "Hush, Rufe. I'll call Dr. Dorsey."

Mother did call her cousin, Dr. Dorsey. My nose was broken. My eye, black, swollen, cut, received damage that refused to heal. The vision in my right eye has never completely returned.

## Seeking Justice

From that moment on I wanted to kill Frannie. The problem was she was so much bigger than me. I pleaded with Daddy to "just go beat her up." I figured anyone Daddy beat up would surely die. But my parents had insisted that these sort of things were best settled in court. We were on our way to DeKalb County Courthouse; my parents hoping to recoup the cost of my medical expenses while I was plotting a murderous act.

Maybe if I stood on a table. It would only take one powerful lunge for her throat. If I could just reach her neck. Height was definitely a problem for me. Weight was another problem—Frannie was so fat, I wasn't quite sure she had a neck. Several freckled chins, but not much neck. I might have to settle for clawing Frannie blind.

My parents, neither of whom had ever committed murder before, sought to settle this with Frannie's parents without legal intervention or bloodshed. Her parents claimed that I had started the altercation with name calling. Admittedly, there had been times when Elizabeth, or Charles, Mrs. Kirby's son, and I would senselessly tease Frannie as she passed by our porch. "Stupid Fatso" we would taunt her. But I wasn't name calling that day. I was only five and I sat on that porch alone. Why have bravado when there is no one around to delight in it with you?

Like most people in Decatur in the 1920's, we did not own a car. It wasn't just a matter of not being able to afford one; we really did not need one. Everything our lives centered on was nearby. Our home, a brick bungalow, was the first house on the right on Feld Avenue. Across the street, set back from the road, was another brick structure, Oakhurst United Methodist Church, where we fellowshipped.

There was a field between our house and the grocery store located at the corner of Feld and College Avenues. Charles, Elizabeth, and I would play in that field for hours: competing in baseball, playing hide-n-seek, or rolling wooden trains over dirt hills left by fire ants.

Mother would walk past our playing field on her way to the corner store. There she would purchase her cuts of meat, breads, eggs, and milk. Sometimes Elizabeth and I would join her for these walks. And when we did, she would sometimes give us nickels to buy a chocolate milk.

Not only was Mother unaware of my urge to kill, she was also unaware of my hidden addiction which forced me to steal—even from her. One day, afraid that she might not treat us, I took a nickel from my mother's purse and pretended that I found it as I walked along. Just to buy chocolate milk; even at five, I was a chocolate addict.

Daddy would walk past the same field every morning, past the corner market, and across the sparsely graveled College Avenue. He would then head east for one block and wait. Standing on a wooden platform that served as the depot, he would often watch the blushing Georgia sun crest the tops of thick stunted oaks as he waited for the westbound train. Every working day the train carried Daddy faithfully to Atlanta to his job as Chief Clerk of Seaboard Railway; then it faithfully brought him back home again every evening.

Mrs. Kirby, a neighbor, lived on the block behind our house. She was my mother's closest friend and had offered to drive us to the courthouse that day. Mrs. Kirby was one of my favorite neighbors, mostly because I was smitten with her son, Charles. He was an only child, who thought I would do for a playmate, but his passion was for older women.

Charles informed me early in the relationship that he intended to marry my sister Elizabeth and I was welcome to live with them. Which may be part of the reason I entertained thoughts of offing Elizabeth almost daily. This act of hospitality on Charles' behalf insured that I would continue to play toy trains with him in the field each day. Elizabeth never shared his love of train sets the way I did.

Fortunately for Elizabeth, my affection for Charles grew cold like a draft-snuffed candle, before I could do any real harm. But I still love trains. Swaying along the rails takes me to new places and to old familiar places, accessible only to my heart, only through my remembrances.

Revenge, and maybe a bit of desire for justice, kept me restless during part of the car ride that afternoon. Which is why I ignored Mother's admonition to sit still. My mind saw Frannie's freckled face in each of the roadside bushes. Even screwing my eyes tightly shut did not take away the vision of Frannie's streaked forehead as she wiped away her bangs and called for me to look at her. I couldn't wait to see, with my good eye, Frannie's face once I told the judge what had happened to me.

Surely, the judge would understand. He probably knows people who've murdered for less. If he's ever gone to Vacation Bible School, I'm sure he'll know that verse about "an eye for an eye." He might hold Frannie down for me; maybe even help me kill her.

*"Hey, Frannie, look up here at me. Quit your crying. This judge don't care about how sorry you are. He's here to make things right. Frannie, you are in big trouble now. You better call on The Rock of Ages to get you outta this mess!"* My mind invented dialogue that would bring me justice.

## Court

Finally satisfied that I knew just the right things to say in court, I sat back on my curled up feet. Riding in Mrs. Kirby's Studebaker was a treat I wanted to savor. Normally I would fall asleep as soon as we left our driveway and not awaken until we returned to the same driveway. This time I planned on staying awake for the whole trip.

Before she had finished parking the car south of the courthouse, I climbed right over Mrs. Kirby and dashed out the door. I thought DeKalb

County Courthouse was the biggest building I had ever seen. I noted the poles bigger than pine trees that held up the face of the courthouse. Stairs led to mouth-like double doors; beyond that was just dark. Even squinting, I could not see into the blackness.

The DeKalb County Courthouse would swallow that wicked girl whole. Yeah!! All good people would be able to get out of its belly, and all the bad ones would stay in the darkness forever. That's how come the whale let Jonah out; Jonah was a good boy.

For someone about to commit murder, I wasn't the least bit scared. Frannie was about to be eaten alive. I wanted to be the first one to see her in the belly. But before I could do that, I had to climb all those steps.

"It'll take Mother all day to climb those stairs in her heels!" I cried back to Daddy as I walked north along the storefront sidewalk.

Daddy, sweat tracing lines in his high forehead, came around to my left, draped his arm around my shoulders and patted me gently. I reached my right hand up and clasped his long fingers. I looked over at the monogrammed "E" cuff link shining in the sun. Taking a deep breath I inhaled his scent—Old Spice.

I adored my father. The desire of my heart was to be just like him. I yearned to ride the train each morning and to work in Atlanta as he did. My father could evoke the blessings of Jacob just by placing his arm around me. His touch assured me that God would give me the dew of heaven, the riches of earth, and that those who cursed me would be cursed. I was afraid for anyone who challenged my father's dominion.

I think Daddy believed murder was justifiable, sometimes, where his family was concerned.

"What time is it, Charlie?" Mother inquired from behind us. She and Mrs. Kirby seemed to be keeping time to some unheard music with the click, click, clicking of their heels against the pavement.

"1:45. We're a bit early."

Early? I didn't think we were early at all. I looked up at Daddy; his eyes were cast back towards Mother. No more waiting for me! I darted off up the stairs, actually not as many of them as I first thought, yanked open one of the double doors by myself and stepped into the darkness.

Inside my first courthouse, I listened. I expected to hear cries for help from within. I heard nothing but a thump, thump. A heartbeat. Was this courthouse alive? Thump, thump. Nope. No cries, no belly, and the only heart in this place was mine. It was my own heart I heard beating in my ears.

Mother took a lot less time to get up those steps than I had thought.

"Which way, Mother? Which way do I go?"

"Hush up, Rufe," she admonished, firmly grabbing my left hand with her white-gloved right one. Whispering something to Mrs. Kirby, she guided me behind Daddy across the spacious hallway through another set of double doors into the courtroom.

Why is it that I can't recall any childhood Christmases, my first grade teacher, or the names of kids I played with daily, but I can remember that courtroom? Most everything in the room was made from the same sullied pine wood: floors, benches, chairs, tables. Shadowed light drifted through the high windows that lined up uniformly on both sides of the room.

A wholesale,"buy 'em by the truckload", antiqued-brass chandelier hung from the core of the high ceiling. Seating was available to the left and right of me. The judge sat at a table at the front of the room. To the right of that table was the jury box, comprised of cane bottom chairs on an elevated platform. Maybe if I stood up there I could face Frannie eye to eye—or at least my one eye to her two.

On either side of the judge's position were two more tables, one on the right, one on the left. Counsel tables. Four cane-bottomed chairs stood aside each of these tables, ready for service. Empty spaces drew boundaries around the judge, the counsel, the jury, and public seating.

Looking back on that moment I am surprised by the simplicity of that courtroom. There was no security check. No one stopped us to frisk for weapons. No buzzers sounded. The only bailiff present smiled and greeted my father. The bailiff was obviously unaware of my murderous inclinations.

Today I am surrounded by buzzers, bells, and armed guards everytime I enter or leave the courtroom. Quite a different atmosphere of security existed in that courtroom. But I never feel the security, the assurance of protection, that I felt that day, in that courtroom with my father there. Is it because I was a child? Did my entire sense of protection rest in the presence of my father?

Although Daddy was the first of the Edward's family into the room, he was the last to be seated. He waited until we were all situated before he finally took an aisle seat. Not that it mattered. The seats were nothing but a long wooden bench—worse than church even. Daddy had directed us to a bench only three rows from the front on the right. Mrs. Kirby, tucking a loose auburn curl up under her champagne colored hat, walked to the end of the bench and sat down. I quickly followed Mrs. Kirby, thankful to be out of Mother's firm grip. Mother sat on the other side of me, next to Daddy. No one talked. There was a case still being heard. Mother motioned for me to remain quiet. I ignored her. Who would I talk to anyway? Just grown-ups all around me.

## Schley Howard

Only one man was speaking. He paced back and forth as he talked, like Preacher Twiggs did during Sunday sermons. This man walked over to the jury box where several men sat clustered together, the way deacons sit when communion is served. Each one of them had on a narrow knotted tie that matched a chestnut-colored suit. Still talking, the man turned away from that group of deacons and spoke directly to the judge for awhile, then turned back to face the deacons again. They all seemed to be waiting for a prayer to finish, or was it they were praying for a finish?

I couldn't hear enough to understand anything the man said, but he reminded me of Preacher Twiggs yelling about a lake of fire. His face was red like Preacher's too. Whatever he was saying must have had something to do with living forever. Tucking my hand down between the jiggly part of my legs and the hard bench, I scooted forward to watch him.

It was then that I realized just *who* this man was—one of our neighbors, Schley Howard. Elizabeth and I often played at his home with his daughter, Jacquelyn. A man of middling height and weight with gray hair, Schley Howard was always dressed in Sunday-go-to-meeting clothes. That day he wore a light-weight bay-colored suit with vest and tie to match. A starched white shirt, no noticeable cuff links and spit-shined shoes.

He walked slowly between the judge and the deacons, but he didn't talk slowly. His voice took on that tone Daddy used when he meant for me to listen. I always listened when Daddy used that tone. Everybody was listening now, even Daddy. Turning on his left foot, military-like, Mr. Howard walked back behind the counsel table and picked up a chair. Then he turned on his right foot and faced the deacons, raised that chair over his head, and with one sudden stroke smashed it against the floor!

Hearing the shattering pieces fall, I ducked for cover. I felt like hollering. Certainly someone would bellow out "Amen." I looked at Mother and Daddy. I think they stopped breathing. Mr. Howard had stopped talking. He went back to the table. Without looking he stepped over the splintered legs, rails and seat of the broken chair and began to gather some papers. The judge said a few words to the men; then all of them got up and departed out a door in the back of the room. Nobody stopped to clean up the chair, strewn about like a pile of broken toothpicks.

After putting his papers into a folder, Mr. Howard turned and headed our way. Walking slowly down the aisle, smiling, Mr. Howard paused to shake hands with my Daddy. I couldn't wait to get home and tell Elizabeth about how Schley Howard busted that chair, right there in front of God and everybody! Court was more exciting than the best tent revival.

## Victimized Again!

Our case was next. I turned around and saw the other family sitting across from us. Frannie wouldn't look at me. I figured she was sorry now that she had thrown that rock at me. If she wasn't, I knew she would be by the time I got to tell everyone in the room just what a terrible girl she was. I felt pretty confident that, if Mr. Howard could throw furniture around the courtroom, I was at least going to get to throw one good punch. Should I break Frannie's nose or blacken her eye?

Daddy stood up and walked to the counsel table on the right. Mother followed. They sat down in two of the three remaining chairs. Our attorney sat in the other.

He was a young, fair-headed, milk-faced man. I don't think I ever liked him much. In my mind I thought anybody wise should have gray hair. He didn't look that much smarter than me. In fact, I would've bet Elizabeth all of my marbles that I was smarter.

The judge asked our attorney a question, something about me.

"How old is she?" the judge inquired looking my way.

I smiled.

"Five, sir," replied our attorney.

"That is too young for her to give reliable testimony."

My father leaned over and whispered something to our attorney.

"We feel that she is capable of giving a reliable account of what happened, Your Honor."

I stood up. Mrs. Kirby jerked the back of my sleeve, motioning for me to sit back down. I stepped around Mrs. Kirby's bird legs and scrunched out a new seat for myself.

"What's he saying?"

"He's saying that you don't have to tell them what happened, Rufe. He says you are too young to testify."

"Am not. I was there; I know what that girl did to me. I wanna tell him what she did." As my insistence increased, so did my volume.

"Hush up, Rufe. He said you're too young. Just hush up and sit still," Mrs. Kirby scolded me.

Daddy was looking through some papers, answering questions about money. If our attorney had been Schley Howard, that judge would listen to me. All this judge wanted to know about was money. The more he talked about money the angrier I got.

This judge didn't seem the least bit interested in justice. What's fair about getting blinded by a stupid fat girl, 400 times bigger than me...well...at least 80 pounds heavier and ten years older than me...okay, only nine years older and the judge doesn't even give me a chance to talk, much less throw a punch? So much for Lady Justice. Give me a chair; I want to knock this stupid judge upside the head!

Why doesn't he want to know what I have to say? I wish I were big enough to make people listen to me. I wish I could look people in the eye. I wish I could reach their throats! Heat was coursing through my body. Murder was in my blood. Or was it the birth of a passion for justice? If only I could pick up that table and throw it at the stupid judge, then wouldn't nobody be telling me what to do. Everyone in DeKalb County Courthouse would listen to me!

## From Victim to Victor

That was the moment in 1924 that I chose my future—a five-year old with a story to tell that no judge would listen to. Schley Howard had just convinced me that there were ways to make people respect you enough to listen to whatever you were saying. I wasn't capable enough then to command that kind of respect, but one day I determined I would be.

I decided that day in the DeKalb County Courthouse to be a person that people respected—an attorney. (Oh, sure laugh, but once upon a time, law was a honorable profession and Lady Justice, a respected virgin.) I wanted to be an attorney like Mr. Howard, one that people listened to—one that listened to them.

In retrospect, I am glad my nose was broken and that we went to court that day.

The anger of injury and injustice that I felt as a five-year-old gave me the resolve to accomplish much with my life. Anger can be a great motivator. Of course, I went beyond anger into determination and resolution. The anger was channeled into something constructive.

I am not sure what would have happened to me that day if, when I complained that I wasn't too young to speak, my mother had stood up and demanded that the judge listen to me, that I had rights, that I was the victim. I suppose I would have gone through my life demanding everything, never resolving anything. Maybe I would have ended up murdering somebody in my pursuit of a vengeful kind of justice. All too often that is what happens.

Forgive me as I moralize a bit. In seventy-nine years I have collected enough material to write a series on morality. I promise to quit before my face turns red the way Preacher Twiggs's used to. Serving as both State Court Judge and Superior Court Judge has given me ample opportunity to hear victim after victim.

Seems to me there is a support group for just about any kind of dysfunction known to mankind. My current favorite dysfunction is PDS—Personality Deficit Syndrome, a temporary emotional state brought on by a lack of purpose in life. I have met many people suffering from PDS. Most people suffering from this disorder end up doing time in either our state prisons or our state offices.

I believe as a people we have lost our respect for adversity. Is it that we no longer value the opportunities that can be ours because of the difficult experiences we endure? There was a time in history when we appreciated adversity for giving our lives clarity. We believed that difficult situations could make us stronger.

Military training, physically, mentally and emotionally stressful, cultivated discipline, respect and appreciation. I don't believe one can be had without the other. Now I am not saying that suffering from a broken nose is the same as suffering from an assault or rape (Although, I have met up with lawyers who could not distinguish between the two). What I am saying is that strength can come from the right intensity of adversity.

We live in a society that teaches us that we have a constitutional right to a life without adversity. We no longer appreciate the opportunities that can be ours because of the difficult experiences we have overcome. Our courts are packed with people frustrated over a justice system that cannot protect them from every adverse situation.

That frustration is what I felt that day in court. No one would listen. It wasn't fair. I had been physically hurt; and the only just thing my young mind believed was that I should be able to hurt that fourteen-year-old back. Which is why I had pleaded with Daddy to go beat her up. Which is why I wanted to tell everyone in court that day about her. I wanted Frannie to be disgraced publicly and to be hurt the way I had been...or even worse. I definitely would have voted for the worse scenario. Lots of blood and screaming and pleading on Frannie's behalf for me to stop before I truly killed her.

I could have clung to that frustration for the rest of my life. I could have taken on an attitude of "nothing's fair, nobody listens." That attitude would have directed my life in a completely different path. Why didn't I?

My parents. They did not allow me to carry through my early years with such a self-intimidating view. Mrs. Kirby told me to hush up in court because it was not the proper place to debate the issue. But at home Mother held me in her arms, stroked my hair, and said, "Rufe, you tell me about it all you want. I'm listening." And when she tired of the story, Daddy sat at the foot of my bed before nighttime prayers and listened.

My parents listened to the story, to my hurt, for as long as I needed tell it. Their nurturing healed my wound. Instead of fueling my anger, they encouraged me to forgive. My parents transformed me from a murderous, revenge-seeking victim into a person who has learned to see adversity as life's scalpel. Adversity scraped away all the externals of my life until only an exposed heart was left. A heart that beat with the passion of justice.

The judge ruled in our favor that day and my parents recouped the cost of my medical care. But I believe that day was in my favor, no matter what the judge had ruled. That was a day that gave me vision. The kind of vision that isn't affected by the rocks that people throw my way. A vision like Paul received on the Road to Damascus. From that day on I had a goal.

Today, I appreciate the people who showed me ways to achieve my goal, ways to make my dream reality. I am thankful for Schley Howard and his broken chair summation. My parents and the stable, secure childhood they provided for me. Their commitment to surround me with that kind of childhood is probably what kept me from entertaining any further thoughts of murder. And I am also thankful for my bad eye, having an eye that cannot see has focused all worth upon the one that can. I treasure the eye that sees.

So Frannie, all is forgiven on my behalf. I hope you'll forgive me for all the times I called you "Fatso."

# 2

# IT ISN'T JUST A NAME

## Mother & Daughter

If my mother had known that I called Frannie fatso she would have put on sackcloth and entered into mourning for the disgrace that I, the rebellious child, had brought to our family's name. Fortunately she never knew.

My mother, Lula Claude Dorsey Edwards, cared about names, enough to even alter her own name. Although named Lula Claude, Mother insisted upon Cla*udia* as her Christian name. A person's name could determine one's worth to Mother. Money didn't matter a hoot to her without a name to be proud of. In her day, in her world, a name could take you places money could not.

In my service as Superior Court Judge I once received a letter from a third-grade boy that told me just what he thought of the name Mother had given me:

> Dear Juge Rufe:
> My name is Rufus. Eferone kids me about my name. When I was in your courtroom I saw thet your name is Rufe, and I no you don't got iny frinds. You can writ me.
> Your frind,
> Rufus

I understand young Rufus' concern. I've often thought that if names were so important to our family someone should have come up with better ones than Rufe and Lula Claude!

I believe Mother was right about a person's name being better than money; I don't think I could have ever bought anything more precious than Rufus' offer of friendship. I have come to understand that names were important to our family because they linked us to a history that Mother was proud of; a family history whose pride has become the legacy Mother left to me.

Mother's pride in her name extended to other areas as well. Like her appearance. Other than when she was gardening, my mother never left the house without first adjusting her elastic-stocking garters and positioning a hat of current fashion a top her head. She would then slip on gloves of the same color as her hat and shoes and grab a purse to complete the ensemble. My mother would not even walk to the corner drugstore, a block away, without first performing this ritual.

Mother had hair that absorbed light. Sometimes while shopping I am reminded of her hair. Taking a dark dress off a rack, I hold it up to the light to determine its color. I think one minute, "It's black." Then a shift of light and I say, "No, it's blue." A moment later I might nudge my daughter, Beth, or a sales clerk, and together we all decide that the dress is, "Black, definitely black."

It is then that I recall the color of my mother's hair. Black, dense hair.

Whenever her hair wasn't pinned up in a bun like a Pentecostal's, it rippled over her shoulders and down her back until it reached her waist. When I was ten years old, she cut it short, like flapper dancers wore, and Pentecostals didn't.

Mother's eyes seemed as big as half-dollars. Large and round, they held stars at their center. Periwinkle stars. Her wide eyes seemed to bring out hues of indigo in her hair. As a child I used to sing "Be careful little feet where you go, for the Lord up above is looking down in love." Well, I don't know how much the Lord saw, but I was convinced there was nothing my mother's eyes couldn't see. The cross way my mother looked at me was all the discipline I usually needed. She might on occasion feel the need to emphasize that look with an elevated tone of voice. It wasn't often necessary though.

The only memory I have of ever being physically disciplined was for sassing my mother. When I was about twelve-years old, Mother instructed me to do something and I popped off a smart answer to her whereupon she slapped me right across the face.

I believe that was the only time Mother ever hit me. And Daddy never did. My own parenting style reflected what I had experienced as a child—I never could bring myself to physically discipline my daughter, Beth.

But not all my parenting skills reflected the way I was taught. My own mother was a talker, who possessed a strong sense of right and wrong. Mother's rules were based upon what she deemed to be socially acceptable. Slang, as Mother called it, was not acceptable. The first time

I ever heard profanity was as a law student. It was the *"s"* word and I didn't even know what it meant. Because of the way Mother raised me I have never felt comfortable with profanity.

Yet, I never took the opportunity to instruct Beth the way Mother taught me. I rarely employed talking as an instructional tool. By nature a private person, I often found it difficult to tell Beth, or others, about my own feelings or expectations. Unlike my own mother, I never said to Beth, "Don't do that. It isn't ladylike." But maybe this was a disservice to Beth. I have my regrets—I should have talked more with her. I thought children learned best by example.

My assumption was that Beth would embrace my own respect for "ladylike" ways. Mother's values had taken root in my own life. Taught by the old ways, I've always believed that a real lady keeps a composed demeanor about her. Never have I been prone to outbursts of anger. I can't release my frustrations by swearing. If I ever hollered loudly at Mac or Beth I think they would wonder if screaming was the first sign of senility for me.

Sometimes this composure has shut me off emotionally from others. Beth has at times felt distanced from me because of my reticent demeanor. She has chosen to relate to her own children and others in a much more independent fashion than I ever dared. Beth has never embraced the quiet demeanor that my mother expected of a lady, but she is a much more emotionally honest person than I, or my mother, ever were. Unable and unwilling to let go of the old teachings, I still prefer a certain amount of distant composure. I have come to believe that successful parenting requires both example and instruction

I know I once had the potential to instruct others in the ways that they should live but it was squelched at age five. One Sunday evening our family attended a fellowship meeting at Oakhurst Methodist Church. It was a dessert get-together because Pastor was retiring. At that time, all church meetings were held in the sanctuary. As the people milled around the tables getting their food and visiting I thought to myself, now would be a good time to tell the folks how to live rightly.

So I quietly carved my way to the podium at the front of the room. Quickly realizing that it was much taller than me, I pulled over a straight back chair. After climbing upon that chair, I began banging a glass paper weight upon the podium's surface. And even though I remember feeling very self-conscious, I began to speak with the voice of authority, *"I wanna tell you that none of you should do evil things. You should not smoke. You should not dip snuff. You should not chew tobacco. And what's more, You should not whip chil...."*

About the time I got to the point of my message, my daddy grabbed me from behind. He carried me out the door, across the lawn and Feld Avenue, up our front porch, and through the screen door of our home where he firmly sat me down on the couch. Daddy didn't spank me, but he told me that he sure was embarrassed by what I had done. That was all the discipline I needed; knowing that Daddy was disappointed in anything I did always drove me to tears. After our talk, he carried me back to my mother at church and told her, "Make Rufe sit down and *don't let her move.*"

Mother never again lost sight of me and never again did she allow me to exercise my freedom of speech in such a public forum. From then on all our conversations were initiated by her and only about subjects she felt worthy of a lady's consideration. Sex was off limits. Jokes were told only by Daddy. Politics were only discussed with someone she knew would agree with her. I became afraid to ask her things. What if my questions weren't appropriate, ladylike, questions? My mother had not only been successful in putting the fear of the Lord in me, but she had me convinced that *God Himself* was afraid to upset her. I thought *He* knew what I did—she was watching *Our* every move.

And often as a small child I watched her moves. My mother's figure cast a soft shadow throughout my youth. On family walks around the nearby campus of Agnes Scott College, I would try to hide within the shadows of my mother's skirt.

Admiring the length and curves of her silhouette, I would step out of the shadow of her skirt into the full sun and arch my back until my shoulder blades seemed to touch. Then I would take a breath, hold on to it, and glance sideways and down at my own puny profile.

My shadow would always be puddled around my feet. I would look for something to define myself. Anything that would give me form. There was nothing. Embarrassed by my efforts to be like Mother, I would look around to make sure she hadn't noticed, then I would do two skip-hops to take my place again in the shadow of her skirt. And like little girls everywhere, I have never lost the sense that my mother still overshadows me.

## Family Names

My mother, Claudia, was a descendant of the Dorsey family of Fayetteville, Georgia. John Dorsey was the first of the Maryland Dorseys to settle in Georgia during the early part of the nineteenth century. He devoted his time to agricultural pursuits, and became known as one of the most successful planters in the region.

Solomon, son of John, himself a farmer, served as mayor of Fayetteville, trustee of schools, Colonel of the Georgia militia, and as a Lieutenant in the Seventh Georgia Regiment during the Civil War. He was the first of the Georgia Dorseys to serve in the public forum. Solomon was the father of eight children.

My mother's father was Edgar Favor Dorsey, son of Solomon. Edgar's brother, Judge Rufus T. Dorsey, was one of Fayetteville's most celebrated citizens. Rufus was the first of the Georgia Dorseys to enter the legal profession. Rufus was also the first stump speaker in our family. Rumor has it that while working the fields young Rufus would step upon the stumps and give speeches.

This practice must have served him well for Rufus T. Dorsey Sr. became a great lawyer. He seldom left the courtroom defeated. Because in his early career there was no legal distinction between civil and criminal law, Rufus practiced both. I believe that I have not only carried the name of this ancestor, but his spirit as well. Judge Rufus T. Dorsey Sr. was elected to every position he ever sought, as I have been elected to every professional position I have sought. Of course, being a female in the South, meant that I might have worked a little harder at getting elected than Judge Rufus Dorsey. Besides Rufus always had the luxury of running unopposed for his positions.

Mother's childhood was spent in Fayetteville, where she grew up with her cousins, Rufus T. Dorsey Jr., and Hugh Manson Dorsey, both sons of Judge Dorsey.

I think everybody in my family is named after someone else from the family. Rufus T. was named after his father. Hugh Manson was named after an uncle, John Manson Dorsey. This might be why Northerners think Southerners have horizontal family lines—we all have the same names.

Throughout her life my mother remained close to her cousins, Rufus and Hugh. As children they spent many hot afternoons hiding from one another and their parents in the cool dark corners of the chiffarobe at Grandpa Solomon's ante-bellum home. The parents would gather on the wide verandah of the family home, some on the steps, others in rockers, swatting at the flies, and the children, often speaking of the crops, the neighbors, the church or the town affairs, and sometimes the Civil War.

Many of Mother's relatives were involved in the war. Mother's grandpa, Solomon, would often repeat the story of his son, John Manson Dorsey. Uncle Mannie served with Company 1, 10th Georgia Regiment, Longstreet Corps, with the army of Northern Virginia. Like many

Southerners, Uncle Mannie took along his slave during battles. When Mannie was badly wounded at Cold Harbor, Virginia, it was this slave who made a stretcher and placed Mannie on it.

*"Then that colored boy walked all the way back to Fayetteville, pulling Mannie behind him. Took care of Mannie till he had his health back. Even when he was told that the war was over and he was a free man, that boy refused to leave. Stayed right with Mannie till the day Mannie died. See, it weren't the coloreds who wanted war; it was those Yankees."*

In the retelling of this story my relatives would say "Yankees" with such disdain that for many of my growing up years I thought "Yankees" was a swear word. Others listening would nod their heads in agreement or mumble, "That's right."

For years this was the story proclaimed from the steps of Great-grandpa Solomon's porch. This slave was always spoken of with respect and admiration for the loyalty he had given Uncle Mannie. But this story was always told with a blinded conviction that claimed everyone had been better off before the war.

It grieves me now that no one ever told me the name of Mannie's slave. The owner of a faithful heart is always known by a worthy name. I hope this slave had a strong and proud name. And I hope that someone, somewhere, was blessed with the heritage of his name. A legacy to his faithful heart.

My own name was a sign of the affection that my mother had for her cousin, Rufus T. Dorsey Jr.. Their friendship, rooted in childhood, was thicker than the trunks of the oak trees they had run around as children. By the time I was born in 1918, Rufus T. Dorsey Jr. was a prominent Atlanta physician.

## Dr. Dorsey and Other Notables

When Mother visited her family in Fayetteville, my sister, Elizabeth, and I would accompany her. Elizabeth, with her thick and naturally curly dark hair, porcelain skin, and fine features, drew attention with nothing more than a glance at others from under her dark lashes. But because of my damaged eye, which seemed to wander to objects beyond my immediate focus, and my stringy, fine hair, I often felt slighted. I wanted people to notice me with that special affection they bestowed upon Elizabeth. Dr. Dorsey was the one person in my life who made me feel like I was more special than Elizabeth. I think Mother knew this which is why is why she took me to visit him so often.

Dr. Dorsey never paid Elizabeth much attention, but he was always doing memorable things for me. Taking me to lunch or slipping money into my grimy palm. Dr. Dorsey expressed interest in me and my future.

"Rufe, what do you want to be when you grow up?"

I knew my plan. " I'm gonna be a lawyer."

Dr. Dorsey encouragingly responded, "That's good."

But my mother cast a dissenting vote, "I don't know about that—with her bad eye. Law school takes a lot of reading."

"Sit down, Rufe," Dr. Dorsey instructed. "Don't you ever forget that you can take in so much through your ears. Learn to be a good listener. It'll save you a lot of reading. Just listen. Be a good listener." When I later lost full sight in my eye due to the effects of tuberculosis, I remembered Dr. Dorsey's admonishment. I was glad I had listened to him.

Sometimes I wonder if Dr. Dorsey felt great affection for me because he knew first hand my emotional pain as I struggled with envy of Elizabeth. For although Dr. Dorsey was a well known Atlanta physician, admired by Mother and many others, he was eclipsed by the reputation of his own brother, Hugh Manson Dorsey, Governor of Georgia, 1917-1921.

Hugh has not generally been remembered by Georgia historians for his legacy of leadership as Governor, but for his tenacious prosecution of Leo Frank while serving as Solicitor General for the State. Frank, a Northerner of Jewish descent, was charged with the murder of a thirteen-year old, white, Southern girl. He faced a jury of Southern white men.

Leo Frank was convicted and sentenced to death for the murder of Mary Phagan in 1913. Hugh Dorsey successfully fought off all of Frank's appeals but Governor John Slaton finally commuted Frank's sentence to life imprisonment in June of 1915.

On August 16,1915, twenty-five armed men entered the state penitentiary in Milledgeville, seized Frank, drove him back to Marietta and then lynched him. Seventy years later an eyewitness to Mary Phagan's murder stepped forward and identified her murderer. It was not Leo Frank.

Historians have stated that it was this case that propelled Hugh Dorsey into the Governor's seat. It has been argued that during the early part of the twentieth century a person could not get elected in the State of Georgia without the backing of political machinist, Tom Watson, who was rumored to control several thousand of the rural votes that could be crucial to any election. Initially, Tom Watson was perceived as a crusader of human rights, eventually he became renowned as one of the

South's most verbal racists. Tom Watson backed Hugh Dorsey for Governor of Georgia.

Did Hugh Dorsey deserve the racist label so often attributed to him? Perhaps the Frank case could be categorized as much by North vs. South as by racial issues. When one realizes that Leo Frank was not only a Northerner, but a Jew, it is easy to label Hugh as a bigot. Many did so even during those years. Tom Watson waged a ruthless campaign of anti-Semitism against Leo Frank, during and after the trial. It was my mother who had taught me that a man is known by his friends. If Tom Watson was a bigot, and Hugh's supporter, then Hugh was a bigot.

But bigot was never the name Mother used for Hugh. Mother always spoke of Hugh with such respect that I just cannot accept racist as the prevailing truth of the legacy of Hugh Dorsey. I do think it is part of the truth about cousin Hugh, but only part. And part of the truth about anyone, or anything, is never enough.

Another truth about Hugh is that he became very concerned about the mistreatment of blacks during his term as governor. On April 22, 1921, Hugh addressed Atlanta citizens about injustices occurring statewide. In that presentation he provided 135 examples of abuse that had occurred during the previous two years.

"In some counties, the Negro is being driven out as though he were a wild beast," Hugh stated. "In others, he is being held as a slave. In others, no Negroes remain."

Hugh reported that a Negro, suspected of the murder of a white woman, was taken from jail, and among a mob of 3,000 was burned to death by a "slow fire." Negroes who wanted to work the railroad were having their jobs and lives threatened by white mobs, Hugh added.

Hugh made many recommendations to Atlanta citizens that day. He advocated investigations of any reported mistreatments of Negroes, compulsory education for all races, and State Committees to study race relations. He also called for laws that would authorize the Governor to deploy forces to quell disorder and that he be given authority to initiate Superior Court investigations of any mob violence or lynching.

I suppose cousin Hugh could have proposed these changes for political purposes. He did run for a Senate seat in 1920, but he lost to his old friend, Tom Watson. Hugh was the first of the Dorseys to lose an election. As it turned out Hugh and Tom had a parting of ways and positions.

I believe that Hugh Dorsey, like so many of his generation (and ours), had almost a schizophrenic approach to the issue of race. I think Hugh had a desire to treat others as equals, or at least in an equally humane fashion. I don't think he supported injustices by anyone. As Tom Watson became more verbal about his racist views, Hugh withdrew his associations with Watson.

And though I think Hugh was genuinely concerned about the black Georgian, I also believe that Hugh felt that God had ordained blacks to an inferior position in society. In the early part of his political career, Hugh took a firm stand against the administration of Woodrow Wilson when black leaders were appointed.

"I hold in my hand a picture of Negro appointees in the Interior Department who drew salaries from $600 to $1200 a year, when the farmers of Georgia were eking out a miserable existence, raising cotton at four cents a pound."

Hugh did not support the appointment of blacks to public office. Hugh might have attended a black peer's funeral, but he would not have invited him to dinner on Friday night.

## Southern Pride

Maybe Hugh's tenacious prosecution of Leo Frank speaks to this double-minded approach he had towards blacks. Possibly in Hugh's mind it was easier to believe that a Jewish northerner killed a thirteen-year old white southern girl, than it was to believe that the only other suspect, a black Southerner killed her. Hugh had more in common with the black man. They were both Southerners. Both had complex heritages.

That complexity continued to manifest itself in the prejudices of my mother. Lula Claude, bless her heart, was a prideful Southern woman. She never would have anything to do with a Northerner, a Catholic, or a Republican. God curse the person that was all three of these! As a high schooler I once attended a social at a Catholic church with a classmate. I came home excited over an event in my life that I did not have to share with my sister, Elizabeth.

"I've found the church for me, Mother. You should meet these people. They're the best people in the world. They listen to me. I even preached at them a little," I exclaimed. "I'm going to join the Catholic Church."

"Oh, no you're not!" Mother replied. "You're not joining any kind of Catholic Church."

My mother's Aunt Lou, who was visiting us at that time, listened to Mother and me fussing. A firm Methodist, who was annoyed with Mother for leaving the Methodist Church, Aunt Lou contributed her own assessment, "Well, really, Claudia. If you can leave the Methodist Church to become a Presbyterian, I see no reason why Rufe shouldn't leave the Presbyterian Church to become a Catholic!" Mother walked out of the room and I remained a Presbyterian.

It never would have occurred to Mother that others might label her as prejudiced. In her mind labels were not an issue of prejudices; they signified common interests. Mother would just assume that Catholics, Republicans and Northerners had very little in common with her. Of course, she felt this way about motorcycle gang members as well. Mother did not know how to approach a relationship without a foundation built upon similar interests.

Most of Mother's interests centered upon her family, a source of great pride to her. Actually there was very little in her life that Mother did not take pride in. She was proud of her heritage, her husband, her children, her church, her home. "Rufe, your teacher called and said you did real well on your test," or "Take a look at this rose, Charlie," or "Elizabeth, you're just as smart as anyone!" Mother's voice was like butter on a hot biscuit; a sweetness that flowed and flavored all our lives.

## Family Shame

But Mother would not speak about anything or anyone she was not proud of, which is why she never spoke of her own father, Edgar Favor Dorsey, a source of personal humiliation. Edgar, son of Solomon, brother of Judge Rufus T., was a farmer in Fayetteville. At age twenty Edgar married Elizabeth "Lizzie" Clark. She was nineteen. Fourteen months later, on January 15, 1881, Lula Claude Dorsey was born.

Lizzie had named her first born after her sister, Tallulah, or Aunt Lou as she was known. Lizzie gave birth to seven more children. She lost three of them in childbirth. With the third stillborn she lost her own life. At the time of her death Lizzie was a thirty-eight year old mother of five. The oldest girl was eighteen, the youngest was three. My mother was that eighteen-year old. Within six months of Lizzie's death, Edgar had remarried and moved to Dry Branch, Georgia, in Twiggs County. And against her father's wishes, my mother had moved to Atlanta to live with Lizzie's sister, Aunt Lou.

Beth, my daughter, has been the only one besides my sister, Elizabeth, and myself, to know why Mother went to live with Aunt Lou. My family's secret has not been shared with casual friends from church or the Professional Women's Club. Even Irene, my secretary of twenty years, and a dear friend, doesn't know this story of my family.

I, myself, did not know this secret until I was almost thirteen. We were living in Jacksonville, Florida, in September of 1930, when my mother received word that Aunt Nola, Mary Panola, had died. My father was unable to leave his job to travel with Mother to Fayetteville for the funeral. My parents decided that my sister, Elizabeth, who was struggling academically, could not afford the time off from school; so I, alone, traveled with Mother to the funeral. It was the one and only time I ever met my grandfather, Edgar Favor Dorsey.

Well, I didn't actually meet my grandfather but Aunt Nola's burial in Fayetteville's City cemetery was the only time I ever saw my grandfather. However, no one ever introduced us. My mother's sister, Carrie, approached Mother and said, "Papa is here." I waited for Mother to go over and speak to her father as she had done with so many of her other relatives, but she never moved toward his direction. So I did.

I walked over to where he was standing with the other men. I recall thinking that his face had that crinkled look of an overused leather purse. Tanned leather. Full pockets formed underneath his eyes. I don't know if Mother's periwinkle eyes were from her father. I never saw the color of his eyes; he never cast them my way.

I stood in front of a granite headstone and feigned interest in the life of someone whose name I could not read. Years had erased away a life and a name. The only inscription I could make out was, "Beloved daughter, asleep in Jesus, never more to wake." I hoped I would never be that tired. I listened as the men talked of their harvest. They spoke as in unison. One voice indistinguishable from another.

I glanced up, looking at my grandfather, who would have faced me if I had moved right four feet. He kept his head down, concentrating on the blade of grass he was toe-kicking. I thought he looked liked he could have been one of my daddy's railroad buddies—someone who would take his hat off when he came in the house; someone who might bring me a model train for a gift. He looked like someone who might be happy to know I was his granddaughter. But he did not know me that day in the Fayetteville City Cemetery and he never did.

The Sunday after Aunt Nola was buried, Mother and I headed back towards Jacksonville. As Mother turned the Nash south towards Jacksonville, (the first car we owned, salvaged from a wreck, Daddy paid $500 for it) I demanded to know why Mother did not speak to her own father, my grandfather. Mother ignored me at first.

I kept asking. Finally she told me that Edgar had been a good father while Lizzie, her mother, was alive.

"He drank some though. Then when Mother died, he was left with all us kids to care for. Since I was the oldest I took care of the younger ones," Mother answered with the hesitant voice of recall.

I looked out the window for a distraction: a leaf with the first golden hue of fall, ashen fence posts that someone had built; sharp wire keeping things in and out.

I waited for her to continue.

She was silent.

It wasn't enough for me. Bold, demanding, careless, I ignored her "keep out" sign. "Well, what's that got to do with me? You don't want me to know my own grandfather because your mother died and he drinks? Minnie drinks and she's nice."

(Minnie had been my caretaker when I was a pre-schooler. Daddy was always having to bail her out of jail for public drunkenness. Every time he threatened to fire her, I would wail so loud he would relent.)

"All people who drink aren't bad. Why won't you let me be with my grandfather?"

Oxygen suddenly diminished. Mother turned pale. I wished I had never asked my last question. I needed air. I wanted to roll down the window. Air. Bursts of air, the whipping kind. Wind that would take the words I had just spoken and carry them to the skies, to that silent place where children's red balloons and human souls go, to that place where sorrows are forgotten.

"Father began to drink a lot after my mother died. One night as I slept he came into my room, into my bed," my mother's voice trailed off. Or was it that I stopped listening?

I found myself unable to look at Mother as she spoke. To look at her was to see her naked soul; my looking would have dishonored her. Mother told me that this was called "incest," and that her father, who had been very drunk, never even remembered it later. He was angry at her for making plans to move to Atlanta. He wanted her around to care for the children in Dry Branch.

"If you leave now, don't bother to ever come back. You'll no longer be my daughter, " Edgar decreed.

Grandfather Clark, Aunt Lou's father, came to Fayetteville for my mother. In a horse-drawn carriage, Mother and Grandfather Clark made the trip from Fayetteville to Aunt Lou's boarding house in Atlanta. That year, 1899, was the year that Mother lost both her parents—one to childbirth and one to a sickness.

It took me a long time to share my mother's disgrace with anyone. I never wanted that suffocating feeling to return. Grandfather Edgar had shamed my mother. He had disgraced her in a manner that had forced her to leave. If she stayed and ignored the dishonor, she risked the possibility that this violation could occur again. The possibility was too much of a risk. But her leaving brought unwanted attention to a situation she wanted to forget.

Mother never forgave Grandfather Edgar for forcing her into a silent humiliation.

I am not sure she ever should have. When in September of 1937, Edgar Favor Dorsey died in Dry Branch, Georgia, Mother, claiming that she was no hypocrite, refused to even attend her father's funeral.

## Restoring Family Honor

My mother saw in her children the opportunity to restore a family and personal honor that her father had taken from her. She kept us from Grandfather Edgar and anyone else who might threaten that honor. She did not believe a parent could be overprotective. Her children were irreplaceable treasures. She felt there could never be enough insurance to cover that which could not be replaced.

So she grasped tightly the reins of parenting. Never did she allow us to befriend anyone whose families she did not know. We were rarely without adult supervision. Minnie, our nanny, provided that supervision in Decatur. When we moved to Jacksonville and Minnie stayed behind in Decatur, Mother became our constant supervisor.

Her first goal was to shield us from harm, but she did not limit that protection to her own ability. Mother wanted us to be strong enough to protect ourselves. She believed the best protection, the best insurance, for her daughters was an education. It alone would provide independence.

A good education would bring about financial security and, hopefully, emotional security as well. Mother hoped her daughters would be confident enough to stay out of vulnerable situations. She never talked to us about dating, about men, or about sexual relationships. By keeping us busy academically and by controlling our social contacts, Mother was able to avoid subjects she felt too delicate to address. So from very early on Mother took pride in any academic achievements that we obtained. Later she was just as grateful for our professional accomplishments. It was her assurance that no one could disgrace us. We would be much too smart for that.

When we were in high school, Mother told us that she wanted us to spend as much time as we could studying. With prophetic guaranty she told us that in our day women would finally take their place in the work force and become equal to men. She believed that we would be able to support ourselves. Mother would often repeat her desire for us to achieve academically. If Elizabeth or I went to the kitchen to watch her cook, she would send us away. "Anyone can learn to cook," she would tell us, "you go and study." She was wrong. Neither of us can cook a lick.

She once asked my husband, "Mac, when was the last time Rufe made you biscuits?" Too embarrassed to tell her that I had never made him biscuits, Mac said he couldn't remember. Mother told Mac it was her fault that I had never learned to cook. Occupied with hopes that I might find something better to do besides cook, she never taught me how. Like mothers everywhere, she had her regrets. I think Mother regretted overlooking some of the basics. I know she did whenever she came to our house for dinner.

Although, she didn't teach me how to cook, Mother did teach me more important things. I have often thought about what I should write back to my third grade friend:

Dear Rufus,

Thank you for your letter. You are a very observant young man. I am sorry that the kids at school make fun of your name. It must hurt very much.

I don't think the kids at school realize what a fine name Rufus is. My mother named me after her cousin, who was a well liked doctor. He was named after his daddy, who was a lawyer and judge.

When I was little, kids made fun of my name too. But you know what? My mother had already taught me that my name was something to be proud of.

Rufus, all families have good and bad things about them. People that we are proud to know, and people we are ashamed to know. It isn't our name that is our honor or dishonor. We are not worthy because we have a good name. Any name can be a good name. What makes a name good, or bad, is the person behind the name. We choose whether our name will be a good one or a bad one by the people that we are.

I hope you will ignore those hurtful remarks kids say and choose to be a person who brings honor to your name. Then when you are old like me, people will say, "That Rufus is sure a fine man. He's my friend and I'm proud to know him." I know Rufus can be a good name. Make others respect the man who bears the name. And thank you for wanting to be my friend. Now days an elected official needs all the friends they can get.

Glad to be called your friend,
Judge Rufe McCombs

Mother taught me old Southern ways. Someone once said to me that they could not figure out why Southerners were so proud to be Southerners.

"Don't you realize that you live in the armpit of America?" he asked.

Smiling and composed, I responded, "We, Southerners, are proud to be Americans, soldiers, Jaycees, Baptists, Dawgs, Braves and Democrats. And if you are lucky enough to befriend a Southerner, we'll even be proud to know *you*."

And my dear Mac, I am glad your mother taught you how to cook!

# 3

# RANDOM ENCOUNTERS

## Life in Atlanta

As 1899 ended and the 20th Century started, Mother began a new life in Atlanta. Wounded from her mother Lizzie's death and a trust betrayed by her father, Edgar, Mother won the affection of Aunt Lou simply because Mother needed her. Aunt Lou had waited a long time to be needed. Lou found in Mother the means to overcome her barren womb, being needed was a good feeling. Besides Mother brought Aunt Lou a new kind of companionship.

Aunt Lou hadn't had a sober confidante for some time.

"Claudia, I don't want you to worry," Aunt Lou said climbing from Grandpa George's carriage," but you should know that Uncle Bud has a small problem."

"Uncle Bud?" Claudia asked. "Is he sick?"

Taking a bag from the back of the carriage, Aunt Lou replied, "Well, yes, Claudia, Bud is kinda of...sick. His mind isn't quite right...not all the time...like when he drinks. He doesn't drink too often though. Well, maybe he does. But it isn't how often he drinks that makes him sick; it's how much."

"Uncle Bud drinks?" Claudia felt her stomach flip, remembering the rancid smell of alcohol from the night her father had visited her bedroom. Shivers crept up her arms and neck like a swarm of South Georgia gnats. Claudia trembled.

Noticing Claudia's shivers, Aunt Lou replied, "Now, don't you worry none. Uncle Bud never does anybody any harm, 'cept maybe the horse. Every time he gets drunk he climbs up on that old mare of his and rides her through town shouting at everybody, 'Fire! Fire!' All the neighbors have just learned to ignore the old man.

"I been ignoring him myself for years," Lou laughed. Almost in a whisper she added, "But he'll probably fall off that fool horse and kill himself some day."

Realizing that Lou might feel even more afraid and lonely than she did, Claudia felt a surge of pity for her elder. Reaching out, Claudia squeezed Aunt Lou's forearm and said, "Thank you, Aunt Lou, for bringing me here."

Watching the carriages and horses sashay around Atlanta's streetcar, Claudia's anxiety filtered through a wave of excitement. "I've always dreamed of living in the city, Aunt Lou," Claudia called over rattles, screeches, and clops. Atlanta's street sounds were like those of a beginner's band—individually they sounded bad, but together, playing off of one another, a tolerable rhythm developed.

The chance to live in the city of Atlanta was a country girl's dream come true. Claudia's heart picked up speed as she thought of all the men she might meet. Lawyers and doctors like cousins Rufus and Hugh. Important, intelligent men, who led lives of purpose. "Perhaps," she thought, "I'll meet someone who will desire me for more than just my ability to birth children. A man who might share his vision and purpose in life with me? Maybe he will need me to help him achieve some goals?" Aunt Lou had unwittingly provided Mother with more options than her life had ever held before!

Boarding houses were quite popular at the turn of the century. (Scares me to say turn of the century. I just barely made it around the last bend, the next turn is fast approaching, the driver is speeding and I'm not as young as I was before. Odds are not in my favor.) Aunt Lou's two-story Victorian boarding house, located on Pryor Street in downtown Atlanta, appeared protected by black wrought-iron fencing and a wide embracing porch.

Two blocks east of the house was the new state capitol building. One block west was the new county courthouse. The Union Station Depot, north of Aunt Lou's boarding house, was located between Pryor and Lloyd streets. This central location determined the clientele Aunt Lou served—mostly lawyers in town for business. They enjoyed her close proximity to the courthouse and the train station.

It appears to me that the location of Atlanta's railroads held sway over the kind of beau my mother might meet. Centrally located, the depots made connections easy for travelers. Electric street cars had been established in Atlanta in August of 1889 under the direction of Joel Hurt, President of the East Atlanta Land Company. Yellow with gold trims, oak interior and cane seats, the motor cars rode as if the rails were greased better than fried okra. The main line ran the length of Pryor, the street that intersected with Alabama Street where so many of the depots were located. Atlanta's streetcar took many travelers right past Aunt Lou's boarding house and sometimes right up to the front door.

Atlanta, like Mother, was in many ways a young woman herself. Although not quite ready for the commitment required for birthing offspring, Atlanta did allow herself to be courted by many. By 1902 Atlanta had established herself as the faithful mistress of the railway industry. Southern, Georgia Pacific, Western Atlantic, West Point Central, the East Tennessee, Virginia and Georgia lines called upon her as often as they could. If there was anything she needed, anything she wanted, these trains would travel all hours of the night just to bring Atlanta her desires.

And because they were so faithful to her, Atlanta kept a special place near her heart for each of them. The Union's Depot was centrally located, right off Alabama, between Pryor and Lloyd streets. The Western Atlantic's Freight Depot was only three blocks west and slightly north, but still on Alabama Street. The East Tennessee, Virginia and Georgia Depot were southwest of Western Atlantic's facing Peter's Street. Atlanta accommodated each of her suitors as best she could and they each in their own way carved out a place in Atlanta's life. Just as Mother had etched out a new life for herself with Aunt Lou.

Because of Lou's small frame, long neck, high contoured cheeks and thin lips that turned up ever so slightly, Mother thought Aunt Lou a regal looking creature. Whenever Lou was present, a natural aura surrounded her like the fragrance of springtime lilacs. This illusion of royalty permeated everything about Lou.

Inside the boarding house Lou had selectively arranged heavy-framed Victorian furniture. Gold brocade pillows rested in the curved nooks of sofas and chairs. Hand-woven tapestry rugs covered hardwood floors. The dining area was set with white linen and silver. Lou never cooked the meals her patrons ate; she hired a capable Negro woman to do that. This same hired woman also served the meals.

Lou, her long neck cradled by pearls and her chestnut hair, sat at the table with her patrons. Where she might have asked, "What do you think of those machine guns the Army has started using at Santiago?" or "Have you read Mr. Well's War of the World? There's a copy of it in the sitting room. Perhaps you'd like to take a look at it during your stay here."

Because of Aunt Lou's attention to detail her boarding house was a financial success. And since she was able to do so Aunt Lou sought to provide for my mother in all possible areas.

"Listen, Claudia, I couldn't do this for all my nieces, but since you are here with me I would like to help you with your schooling," Lou said across an empty parlor.

"What schooling, Aunt Lou?" Claudia responded. "I finished school last spring."

"Well, what about college?" Lou pressed.

Fixing her eyes upon a cabbage rose in the rug, Claudia cautiously replied, "Aunt Lou, I couldn't let you do that. You're doing more than enough just letting me live here. I appreciate it, really, I do. You've been far too generous already."

"Listen, Claudia," Lou persisted, "Don't refuse my offer; think about it awhile."

"I do hope you won't think ill of me, Aunt Lou, but I don't believe I want to go to college," Claudia spoke with quiet conviction. "I believe I'd most like to get a job. But thank you for the offer."

Mother did find a job selling ribbons, the current fashion in the early 1900's, for the well-heeled department store, J. M. High's, located on the corner of Whitehall and Hunter streets.

Every morning Mother walked one block to High's and entered the four-story brick and stone building. She loved the elaborately-carved wood that gleamed under hand-rubbed wax and low-hung chandeliers. High's had been founded in 1880 by Joseph Madison High, who had come to Atlanta from Madison, Georgia, with the intent to establish a quality dry goods store.

Mother turned nineteen in January of 1900, the year she began working for High's; the first and only job she ever got paid for. Prior to this she had helped her own mother with the caretaking of her three younger sisters. She had stood by helplessly as her mother suffered through the birth of two dead babies. When the last born caused Lizzie to lose her own life, Claudia was there. Eighteen at the time, she was old enough to grasp the loss for herself, her sisters, and even for her father.

By taking the job at High's, Mother refused Aunt Lou's offer of a higher education. I often wonder if she later regretted that decision. If she did, she never said. But Mother continually emphasized the importance of a college education to Liz and me. Mother, I think, was tired when Aunt Lou made the generous offer for further schooling—tired of grieving, tired of trying to please everyone, tired of trying to fix things that could no longer be fixed, and too tired to face another challenge.

I believe that a college degree would have just consumed more energy than Mother had available. Later, when Liz and I were born, Mother returned to the nurturing way of life that had been second nature for her throughout her formative years. But while she lived with Aunt Lou, I think Mother wanted simple work that brought her a sense of achievement, a sense of self, and a sense of security.

Perhaps Mother refused the education because she was not prepared to assume such a task or commitment. But I also believe that, as the oldest child, Mother found it difficult to receive from others. She just would not agree to letting Aunt Lou support her financially. Mother was much too independent to allow that. The fact that Aunt Lou had taken her in at all was more than Mother had expected.

Looking back on my mother's life I am struck once more by how much of life *is* affected by small details and random encounters. The location of the boarding house did determine the men my mother would meet. Mother's refusal of a higher education probably affected the passion with which she later emphasized education to Liz and me.

Was she trying to correct what she might have viewed as a mistake? Did she worry that she had disappointed Aunt Lou by taking a job instead of pursuing an education? Mother did not grow up in a time when *self-fulfillment* was a buzz word. She may never have gotten over trying to live a life that would please others.

There is that point one reaches in life where more time is spent looking back over life, rather than looking ahead. It happens because there is more to one's past than there is to one's future. I am at that point. And as I look back I see that the random events of life have too much rhythm in them to be void of a Creator.

Poetry doesn't just happen. Its rhythms are designed to flow in an orderly manner that only appears to have just naturally occurred. The beauty and horror of life may seem by chance, but life's rhythm and order expose a Creative Hand.

I believe *life is poetry*, but I am a bit anxious about meeting the Poet.

## Rob Welch Takes the Gravy Train

I just don't believe our encounters are random ones. For instance, after I was elected State Court Judge in 1978 I was called upon by the courts to fill in for Municipal Court Judge Ernest Britton who was very ill. Municipal Court handles misdemeanor cases. In most cases fines are levied and then paid by the defendant to the Court Clerk. My first day in for Judge Britton had been a very full one and our Court Clerk, someone I'll refer to as Rob Welch, had taken in several hundred dollars in fines.

As I stepped into the elevator on my way home that evening I was greeted by the Deputy Clerk, the person responsible for the accounting of monies collected by the Court Clerk.

"Well," I said smiling, "they kept me busy today. I reckon we made enough money to pay both of us and still bank some." Since I was just making elevator talk, I had expected nothing more than a nod of agreement back from her.

"We didn't receive any monies from Municipal Court today, Judge McCombs," she stated with a professional voice as flat as the last sip from a warm can of Coca-Cola.. My stomach convulsed.

"Are you sure?" My mind raced over the events of court that day.

"I sure am, Judge. Rob didn't turn in any money today. At least not to me, he didn't."

The door to the elevator opened in the lobby, quickly I turned and said, "Please don't mention this to anyone."

"I won't," she assured me.

That was on a Monday. On Wednesday I was due back in Judge Britton's courtroom. I decided to trace the money disappearing from Municipal Court by keeping a written log of all fines assessed that day. Little details could have significance. So each time on Wednesday a defendant was charged a fine, I would watch as the defendant walked over to Rob Welch to pay the fine. Then I would write the amount down. The fines Rob was to have collected amounted to $390.

When I finished my duties, I stopped by to visit with the Deputy Clerk, "Am I earning my keep?" I joked to lighten the intensity I was feeling.

"Well, you did good today, Judge," she replied, flipping through a stack of receipts. "We took in $40."

"Good, good," I said. "Glad I could help." Then I took the elevator back to my chamber, hoping my countenance had not betrayed what I now knew to be true—Rob Welch was stealing money from the courts.

Rob Welch was my friend. He had worked with me during my previous tenure in Municipal Court. Confronting someone I knew about stealing from the city was not what I had bargained for when I sought my position. My palms were sweaty, I heard my pulse swish-swish inside my ears. Picking up the phone receiver, I dialed the four digit number that put me through to Chief Superior Court Judge John Land. "Hey, Judge, how're you?" I began.

"Fine, Rufe, how 'bout you? How long you gonna be in for Britton?" Land inquired.

"Not too long, I hope. Things are piling up around here. Listen, Judge, do you mind if I come down to see you?" I asked, twisting my chair around to the right.

"Now?" he asked.

"Well, if it wouldn't be too much trouble. There is something I need to discuss with you," I answered.

"Why, not at all, Rufe. I *always* make time for the Judge favored by the Junior League!" he bellowed back.

"I appreciate that about you, Judge," I remarked, with more than a grain of sarcasm. "I'm on my way."

Explaining my dilemma, I leaned forward, sighed and looked at Judge Land.

I was hoping he would just tell me to forget the whole thing and to go on home. Perhaps we both could forget about the monies Rob was skimming from the court. Let someone else figure it out. Let someone else turn him in. I had a political career to think about. So did Judge Land. I wanted people to continue thinking I was "just the nicest person." What "nice" person betrays a friend? Now I'd be known as that "woman who won't mind her own business!"

"Rufe, I hate to say it. But I don't think the voters would forgive you if you walked away from this one. How many people already know about it?" Judge Land unconsciously tapped out a rhythm with the heel of his left foot.

"I haven't told anyone but you. The Deputy Clerk has her suspicions, I'm sure, but only because of our conversation in the elevator. I didn't say anything more today," I assured him. "I'll tell you one thing, Judge Land, I'm keeping my mouth shut on the elevator from now on," I smirked.

"That's not a bad idea, Rufe. Perhaps you should take the stairs; they'll take the wind out of you!" he laughed.

"Judge," I replied, "eleven flights of stairs would leave me breathless forever, I'm afraid." And we both laughed.

I wasn't just afraid of the voters not forgiving me if I walked away from this—I was afraid of my own conscience. I have never desired companionship with guilt. When invited to stay for dinner, guilt often finds a way to sleep over, then makes so much noise no one gets any sleep. If there had been another option for me than to report Rob Welch for theft, I probably would have taken it. But I felt, and still feel, that if I did not report the theft, then I would be Rob's accomplice.

I knew beyond a doubt that he was stealing. There was documentation that would certainly convict him. I wanted to overlook it. I wanted to go back to State Court and forget about my fateful, seemingly random encounter with the Deputy Clerk that day on the elevator. But I knew that if I didn't report Welch, I might as well have been stealing the money myself.

So I turned Rob Welch in for theft. Sheriff Gene Hodge and his department followed through with an investigation that found Welch guilty of 42 charges of theft which involved approximately $3,000. But court records revealed at least 600 potential instances of theft for a total amount of about $32,000.

The *Columbus-Ledger Enquirer* summed it up this way:

"Columbus citizens take no pleasure in seeing an elected official sentenced to spend time in prison. But the drama that unfolded in Muscogee County Superior Court Wednesday afternoon was both important and necessary.

It was necessary, first of all, because a law had been broken and punishment was called for. It was necessary because Municipal Court Clerk, by his own admission, had violated the trust of office by taking funds paid to the court and converting them to his own use.

...It was necessary to protect the reputation and standing of our courts. In recent years a number of events—some local, some occurring in Georgia and Alabama and some happening elsewhere—have tended to undermine public confidence in the judicial system.

Judges have been forced to resign for improper conduct. Others have been charged with criminal offenses. Prosecutors have been accused of favoring their friends. Court funds have been mishandled.

The prosecution of Welch was a way of proving that such abuses will not be tolerated. Judge John H. Land's sentence of five years in prison was, we think, fair and reasonable. A lighter sentence would have minimized the offense. A much longer one would have been harshly unfair.

As unpleasant as the whole affair may seem, there were some heroes...Judge McCombs—sitting on the Municipal Court bench of the ill Britton—kept record on the $390 fines she imposed on defendants during one session. A later check revealed that Welch turned in only $40 in fine money that day.

On the basis of McCombs' detective work, Sheriff Hodge obtained a Superior Court order to seize records. The charges resulted.

This story is encouraging because it demonstrates that although a few officials may be dishonest, there are others who can be depended on to uncover the dishonest conduct and to take action to correct it.

Citizens should be grateful that they have public servants like Judge McCombs and the watchful employees of the Municipal Court clerk's office." (*Columbus-Ledger Enquirer*, August 28, 1981)

At the time the events that led to the conviction of Rob Welch seemed to have just happened. Was it by chance that I met the Deputy Clerk on the elevator that day?

I often ride in elevators and never say a word. What were the odds that a casual conversation in an elevator would led to the drama that unfolded? Would Rob Welch have been convicted if I had not been called away from State Court and been on the elevator at that particular moment? And finally, how was my own career affected by this incidence? Did the conviction of Rob Welch convince voters that I was an honorable person, someone they could trust, an honest elected official?

If so, I am glad, but I don't take any credit for it. As I said before, I would like to have avoided the whole situation. From my perspective it appears to have been planned by Someone who knew far more about what was going on in that courtroom than I did. Someone who intended for me to be in Municipal Court at the time and on the elevator that day. Someone who knew that a situation I would prefer to avoid would one day prove to benefit my life. A Poet who plans and creates lives with such detail that even the pauses in rhythm have a purpose.

Of course, my longest pauses are on the landing before climbing the next flight of stairs.

## Charlie Edwards—Runaway Farm Boy

It was an April evening in 1903 when Mother paused on the front porch of Aunt Lou's boarding house. There she was, relaxing in the rocker, consciously breathing in the fading fragrance of white-bearded irises, unaware of the people who passed by and the one who didn't.

" 'Scuse me, Ma'am," he called from the street.

"Sir," she responded, fixing those periwinkle eyes upon a lanky and somewhat disheveled figure.

"Well, ma'am, I see that sign there. And I was wondering if there might not be a room I could let?" he twisted the brim of his gray felt hat between his thumbs.

Normally, she would have just excused herself and called for Aunt Lou. This time Mother gave pause. Focusing once again on the young man, she saw that he was as long and thin as a willow's switch. His brow was furrowed over his eyes, casting shadows that hid their color. She knew immediately that this man was not a lawyer, or a doctor. His hands were stout, weather worn. Farmer's hands, she thought.

"Ma'am?" his voice, quiet as a mountain stream, stirred her from her gaze.

"Yes, sir . . . well . . . no, sir. I mean I don't really know, sir," she stammered. "If you'll wait here I'll get my aunt. She can help you." Claudia grabbed up a handful of her skirt, rose, nodded once again at the young man, turned, and disappeared behind the partially leaded-glass door.

Lula Claude Dorsey was right about one thing that evening—those farm hands. Dried and splintered, they had ably performed the work required of them. And would have continued to do so if C.E. Edwards had not hopped a ride on the East Tennessee Freight that very morning.

It didn't matter that the Georgia Pacific could have accommodated him in a more courtly manner than the boxcar of a Tennessee freight train; the Georgia Pacific didn't run the back alleys of Morristown, Tennessee. C.E. Edwards, Charlie, 21, a recent graduate of the University of Tennessee, was running away. And the Tennessee freight, as far as Charlie could see, ran a lot faster than he did. The only destination he had in mind was some place else . . . any place else.

Charlie hadn't exactly intended to leave the family farm that morning when he asked his father, Joe, for permission to visit Knoxville.

"Aw, Daddy Joe, let him go. Just for the day," Charlie's mother, Patsy, pleaded.

"Patsy, there's work to be done. What's he wanting to go to 'Noxville for?

I been carrying his weight 'round here while he was off at school. Well, school's done and I could use the boy's help," Joe declared.

"Tell ya what," Patsy offered, "let him go just for the day. I'll help with the chores. The boy needs a break after all that studying he done."

"Yeah, well, any more of us wanting to take breaks around here we're likely to find ourselves broke. Go on, Charlie. Have yourself a good time. But you'd better get back in time to get some sleep; them cows wake up awful early," Joe instructed.

Charlie's parents, Joseph Norman and Patsy Thompson Edwards, owned a farm located on both sides of the road where Highway 25 led to Knoxville, known to me as the Knoxville Turnpike. It had been over twenty years since Joe and Patsy had relocated from Virginia to the fertile valley enclosed by the Clinch Mountains. Patsy's father, Luke, a Virginia farmer, fronted the initial cost of the farm.

Migration to fertile East Tennessee was not uncommon. Pioneers had originally taken wagon trains from southwestern Virginia and over the mountain passes from North Carolina. Charlie's ancestors were hardy farmers, who grew weary of farming clay hills, so they began to press on for a land that they hoped would be richer. And the land had not disappointed Charlie's ancestors the way it had him. Morristown, located in Hamblen County, was named after three such pioneers: Gideon, David, and Absalom Morris, who had settled the area in 1783. But neither land nor family had hold of Charlie now.

Charlie's disappointment was not tied to the productiveness of the land, but the unproductiveness of the people who farmed it. Most of the farmers Charlie knew were not landowners, they were land owers. Every farmer owed the land for sustaining them and their households. The land dictated the lives each family led, the people they met, the food they ate. The land that sustained their lives would cradle these same families in death. Charlie knew Morristown's cemetery was home to more population than all the city proper. Perhaps Charlie's escape that day was not so much from the land as it was an attempt to escape his own mortality.

Annual summer trips with my father—who had by then escaped the claims of the farm, were the only times as children that Liz and I spent in Morristown. I have a hard time recalling the farm of my grandparents. I don't know if the memory is like air spun cotton candy, sweet but hard to grasp, or like the tales of an inebriated co-worker, exaggerated dribble. It is probably both.

But pictures remind me of the expansive two-story farmhouse, white, with a wrap-around porch, and a widow's walk above the front door, crested by gingerbread trim. By the time I was old enough to wonder why my father ran from this picturesque farm, I was old enough to know that the passions of youth are often nothing more than a fleeing from mortality. My grandparents explained their son's running as the impulsiveness of youth, but perhaps Charlie was intently aware of how routine can lull one's senses into a false sense of security, a sense that death is not an enemy, and that this life is eternal, not temporal.

After Charlie left, Daddy Joe employed several people to help him with the business, primarily a dairy farm that encompassed over 100 acres. Along with dairy farming, Daddy Joe grew tobacco, vegetables and fruit. During our summer trips there Liz and I would set up a makeshift stand at the end of the dirt road that led to the farmhouse. From this stand we sold watermelons or cantaloupes to the people headed to or from Knoxville.

Sometimes we would fish in the pond located on the slope to the left of the house. Or we might climb up the loft in the brick-colored barn. Daddy Joe kept about six horses in that barn. One of them he gave to Liz and me. Tip, an Arabian, she was the only white horse Daddy Joe owned and the only horse I've ever owned. Liz and I loved to saddle Tip up and ride her on the only course our mother allowed us to, the one that circled the farmhouse.

Daddy Joe and Grandma did not live alone at the farm, even after my father, Charlie, their only child, left. Uncle Ab, Albert Thompson, Patsy's spinster brother, lived upstairs. Other than Uncle Ab, no one ever went upstairs. I remember once as a child standing at the foot of the stairs that led up. I desperately wanted to see them from the top looking down. Mostly I wanted to experience forbidden adventure.

As I lingered and debated my first step, Grandma Patsy stopped me, "Rufe, get on outside. You got no business here." I never knew what went on up there, or why we weren't allowed there, but I never did see the second story of my grandparent's home, except from the outside.

Uncle Ab put meat on the folklore bone that claims, "any man that will talk to himself has money in the bank." With his pudgy frame squared by oversized jackets, which he wore even in July, and likely the same pants on that he had worn the day before and the day before that, Uncle Ab was often mistaken for a man without means. In truth, Uncle Ab owned a lumber business in Morristown, near what came to be Southern's railroad tracks.

These railway areas were often populated by hobos, nomads of the industry. They would ride from town to town, freight car to freight car, gathering up whatever job they could find, whatever meal they could hustle and whatever warmth a life of that nature had to offer.

Once a yard man spotted Uncle Ab perched upon a stump in the lumberyard, "You see that hobo over there on that stump?" he said pointing at Uncle Ab.

"Yeah," a co-worker replied.

"Well, that hobo is out here mostly every day. Just sitting on that stump. Reckon' we oughta do somethin' about 'im?" the yard man inquired.

"Naw, I don't reckon the boss would want us to," his co-worker said, laughing. "That hobo's the one who pays ya when ya wants to be's paid."

And it was Uncle Ab who paid for Charlie's college education. Daddy Joe had wanted Charlie to finish high school and start in full time at the farm. As the only child, Charlie would one day inherit all that Daddy Joe had spent years building. But Uncle Ab had reasoned with his brother-in-law, telling him that farming was a more complex business and that Charlie would be able to run the farm better with an education than without one. What neither Uncle Ab nor Daddy Joe had considered was the possibility that Charlie might want something entirely different for his life.

It is possible that Charlie hadn't even considered it himself. Not until that April morning when he hopped some freight, like the Pea Vine, for the fifty some mile ride to Knoxville. But by the time he got to Knoxville, Charlie had made up his mind that he wasn't going back. At least not yet. I guess Georgia country girls weren't the only ones who dreamed of a life in Atlanta; Tennessee country boys dreamed too.

So Charlie continued on through Knoxville, through Chattanooga, on to Dalton, and into Atlanta. Upon arriving in Atlanta, Charlie took the motor car southeast from the downtown area to Grant Park which held public bathing facilities. There he cleaned up as best he could without a change of clean clothes. "I'll let the folks know where I am as soon as I get a job," he resolved as he wiped dirt from his shoes. Then he boarded the electric cars that ran past Aunt Lou's on Pryor Street.

Whenever Daddy told me this story of how he met Mother I would imagine that I was hiding in the shadows nearby when his quiet but rushing voice stirred the stillness of Mother's evening. "As soon as I saw your mother on that porch, I said to myself, 'There's the woman I am going to marry. Might as well get a room here.' So I did what I set out to do, got me a bed and someone to help me keep it warm."

In reality, it was quite a long time before Daddy got the latter. The old saying, "You know why men like Southern girls better? 'Cause it takes them so long to say 'No'," was never true of Mother. "No" came naturally to her once she knew those were indeed farmers' hands.

Charlie had to find some way to convince Lula that he didn't plan on taking her back to Morristown to populate the family farm with male heirs. Charlie may not have intended to migrate south the day he left Morristown; he certainly wasn't comparison shopping for brides the day he met Mother; but once he got settled in Atlanta he began to plan a future.

On April 16, 1903, Charlie became a messenger boy for Atlanta's favored Southern Railways, but after he abandoned the family farm tradition he lost favor with Daddy Joe. Farming had been the only livelihood that Daddy Joe knew. Phillip Edwards, Daddy Joe's father, had farmed in Carroll County, in southwestern Virginia. And his father before him, Isaac Edwards Jr., had farmed in the Hillsville and Piper's Gap areas, foothills of the Blue Ridge of Virginia. Isaac Jr. was the local auctioneer of the area, known for his ability of "crying the sale." Little Reed, the family farm, near Hillsville, was first farmed by the Quaker family of Isaac Edwards Sr..

Charlie had not just rejected a way of earning a living to Daddy Joe; Charlie had rejected his family's life. Farming was what defined the living. The farm had sustained their very lives. Farms had nourished

Daddy Joe's people for more years than he could remember. Farms were heirlooms for the next generation.

An eternal heritage that would outlive caretaker after caretaker. Like the Hebrew father who believed that personal eternity was lived through the lives of his male heirs, Daddy Joe believed his eternity was bound to the farm he would leave to Charlie and then to Charlie's son.

So Daddy Joe did find himself broke after Charlie took the trip to Knoxville that day but it wasn't family finances that broke Daddy Joe; it was his heart. From the moment that he received word from Charlie in Atlanta, Daddy Joe knew Charlie would never return home to farm.

It was Grandma Patsy who encouraged Daddy Joe not to build a fence of resentment, "How can we turn out our only boy, Joe? I hate that Charlie has gone and done this. I miss my boy. But I am not going to let anything but miles distance me from him."

And it was only the miles that ever did distance my father from his family. Daddy Joe continued to work the farm for many years, struggling to make it last a lifetime and then some. In 1938 when Daddy Joe died he left the farm to Charlie, which was later sold to pay for college tuition for Liz and me. But it was while he was still living that Daddy Joe gave Charlie the gift Charlie treasured most—forgiveness.

Daddy Joe's love had proved to be our family's eternal heirloom.

## Thirteen Years of Planning Pays Off

Mother was always glad for the miles that separated Charlie Edwards from the farm and his parents. Her hope was that Charlie would so enjoy his work with Southern Railways that he would never return to the farm. After all, she had not come to Atlanta to hitch up with some farmer; she could have done that in Fayetteville. It didn't appear to Charlie that Mother was inclined to hitch up at all. For although they met in 1903 and Daddy said he knew then she was the one for him, my parents did not marry until thirteen years later, on April 15, 1916, in the Fulton County, Atlanta, Georgia Superior Court. Southern girls are never easy pickin's.

Today it seems unfathomable that my parents would have courted for over twelve years. And though they did reside at the same address, they by no means "lived together." Considering the time period, it now seems unreasonable to have waited until Mother was thirty-five and Daddy thirty-three before they married. What about children? Unlike today's society, women rarely postponed marriage in lieu of a career. Working at J.M. High's was a good job, but certainly not a career.Why did they wait?

I am not sure I know all the reasons why they waited. Maybe they both were enjoying a season of life that was free from major responsibilities. Mother had helped raise one family. As long as she was working and living with Aunt Lou, the only person she was responsible for was herself. Maybe she enjoyed freedom from worrying about others and her independence.

I believe Daddy was just beginning to enjoy his freedom. Making the break from the farm was the most independent thing he had ever done. He had been willing to sacrifice the esteem of his father just to gain some independence. Getting married would have required that he sacrifice the freedoms he had just won.

They may have postponed marriage for money. Daddy's favorite phrase as I was growing up was, "Time is getting short and money shorter." No matter how much money Daddy made, Mother found some way to spend it all. I think that he must have known before he married her that Mother was accustomed to living above her means.

I guess he was hoping he'd have enough saved so that they could stay a notch up.

By January of 1916, Charlie had worked his way into the joint auditor's job of the short lines of Southern: the Danville, Western, Blue Ridge, Yadkin, High Point, Randlemen, Asheboro, Southern, Lawrenceville, and Tallulah Falls branches. At the time he worked for them, they all operated out of Atlanta.

Prior to marriage, from 1903-1909, Daddy worked his way up from messenger boy to Chief Billing Clerk. He worked out of the same freight station line located on Peter's Street that had brought him to town. His salary ranged between $40 a month to $100 a month. By January of 1914, Charlie was working as the Ticket Collector for Southern. But by September of the same year Daddy was no longer with any railroad.

Charlie quit this job and left town again. This time he ran West. How far West he got I do not know. But he went—without Mother. While I can speculate on what possessed him to leave; the call of new adventure, to earn more money, maybe just to make sure what he wanted was in Atlanta; the truth is that he never talked about it and neither did Mother.

Daddy headed West in September of 1914 and did not return until December of 1915. I would like to believe it was the journey of journeys for a Tennessee farm boy.

I hope he had moments of awe and anxiety, for these are born from a heart that has never ceased to look at the world with wonder. Whatever Daddy went in search of during that time, he came to realize that what he wanted was still in Atlanta.

So he returned and obtained another job as Rate Clerk with Southern. Within four months of his return he married Mother. The courtiers of Atlanta had been the ticket for my parents' romance. The location of Atlanta's depots and the street railway, the "dummy line," that ran down Pryor Street practically ensured that Daddy would end up at Aunt Lou's front porch. Southern Railways provided the means by which Daddy could pursue the woman of his desires. Rhythmic rails had begun their sway over the lives of my parents and our family.

Another random encounter or the Poet's plan?

# 4

# GOING PLACES

## Atlanta's Big Fire

Much of my life has been influenced by the different aspects of the rail business: where I have lived, people I have met, and places I have been. After Daddy came back to Atlanta in 1915 and began working for the railroad, he never left the railroad business again. He worked in different positions with different companies, but always for the trains. When he retired from his position as Office Manager for Seaboard's Jacksonville, Florida, branch in 1953, he had on record fifty years of service to the rails. His service record included the years he worked between 1903 until the time he left for the West in 1914.

Once they were married in 1916, on April 15, (a poetic emphasis to a bookkeeper's life?), my parents bought a small bungalow home on Feld Avenue in Decatur, Georgia. Elizabeth was born at this home with the assistance of a mid-wife. Mother and Daddy quickly made up for those thirteen years of repressed physical attraction. My sister, Elizabeth, was born in March, 1917 and I was born the following August, 1918.

This was the same house that was located across College Avenue from the railroad depot where Daddy took the train to work every morning. And it was the house that Mother and Daddy lived in when Atlanta's "big fire" devoured almost two miles of northeastern residential areas. Six blocks wide and twenty-four long, the big fire was just one of four fires to have started in widely separated sections of the city on May 21, 1917; all four fires began within an hour of one another.

Mother saw smoke rising northwest of the bungalow on Feld Avenue. Daddy was at work in Downtown Atlanta. Was he in the midst of it? Frightened, Mother, like many others that day, began plans for escape. Evidently the phone service was not working, so she could not consult Daddy. She had no way of knowing how quickly the fire might reach the neighborhood. The eastward billowing of the smoke indicated that the fire was not far away and heading towards Decatur. Mother had already heard three different alarms that Monday morning beginning around 11:30 continuing on through the noon hour.

"Minnie, bring Elizabeth's carriage around front," Claudia hollered. Grasping all the family treasures she could find in her haste, Mother threw them into the carriage.

"What's we gonna do, Mrs. Edwards?" Minnie nervously inquired.

"We're going to Carrie's place, Minnie," Claudia replied, shifting baby Elizabeth in the cradle of her arms.

"Maybe I should go home, Ma'am," Minnie hesitantly suggested.

"Don't be silly, Minnie. Of course, you can't go home. I need you to help me get this baby safely outta here. How could I possibly get to College Park without you?" Claudia responded with a persuasive force that indicated the question didn't need an answer. "I need you. Elizabeth and I need your help to get to my sister's home."

"Yes'm, Mrs. Edwards," Minnie nodded, turning the carriage north on its wheels.

As they approached the corner of College and Feld, Mother caught up with a neighbor who was heading toward Atlanta.

"Where're you going?" Claudia cried out.

"I'm headed downtown. Hoke's at work. I want to make sure he's okay," the neighbor replied.

"I'll join you then. Charlie's there and I'm plum sick with worry," Claudia offered.

In reality, the fire was not near Decatur. Charlie was fairly certain that the fire did not threaten Decatur, but still worried about Claudia and the baby, he took off towards home. Since there was no train to take him, Charlie began to walk.

Charlie's nostrils were irritated by the haze of smoke floating over the downtown area. He could tell from the alarms that there must be more than one fire. Several of his co-workers at the railroad had rushed off to help when the last of the alarms sounded. Someone said something about a fire in an old warehouse near Grady Hospital. But as he walked, Charlie overheard one store owner shouting about homes being burned down on York Street. He stopped.

"Has the warehouse fire spread?" Charlie stepped up to the store owner.

"Last I heard it had just about burned up Niggertown and was heading down Ponce de Leon. They're even calling in soldiers to help contain the fires. Seems that a fire started at Mr. Candler's Warehouse over on

Murphy and while the firemen where there, another fire got started over at the west end near York."

Both men grew silent as a car stopped and someone shouted from within, "We need volunteers to help at the pumping stations. Who'll go?" Within seconds the dusty car was full, some men stood on the running board, grabbing hold of the roof as the car headed away.

"Ponce de Leon?" Charlie looked back towards the smoke. "Can they stop it?"

"Who knows?" the store owner replied. "They got bucket brigades going in every direction. Cars been running up and down this street, carrying people off to help. Guess when the fire truck got to Grady's they found mattresses burning, but couldn't stop it cause there weren't any hoses on the truck. I heard someone say they thought maybe an arsonist had set fire to Atlanta. But I think it's just too many fires going in too many different directions."

"I gotta get home," Charlie looked east toward Decatur. "My wife's stuck at home with our new baby. She's probably figuring I'm burned up by now."

"You walking? No trains headed that way right now."

"Yeah, I'm walking till I find me a ride," Charlie tipped his hat at the man and headed towards home. He knew it would take more than an hour to reach home afoot, so he began to search the streets for a ride. When someone he knew drove by, Charlie waved him down. "Can I get a lift home?" he inquired.

"Hop in," his friend said, opening the door from the inside.

"Claudia's at home with the baby. I need to make sure they're all right," Charlie fretted aloud.

Driving along they passed truckloads of soldiers. People were moving furniture out into the streets. They saw cars and trucks loaded with bedding, silver, lamps, clothing, and food. Piled on top were kids, bawling. As they passed one corner they heard a man shouting.

*"The first angel sounded his trumpet and there came down hail and fire mixed with blood."*

"What's he talking about, Charlie?" the driver asked.

"Stop for a minute and let me listen," Charlie stuck his head out the window.

*"And it was hurled down upon the earth. A third of the earth was burned up, a third of the trees was burned up, and all the grass was burned up,"* the man paused for breath before continuing to quote from a black leather Bible, *"The second angel sounded...."*

Charlie smiled at his friend, "Well, if this guy's right, looks like we'll only lose about a third of Atlanta and we won't have to mow all summer long."

"Guess that means Claudia is safe in Decatur then, huh?" the driver made a left-hand turn.

Heading down College Avenue, the smoke became so intense that Claudia quickly realized that they were not going to make it downtown. Despairing, Claudia and Minnie parted ways with the neighbor and once again decided to push a route south to College Park.

With tears smarting her eyes and fears gnawing her stomach, Claudia cried out, "This way, Minnie. I don't know what's to become of Mr. Charlie. We've got to get out of here." She turned her face east away from the smoke as the car Charlie was in headed towards her.

"Claudia! Claudia! Over here!" Charlie hollered as he spotted Minnie pushing Elizabeth's carriage. Opening the car door and hopping out, he assured his friend, "Thanks for the ride; I see her now."

Daddy took Mother back home that afternoon. "Don't worry Claudia, the fire isn't going to make it out here. They've called in soldiers to help. The fire departments got the whole city of Atlanta at work. We'll be fine."

"Are you sure we's gonna be okay, Mister Edwards?" Minnie asked. "Can I go on home an' see about my folk?"

"Of course, you can, Minnie. But could you help me get Mrs. Claudia home first?"

Mother was never the same after that day. Nervousness lit upon Mother with the fury of mountain lake mosquitoes, annoying her most relaxing moments. Whenever she told this story she would comment, "My hands shook for months after that fire. I can't sit still to save my life."

The biblical prophecy Charlie heard appeared to be true. Atlanta's big fire blistered over 300 acres, left 2000 homes in ashes, and over 10,000 people, mostly blacks, homeless. Property loss reached an estimated $5,500,000. And over 3000 soldiers were called in for service before the fire was stopped by dynamite halfway between Ponce de Leon Avenue and Piedmont Park.

From the time I was born the following August, 1918, the mother I knew was strung tighter than a new clothesline. She was always just a bit on edge, not necessarily in need of therapy, but I wouldn't have wanted her to work a postal service job.

Because of this nervousness, my parents decided that two children fulfilled their nurturing instincts. So Mother underwent a tubal ligation. I suppose Mother's nervousness wasn't the only reason; Mother was thirty-seven and had never really desired a large family. But nervousness was the reason she often used to explain why she did not have more children.

# Minnie

Yet, it never was Mother who did the mundane duties of childrearing prior to our starting school. It was Minnie who followed Elizabeth and me throughout our early childhood: picking up books and wooden trains we tossed aside in childish abandonment; wiping our grimy marks off doorway moldings and bathroom mirrors; finding time each day to tell us a special story; taking us to the empty lot for another ball game.

Minnie was tall, 5' 8", skinny, 122 lbs, young, 17, and black, no cream.

I always knew she was black, a Negro, as we used to say. She was the only black person I knew as a child.

Looking back, I think that I should have had an awareness that we were different, very different, but I never did. Minnie was family to me and I loved her.

I saw her with my heart, not my mind. Hearts are rarely as confined as the brain. Minnie was my much adored nanny.

I was only six or seven years old when I learned just how severe the limitations of the mind can be. Early one fall evening, our family rode the streetcar from Atlanta to College Park. My Uncle John and Aunt Carrie lived in College Park with their two children, Lula Lee and John Jr.. We often made the trip to visit with my mother's sister and her family.

On this occasion, we had taken the train to Atlanta and the streetcar from there. We had just passed East Point; our next stop would be College Park, or so we thought. But we had not even gotten half a mile from East Point when a loud explosion reverberated through the streetcar.

"What was that?" Mother turned to Daddy.

From where we sat, two-thirds way through the car, Daddy could not readily see up front, so he strained forward, peering over my head and those in front of me. The streetcar jolted. Daddy jerked forward then backward. I was thrust to the empty space between the seats.

Someone screamed, "Get down." I looked out the window of the car and saw blacks— men, women and children—running in every direction. Rocks were being hurled at them. I saw one man struck behind his ear. He lost his balance and stumbled, then righted himself and began to run faster. Looking to my left, I followed the path of the rock backwards to a mountain of white. They were grouped together, some on horses, a few on foot. Their heads formed a tier of jagged points. I wondered why they had on baptismal robes? My childish eyes searched for reasons.

Just then Mother's hand pressed in on my scalp, " Rufe!" she gritted while pushing me to the floor. Another rock hit the side of the streetcar, more to the middle this time, the din was closer. Then I heard a sound like wood crackling in a fire but the crack was so loud I jumped in alarm.

"STAY DOWN," Daddy yelled. I crawled back under the seat and began to cry. Elizabeth and Mother huddled in the aisle around me. Daddy was behind them. The crackles continued, one right after another. Everyone searched the car's crevasses for safety.

It had been dusk when we first pulled out of East Point but we stayed in the streetcar on the floor until it grew darker and darker. Finally it was pitch black outside. It seemed like hours that I stayed underneath that seat. I felt the condensation of my own breath upon my arm. My legs ached with cramps and both my feet tingled with numbness. Scrunching my toes within my shoes, I tried to restore circulation. The screeching from outside had moved to another area, further away.

Daddy was the first of us up. "I'm going up front, Claudia. Stay put," he instructed. I watched the heels of his shoes as he walked to the front of the streetcar.

A few minutes passed and I felt the vibration of a motor. Daddy returned. He took Mother by her elbows and helped her to her feet. People around us began to stir. Elizabeth stood and pulled me from under the seat.

The car was slowly moving forward. My feet burned as blood rushed known pathways. I looked over Elizabeth's shoulder, out the window, and watched fading embers drop from the remains of a charred cross.

Today, I don't recall any discussion that my parents and I had after this incident.

I remember that I thought the blacks were being harmed for no other reason than they were black. I thought the men with pointed hats were horrible. I was afraid of them. The word "Klan" was not mentioned by my parents.

Looking back on that moment, my parents seemed to have expected Elizabeth and me to act as if nothing had happened—so we did. The only comment I recall was my mother telling Daddy, "I'm ashamed of white people who behave like that. Why those could've been some of Minnie's folks!" We continued on that night to College Park, but we did not stay because it was so late. Uncle John gave us a ride home in his Model T Ford. I slept all the way.

It was this incident that led me to worry about Minnie. I worried because I knew she was black and I realized then people might mistreat her because of that. But also because Minnie for as long as I could remember had a drinking problem.

The routine was that every Friday night Minnie would call Daddy from jail, where she sat for public drunkenness.

"Mr. Edwards," she'd cry, "would you help me? I need some money."

And Daddy would fume every time and shout, "This is the last time I'm going to help that girl get out. We can't afford to keep bailing her out every week." Then he would decide, "I'm not going to do it. By golly, this time that girl can just stay there!"

At which point, Elizabeth and I would begin to wail with the feverency of praying zealots. "Daddy, you can't leave Minnie," we'd plead. "Here you can have our money," bargaining we'd hand over hoarded pennies. As always Daddy would relent.

As a child, I believed that if the men hurling those rocks, burning those crosses, had the opportunity to know Minnie, they would never again want to hurt a person just because of skin color. Minnie was my caretaker, my nanny, my playmate, my friend. And I knew that in many ways Minnie needed someone to take care of her. I wanted to be that person.

But Mother would never have allowed me to help. She never even allowed Elizabeth or me to help Minnie with the household duties. We'd idly sit on the couch as Minnie dusted the dark cherry wood of the buffet. Pressing our snub noses against the mesh of the screen door, we would watch as she and a broom danced around the corners of our front porch. And as soon as Minnie was finished, we would drag her away to the empty lot between our house and the corner already marked for games of dodge ball and baseball. I realize now that Minnie was my first friend. In some ways I trusted Minnie more than I did my sister.

As a child, I was always too jealous of Elizabeth to feel very safe with her. Some of my earliest memories are of the jealousy I experienced over Elizabeth. The way neighbors always commented as to what a beautiful child Elizabeth was, while staring at me as if searching for some conciliatory words to explain my lack thereof.

I could see it, too. I knew that from a physical standpoint Elizabeth was a beautiful child. Just as I knew I wasn't. Elizabeth had dark, thick, curly hair. She looked angelic. My own hair was like angel noodles— thin and limp. Elizabeth learned early on to use this to her advantage.

"Rufe," she would chide, "did Momma tell you that you were adopted?"

"Nuhu, was not!" I declared.

"Yes, you were. How come you don't look like Mother or Daddy then, huh?" she would reason.

"Minnie," I would cry, "make Elizabeth stop. She's saying hateful things."

"What'd she say to you, Child? What you be saying to her Miss Elizabeth?" Minnie patted me on the back as I buried my face into her meatless thigh.

"I didn't say anything, Miss Minnie, " Elizabeth would reply. "You know Rufe is just a cry baby."

Elizabeth was also adept at using her position of authority to control me. She gave more directions than a made-in-Japan bicycle manual: "Rufe, pick up your socks. You can't have another piece of cake. I'm telling Mother you stuck your tongue out! You better not go out without your shoes on. You can't wear that dress today!"

I resented Elizabeth's looks and her position of power over me.

Today, of course, we are friends. I am no longer jealous of her looks—when you reach seventy-plus years everyone pretty much looks the same—old. Eventually, Elizabeth found more pleasure in doing her own job than in telling me how to do mine.

But I think those feelings that I embraced as a child helped me to bond even more with Minnie. My self-esteem was not threatened in Minnie's presence the way it had been with Elizabeth. I knew Minnie accepted and loved me.

Which is why I was so broken when we had to leave Minnie. In 1926, my parents and Mrs. Kirby's family had decided that we all would move out to a newer housing area—Avondale Estates. My parents had picked out a new home, Tudor style, which I thought grand because I would no longer have to share a room with Elizabeth. They had borrowed $500 to pay down on the new home. The plan was to trade in the home on Feld Avenue, and finance the new home at a higher mortgage.

Right after making the down payment, Daddy was promoted and transferred to a position with Seaboard Railways in Jacksonville, Florida. So we had to move. Daddy was glad for the promotion and Mother was proud for him. But overall it was a difficult, reluctant move for us all.

We had planned for Minnie to join us in Florida. Keeping Minnie was going to be financially difficult for my parents, but no one wanted to leave without her and she had agreed to go. On the night we were to board the train for Jacksonville, Minnie called to say she had married and could not go with us.

My parents' finances were diminished by the move, which occurred before we could get the home on Feld Avenue sold. They lost the $500 down they had borrowed for the home in Avondale, and Elizabeth and I lost Minnie.

Throughout the train ride to Jacksonville, I worried about Minnie. Who would get Minnie out of jail now? I fretted and then resolved that night that I would grow up fast so that I could always be around to help Minnie.

It didn't take long for me to figure out that worry-induced resolutions produce very little results. I was only seven years old when I left Decatur for Jacksonville and in spite of my decision to "grow up fast"—I didn't. I never saw Minnie again. But I believe the affection I felt for Minnie produced in me a lifelong desire to help others in trouble, a desire that continues to motivate me to this very day.

## Jacksonville, Florida

While the move to Jacksonville was a promotion for Daddy from a career standpoint, it was more like a sidestep financially. Daddy had gone ahead of us and found a temporary living situation at a boarding house. Our furniture had been placed in storage in Decatur until there was space available on the train to transport it. We lived at the boarding house for a month. For Elizabeth and me it was like being on a permanent vacation. Since it was a boarding house we never had to do dishes and chocolate sundaes were served for dessert most every night.

When the furniture did arrive my parents found a duplex in an area known as Springfield, and our vacation time ended. The furniture came from Decatur free of cost, but not without freight damage. Our home in Decatur had a buyer, but we were going to stay in the duplex until the paperwork was finished and the Feld Avenue house was out of my father's name.

Daddy no longer had the luxury of walking across College Avenue to hop a train to work. Now he had to walk thirty blocks to and from work everyday. Mother missed being close to the corner market and a home church. Commodity prices were higher in Jacksonville and money for necessities seemed non-existent. Mother took us to the Public Health Department for health and dental care.

We had been in our duplex only a few months when Daddy learned that the new owner of our home on Feld Avenue had moved out without paying on the mortgage, leaving Daddy with a past due owing. Then we received word that the duplex we were living in was to be torn down to make way for a new synagogue, so we moved back to the boarding house and then to an apartment in San Marco, near the St. John's River.

As I look back now on all the moves we made that first year in Jacksonville I am surprised at how little I was affected by the stress my parents must have been under. We had gone from a very established neighborhood to very transient ones, but throughout our moves I recall Mother stating, "God did not bring us to Jacksonville without a purpose" and as trite as that may seem today, I believed it. Of course, I realize that Mother was probably trying to reassure herself as much as anyone else.

While living in this last apartment, my family bought our first car, a Nash. Daddy paid Seaboard $500 for the car which had been damaged while being shipped.

A neighbor taught Daddy to drive it and Daddy, in turn, taught Mother. But Mother never quite got over her farm background; whenever she would press the brakes to stop the car she would pull back on the steering wheel and call out, "Whoa! Whoa!"

After a year in Jacksonville, Daddy tired of paying for an apartment and a home in Decatur. He made a deal with a contractor to accept the home in Decatur as a down payment for building us a new home in Jacksonville. That home, located at 1725 Belmont, cost my parents $7000. We moved into that home in April of 1929 and my parents did not move again until after Daddy retired in 1953.

Our Belmont home was a mansion to me. Mother had gone to the building site everyday to assure that only the best quality of materials was being used. The contractor could have saved money by hiring Mother as foreman. Styled after Colonial Williamsburg, the brick home was two stories with nine sets of white-shuttered windows facing Belmont Avenue. A screened-porch sat back from the driveway, with a brick walkway leading from the drive around flowering shrubbery to the double-columned front entry. Inside arched doorways opened into each of the eight rooms, which were all trimmed with crown moldings. The arch design was repeated in the living room's brick fireplace.

This was the house that became an art gallery for my crayola drawings, a campground for my slumber parties, a quiet refuge for my daydreaming, and a conference center to plan my moral, religious and educational training. My parents seemed to like the conferencing more than they liked the camping. Of course, it may have been that my performance indicated I was better at sleeping than I was at studying.

While attending Davis Grammar School, I came down with the measles and then pneumonia, which caused me to miss a lot of school. Today we have "no pass no play" rules in school for sports; then we had "no attend, no pass" rules for school. So I was put into a class for slow learners. This devastated me because I knew I would never get to be a lawyer if I didn't perform well in school. I could not bring myself to tell

Mother that I had been placed in a special class and for some reason the school had not informed her. But when Elizabeth told her, Mother marched right down to Davis and in her most civil threatening manner had me transferred back to a regular-paced class.

## Mr. B. B.Williams Sr.

I like to think that Mother did this because she believed in my dream to be a lawyer. Maybe she did it so that I would keep believing. In today's society, with so many teen pregnancies and so many kids at risk for failure, I wonder how many mothers fight for their children's hopes? Is it birth and gun control we need or hope and a vision? Or perhaps people who encourage kids toward their goals, like my mother and Mr. B.B.Williams Sr., of Wilmington, North Carolina?

I met Mr.Williams the summer before I turned ten on a train trip to D. C. and New York. Because Daddy worked for Seaboard and the fare was free, our parents would occasionally take us on educational trips. On this particularly boring ride, I entertained myself by swinging through the aisle of the train. I would place a hand on each armrest, pick up my feet, and swing forward to the next armrest. Elizabeth followed close behind, singing with me as we went: "Two, six, nine, the goose drank wine. The monkey chewed tobacco on the streetcar line...."

When I came to an armrest that was positioned up I stopped. In the seat was an older gentleman, dressed in a tweed jacket, with dark slacks. When he noticed me hesitate he reached up and put the armrest down. As I continued down the aisle, I turned, smiled, and said, "Thank you, sir."

"Why, you're a polite young lady. Where're you going?" he inquired.

"We're going to Washington and New York," I responded with my biggest smile.

"Where do you live?" he continued the conversation as he smiled at Elizabeth who was still behind me...or so I thought.

Elizabeth had already turned and headed back down the aisle. Mother had told us never to talk to strangers and Elizabeth never did anything against Mother's rules, but I shouted back over my shoulder as I moved on, "Jacksonville."

As I turned and headed back down the aisle he asked me, "What do you want to be when you grow up?"

"A lawyer," I stated with an air of importance.

"You do?"

"Yes, sir," I said.

"Why do you want to be a lawyer?" he pursued the topic.

I should have known by this point that he was a lawyer; it had not taken him long to charm the unsuspecting.

"I think it would be fun to argue cases," I answered with the confidence of a child that knew there must be some learned skill that allowed others to win arguments.

"There's a lot to law besides arguing cases," he replied.

"Yes, sir," I conceded, "I'm sure there is, but that is the part I like best." Then he laughed out loud.

It was at this point Mr.Williams told me that he was a lawyer. Now I was as interested in him as he was in me. Sitting down across from him, I began to ask him questions, "Have you ever represented a kid? Do you think children should be allowed to testify?" And I told him all about my experience in court with Frannie. We talked on and on.

Finally he said, "Where's your mother and father?"

"Oh, they're down there," I nodded toward the back of the car.

"I'd like to meet them," Mr. Williams stated.

"Well, c'mon," I said, getting up from my seat.

I went first; he followed. Once there he introduced himself to my father. Daddy didn't even shake his hand. I am sure that he must have thought this guy was a salesman or something. "Your daughter tells me she wants to be a lawyer," Mr.Williams began.

My mother interrupted, "Yes, but she doesn't have good eyes. It might be that she can't do all the reading."

"Oh, I bet she can!" Mr.Williams defended me.

"Well, first we'll have to find the money to send her to law school," Daddy, the pragmatic, reasoned.

"That'll come," Mr.Williams replied. Then he took out his wallet and said, "I'll tell you what I want to do. I want to give you some money—for her. Put it in the bank for when she goes to law school, passes the bar and becomes a lawyer, this money will be hers, with interest. If she doesn't, send this money back to me. I might not be around by then, so send it to my son."

Fumbling dumbfoundly, Daddy thanked Mr.Williams and got out a pen to write down his address. Mr.Williams counted out $300. Daddy put the money in his wallet and thanked him again. When we returned to Jacksonville, my parents opened an account for me and deposited the money in my name.

In 1941, when I graduated from law school, I took another train trip to Washington, D.C.. This time I was reporting for my first job, with the U.S. Department of Agriculture, as a lawyer. When I stepped off the train I picked up the luggage I had bought with the $300 Mr. B.B.Williams of

Wilmington had given me. In my purse was a letter from his son, B.B.
Jr.:

> *"Thank you, Miss Edwards, for your letter. I'm glad to hear
> you have secured a job. Yes, my father passed away some time
> ago. But he left behind many, like yourself, who remembered the
> money he gave them. Many have written to acknowledge the
> sense of purpose and vision, that my father instilled in them.
> Good luck in your career, Miss Edwards. I know Dad would be
> pleased that you accomplished your goals."*

I bet Mr. Williams Sr. seriously studied the teachings of wise men,
like King Solomon. It appears this one ancient king knew more about the
root of social reform than all of this nation's psychologists, politicians,
and sociologists combined. In wisdom, Solomon determined, "Without a
vision, the people perish." Could this be the key ingredient missing in
our current educational and social reform programs?

As a child I thought that trains were the only way to get from one
place to the next. But at this end of my journey, I believe that the manner
in which I've traveled has helped me reach my destination more than my
mode of travel.

I realize it wasn't only the trains that helped me get places throughout
my life.

# 5

# SCHOOL DAYS

## Humility's Sufferings

Maybe God designed junior high and puberty to ensure that every adult will have a memory of true humility. No one escapes puberty unscathed. I compare it to discovering there is a pepper grain stuck between my front teeth—at the end of the day. By that time, I have smiled at twenty different individuals. I'm angry that I didn't notice sooner; I'm embarrassed that so many people did; and I realize not one of them told me. Do they go away wondering about my toothbrush?

That's the kind of humility I suffered for three years at Landon Junior High, always wondering, "What do they think of me?" This insecurity was compounded by a slight stuttering problem. It had bothered me for years, but not really anyone else. Until Landon.

That's another characteristic of puberty. Everyone is experiencing insecurity at the same time and the best way to deal with it is to draw attention away from personal problems by pointing out other people's faults. Come to think of it, that happens a lot in political life too. I guess many politicians never get beyond their pubescent stage, which would certainly explain why so many of them get caught with their pants down!

Miss Wilson called on me everyday to answer a question. Wearing a blonde wig that never sat atop her head, but always leaned a little to the left or right, Miss Wilson instructed us in the ways of our forefathers. Which seemed appropriate to me because I thought she had to be as old as one, with a century's worth of personal historical experience. (Of course, at my current age that doesn't seem like much)

"Miss Edwards?"

"Yeeess...Miss Wilson?"

I looked up from where I sat. Miss Wilson cocked her head to the left, making her wig appear straight. She was waiting on me. I was expected to stand up beside my desk while answering but I knew if I did the class would roar in laughter.

When I stuttered the kids laughed at me, kids who had been my friends at Davis Grammar School, who never once before even indicated they noticed I stuttered. They now would point fingers and howl as I stumbled over my words. A daily occurrence in Miss Wilson's class.

I stood up.

"Miss Edwards, would you please tell the class who helped draft the Declaration of Independence?"

"Thththomas Jejejefferson." Bubbles of laughter began in front of me. Warm blood mottled my downy white skin like water rapids splotching sun dried rocks. Laughter erupted, exploding all over the room, like a hot coke that's been shaken and quickly opened. The class laughed not only because of my stuttering problem, but because of my cohorts, Alice Court and Estella Mae Bowles.

I turned around. Both girls jumped back into their seats, laughing. Alice's laughing created a dime-sized sinkhole in her right cheek—her trademark dimple.

"I didn't do nothing!" Estella held up her hands in mock surrender.

My skirt began to slip. Moving my left palm across the back of my skirt I felt tightly-woven silk instead of coarsely-woven cotton. Frantically grasping with my left hand and pulling with my right, I zipped up my skirt. Hurriedly sitting back down, I covered my head and embarrassment with my long arms.

Alice and Estella, sitting behind me on either side, would often unzip my skirt or unbutton my blouse as I stood answering Miss Wilson. So along with identifying "Thomas Jefferson" as the drafter of the Declaration of Independence, I had to endure a draft on my backside. Those humiliations were worse than pepper grain stuck between my teeth.

After hearing these stories through the anguished tears of a shy teenager, Mother decided something definitely needed to be done about my stuttering. So she hit Daddy up for private lessons with Mrs. Case, who taught speech classes at Jacksonville Conservatory. With a confidence in me, like that of Mr. B.B. Williams, Sr.'s, I credit Mrs. Justine Case for helping me get places in life.

But Mother received the same response she always did when asking Daddy for something extra, "There's no money for it, Claudeia." I think he just gave her that reply because he knew Mother was resourceful enough to figure out some way to pay for the things she really wanted.

This was during the Depression when there was very little money anywhere. It seemed to me every time the radio was turned on we would hear about another suicide. Almost everyday someone would come to our house looking for work and for food.

One day a young man with a dog came asking," Do you have some work I could do for you, Ma'am?"

"No, sir, I sure don't," Mother replied.

"Yard work or something around the house?"

Mother shook her head no but said, "I'd be more than pleased to share some food with you and your dog."

I will never forget the look in that man's dark brown eyes as he tipped his musty frayed hat and said, " No, thank ya, Ma'am. If I don't work, I don't eat."

Then he turned away from our front door and headed back down Belmont Avenue. His was a more naked humility than the one I had experienced at school.

I watched my friend Alice Court go through this same kind of exposure. Alice's father, a C.P.A., lost his job during the 1930's. For awhile the Court family seemed unaffected, but within a year they lost their home. I remember Alice telling me they only ate one meal a day, never any meat, only beans and a snack. Alice never had any new clothes for school, and while the rest of us were attending the Saturday matinee for five cents at the Jacksonville theater, Alice stayed home.

Except once. I felt so bad for her that I placed a nickel of my lunch money on the floor where I knew Alice would find it. She did and that Saturday she went to the matinee with us.

But the next time I tried this, Alice picked up the nickel and threw it at me, shouting, "I know what you're doing, Rufe! Keep it yourself!" Then she ran crying towards the girls' bathroom.

That should have been Alice's worse moment, but it came later—the day she appeared at school, sorrow creasing her forehead and eyes, grief firmly holding back her face from any pleasure.

"What's the matter, Alice?" I asked as I rifled through my locker searching for my literature book.

"Daddy gave Dixie away last night. He said we couldn't afford to keep her." Alice turned her head away, staring vacantly at the near empty hallway. Her voice cracked softly, like a new egg, tears plopped from her chin onto her red cotton blouse, creating blotches of loss.

"Oh, Alice, I'm so sorry," I said. Afraid of her naked emotion, I didn't look directly at her. "Aw, forget it, Rufe. I'm sure Dixie'll be fine," Alice commented, quickly masking her embarrassment and emotion.

Jerking my book from the bottom of the pile, I flipped my locker shut. Silently we walked away from our lockers and from her humiliation. At that moment, I knew it was the loss of Dixie, the family dog, that Alice grieved more than any of her other lost possessions.

## Mastery Learning

How did Mother find the money for me to take Speech classes with the locally renowned Mrs. Case? It seems incredible now, but she did it by taking in a boarder— Mr. McCall. He was Landon's new Assistant Principal, who had just moved to Jacksonville from South Carolina. Elizabeth and I had always felt some equality in numbers with our parents, two against two, but now we were outnumbered.

Mother might have initially taken in Mr. McCall for extra income, but ultimately I think she enjoyed the power she held over us. Now we were never going to associate with people who didn't meet with Mother's approval. Because we were Mother and Mr. McCall's most common subject, Liz and I became the topic of mealtime discussion. Mr. McCall would give a daily school report to Mother. Most parents believe that they need to release the reins of parenting by the time their kids start high school. Not our mother. She had us corralled, at home and at school.

Yet, it was the extra income that provided the means for me to attend The Conservatory, and if I had to pick just one thing that helped me attain self-confidence, it would be the lessons I took from Mrs. Case. Many educators today believe that if you just teach a child to value his/her self that alone will instill confidence. My question to them is what has the child got to be confident about?

Never have I been paid for a job just because I showed up and sat in my office all day. I had to perform, produce. Teaching kids to value themselves purely because they are human is a disservice to them. Society will expect them to perform, or should. I believe the kids of today know this. When they are singing songs and reciting poems about how "great it is to be me," maybe they are secretly thinking, "Why is it so great?"

That is what Mrs. Case did for me; she taught me to achieve.

"Rufe, don't be so frustrated. Mastering anything is a process. First, you set your goals, then you practice."

"But, Mrs. Case, I did practice," I whined.

"No protests allowed, Rufe. Accept honest criticism and then practice some more and then when you think you've got it, practice some more. Practice this page for next week along with the others I've marked," Mrs. Case's blushing pink nails folded down a page in my book.

Never once did she call me aside and whisper, "Now, Rufe, you have just got to believe in yourself. If you would just believe in yourself, you would overcome your problems."

No. Mrs. Justine Case, who was married to an attorney, who played the lead in many of Jacksonville's Little Theater plays, expected laborious efforts, "Rufe, you must practice your breathing. How long did you practice last week?"

Apparently unaware of my self-esteem, she was often intensely demanding.

"If you want to be a lawyer, Rufe, you must first learn to speak correctly. The ability to speak forcefully and well is important to the success of a trial lawyer."

"Ssprring rrides noo horrses doown the hill..." I was hesitating over my words.

"Enunciate each word, Rufe. Project your voice so that I can hear you from here," she would stand in a corner across the room, instructing me. "Try it again."

"Spring rides no horses down the hill but comes on foot, a gooose-girrrl ssstill..."

"Much better, Rufe. Now again."

Mrs. Case taught me the skills of public speaking. When I was successful at enunciating Mrs. Case noticed. Self-esteem was a natural overflow of my achievements. Mrs. Case showed me how I could be successful.

As did many of my teachers—by teaching me I could do something. I could enunciate; I could read; I could research; I could add. It was through these skills that I gained self-confidence. Self-esteem was not considered a subject to master; but it was by mastering a subject that I gained my self-esteem. Perhaps if we actually were successful at teaching kids to read, to write, to research, to add—then they too would have the confidence required to be achievers.

## Testing New Confidences

After two years of lessons with Mrs. Case I felt confident that I would indeed become a lawyer one day. This confidence was boosted by the time I was in high school because of women in the news. Like many families, ours owned a radio. It was over this radio that I first heard of Amelia Earhart, the first woman to fly solo across the Pacific, and Hattie Caraway, the first woman elected to the U.S. Senate. Mother had always taught Elizabeth and me that ours would be a new age for women in the work force. As I listened to the craggy radio voice report the achievements of women, I believed Mother to be prophetic.

In my new enthusiasm and with Mrs. Case's encouragement, I auditioned for many of Landon's school plays. Though I tried out many times, I received numerous rejections. One afternoon I received a phone call from someone who identified themselves as the director of Landon's upcoming drama production.

"Rufe, we've heard much about your ability and our desire is that you play the lead for us."

"Why, certainly, I'd love too!" I exclaimed, projecting much too loudly over the phone. The lead? I was ecstatic. "When do you want me to audition?"

"Oh, no need for that," the director stated. "Just show up for practice after school on Monday. Okay?"

"Fine, fine," I said. "See ya Monday."

As soon as I was off the phone with the director, I was on it again to the neighborhood. I called up everyone I knew, including my Sunday School teacher, to tell them how much God was smiling on me that day. I was right about the smiling part, but it wasn't God.

When Liz came home and I told her of my good fortune, she wasn't just smiling; she was possessed by hysterical laughter.

"That wasn't a director, Rufe," Liz laughingly threw back her head until her dark curly hair fell between her shoulder blades. "It was me!" she shrilled, squeezing my bare thigh with the palm of her right hand, obviously pleased with her own performance.

I was playing a part I didn't want, in a production staged for Liz's entertainment.

I felt enraged that Liz would treat me in such a cruel fashion. Would my esteem always be sacrificed for her benefit?

Determination and sibling pride encouraged me to continue auditioning for plays at Landon High. And sibling rivalry encouraged me to continue seeking public recognition.

## The Coveted Greeley

Which is why as a freshman I competed for the coveted Greeley Cup. Named after the great American Orator and editor, Horace Greeley, the silver cup was offered in a contest at Landon each year to the student who demonstrated superior speaking skills. As a freshman I decided that I wanted my name on that cup.

Each contestant was required to do a performance based upon a famous character from Classical American literature. I choose "Rip Van Winkle."

For several months of my freshman year I would come home from school and sequester myself in my room to practice until supper time. Standing in front of a large mirror, I would recite the words like a mantra chant. Returning to the isolation once more after the meal, I added intonations, varying my voice projection to create drama. Finally, toward the last of the preparation time, I learned each word. Like a spirit-filled preacher I knew just when to speak hypnotically and when to call forth the powers of hell.

I must have done a good job too, because three days before the contest those demons afflicted me. I had the flu, fever gratis.

Handing me an aspirin, Mother advised, "Rufe, I know you've practiced long and hard for this, but I'm not going to allow you to attend school with a fever."

"But, Mother, if the fever's gone, then can I go?" I implored.

"We'll see, Rufe," she answered flatly, as she snapped shut the yellow tinned Bayer lid. "Let's just wait and see."

The morning of the competition Mother greeted me with a thermometer. As soon as she walked out of my room, I grabbed that glass-tipped probe by its end and swished it around in a glass of water Mother had placed by my bed. When she returned to chart my vitals, the mercury beads held at 100.4 degrees.

"Pleeaasse, Mother, I just have to go," I said throwing back my ivory-tufted chenille bedspread.

"All right, Rufe," Mother sighed with resignation. "But first I'm going to make you something to soothe your throat. It'll help your performance, too" she said, exiting through my doorway for the second time that morning.

As I dressed, Mother fixed me a hot toddy, like the ones the doctor had prescribed for my father when he had a bout with pneumonia. Mother was often heavy-handed with the brandy in her cooking and this morning was no exception. The fact that I had not eaten in three days helped heighten my enjoyment of Mother's brew.

By the time I arrived at school students were already filing into the auditorium for the program. Mrs. Case, my mother, and five of her friends came to cheer me on.

As I walked toward the front row, Mrs. Eastman, the Dean of Girls at Landon, stopped me. Of course, Dean Eastman, taut, with a charm school posture that appeared to make her 5'5" frame stretch to a 5' 7" height, and a voice as thunderous as a midnight migraine, often stopped the multitudes in transit.

"Rufe, where've you been? We've missed you for three days now."

"I'm, okay, Mrs. Eastman. I've been sick for a few days," I stammered.

Dean Eastman's nostrils flared. I silently wondered if Eastman was reacting to the Vicks Vapor Rub I had on or if her nostrils always flared when she was mad?

Holding my elbows with sweaty palms, I dismissed myself, "'Cuse me, please, Dean Eastman. I better sit down now." Mr. McCall was walking to the microphone to begin the assembly.

"I suppose you'd best sit down, Miss Edwards." Dean Eastman nodded me on by, breathing in deeply as I pressed past her.

My nylons snagged against the edge of the dingy pine spring-hinged seat as I sat down. Rotating my left ankle, I checked for a run. Luckily there was none. Alice leaned over the armrest and pushed on my shoulder, "They called your name, Rufe. Better get on up there."

"They did?" I asked, reaching behind me to make sure my skirt was still zipped.

"I didn't hear them."

"Honest, Rufe," Alice assured me. Smiling, she said, "Good luck, girl."

It wasn't luck I needed. A shot of New Orleans Chicory coffee would have served me better. I almost fell off the stage three different times during my presentation of ol' drunken Rip. Even if I had never said a word, I think the students would have given me the Greeley Cup for my physical interpretation of an inebriated person.

Ending my presentation, I looked at my classmates; their fingers were rubbing eyes wet with laughter. I looked over at Mother with her red lipsticked closed-mouth smile, her eyes bright with beastly pride, her white-gloved hands clapping. As I stood at the edge of the stage, waiting for the clapping to stop and hoping it never would, I looked in the back of the auditorium and saw Dean Eastman— neither clapping nor smiling.

She was not happy with my physical interpretation. I didn't know why. As I descended the three steps that led up to the stage, Miss Eastman motioned me towards her. Alice turned as I walked past my previous seat. Mother saw me from across the aisle, got up and headed towards the back of the auditorium. I slowed my pace down. Mother reached Dean Eastman before I did. Pressing the brass bar across the exit door, Mother, then Dean Eastman, stepped out into the empty hallway. Leaving behind the laughter of my classmates, I opened the right door and joined Mother.

"Mrs. Edwards, I'm afraid that I'm going to have to disqualify your daughter," Miss Eastman said.

Mother took the news well, I thought. Brushing off her left forearm with her still gloved right hand, she cast those periwinkle eyes straight at Dean Eastman and stated rather than asked, "Because she missed three days of school."

"No, Mrs. Edwards," Dean Eastman spoke with a quiet but still reverberating voice, "because I believe Rufe *is* drunk."

They both looked at me. I grinned at such a ridiculous accusation. How could I be drunk? I was only fourteen. Dean Eastman had obviously been sniffing more than just Vick's Vapor Rub!

"Drunk?" Mother questioned, her mind trying to figure out where I would have gotten liquor from. "Rufe, couldn't possibly be drunk. She's been at home with me all week, sick, like I already told you, Miss Eastman. I'm telling you she's had nothing to eat for three days now." Mother's voice was increasing in volume and velocity. "And not much to drink, except for this morning when I made her drink...". Abruptly Mother stopped.

"Made her drink what?" Miss Eastman inquired.

"A toddy," Mother answered with the hushed voice of a librarian. "For her sore throat."

They both looked at me. I was still grinning.

If I hadn't felt so good, I probably would have felt worse about being disqualified for the Greeley Cup as a freshman. Mother talked with Dean Eastman and Mr. McCall. She rightfully assumed all the blame and kept me from getting expelled.

I did go on to win the Greeley Cup as a senior. Mother put the cup on the mantel in our living room the night I won it so that all who entered could see the Edwards' name engraved on the silver cup.

"We're so proud of you, Rufe," Mother exclaimed. "You've worked long and hard for this special honor." She placed the cup underneath her most prized possession, a reproduction of the Mona Lisa. It looked as if Mona might be pleased with me too; she kept smiling in a twisted fashion.

At three a.m. I found out that Mona had actually been smirking at me. A loud "Gggruggh...Thud" woke the whole house up. Running downstairs, we heard a mellow "Chimmmm" echo throughout the living room.

Turning on the lamp beside the sofa, Daddy bellowed, "My Gracious!"

"Is it broke, Charlie?" Mother shrieked.

Stumbling through the arched doorway, I focused my eyes enough to see Mona casting her eyes back over the top of the frame at me—still smiling. She had propelled herself off the wall onto my cherished Greeley Cup, knocking it against the brick fireplace.

"Oh, Mother! My trophy!" I cried.

I spotted a silver handle broken off and lying next to the claw-footed end table. Mother picked up the cup; Daddy the picture. Mona was fine; Greeley had a side bender.

I never did get to enjoy my Greeley Cup. It cost Daddy $200 to have the handle replaced and the side dent hammered out. Mona was hung right back in her place of honor, nary a scratch on her. Unlike me, I don't think she cared much for competition.

Striving to be noticed in all my endeavors, I flourished in competition. Whether a silver cup or prized role, I sought out opportunities for recognition. Perhaps that is why my classmates voted me "Most likely to succeed" when I graduated from Landon High in June of 1937. I don't think I deserved the title. A more fitting one would have been "Most likely to try."

Mother probably would say I should have won, "Most trying!"

# 6

# ACHIEVEMENTS

## Losses and Gains

I first met Mac in a summer term English class at the University of Georgia. We were studying Homer's *Iliad*, but Mac always told everyone we were studying Homer's *Idiot*. Sitting in class, I tried to pay attention to the instructor, but found Mac far more interesting. Besides his clean shaven appearance, I noticed Mac's chocolate eyes, auburn hair, and a smile as genuine as a preacher on Monday. His long, lean body seemed fitted for even longer legs, but Mac's legs were short by comparison, more calf than thighs. Mac stood about 5'10".

Mac's gentleness and clean-shaven appearance drew me to him. As a little girl, I had been frightened by beards. My mother's grandfather had a chest-length white beard. Mother was very close to her grandparents and when we lived in Decatur we often took the train to Fayetteville to visit them.

"Now, Rufe," Mother turned down the lacy part of my anklet, "it hurts Grandpa Clark's feelings when you scream at him like you do."

"My stomach hurts, Momma. I think I'm sick."

"You're not sick, Rufe. That's fear. Fear will make a perfectly healthy person sicker than a mad dog. Why are you so afraid of Grandpa?" Placing her hand beneath my chin Mother looked into my eyes, like she was staring into a mirror. I wondered who she saw in my eyes—her or me?

"Momma...."

"Mother, Rufe."

"I don't know how come I'm so scared. I don't want to hurt Grandpa. His face scares me. Grandpa looks like a mean old God or something."

"Rufe, you're five years old. It's time you put these screaming tantrums aside. You're not a baby, are you?"

"No, ma'am."

"Well only a baby would be scared of something as harmless as a soft furry beard. Now promise me you won't cry when we get to Fayetteville."

"Yes, ma'am," I promised, crossing my ankles just in case I proved unfaithful.

Every trip to Fayetteville to see my great-grandparents resulted in the same scenario. As the train rolled into Fayetteville's station, I would see Grandfather Clark standing along with Grandmother, watching for us. Forgetting my promise, I would take off through the aisles of the train, screaming and running as fast as I could to the rear of the train. Grandfather Clark's white beard frightened me. As a child I never would go near Santa Claus. Wonder where I'll run to screaming when I get to heaven and find God with a flowing white beard?

Years later the old Fayetteville depot was moved closer to town, all the rails were taken up. But I've heard people say that sometimes they can still hear the old whistle blow and if they are really quiet, they can hear the piercing cry of a child. "Sounds like the child's scared to death," they say. I know just how that child feels.

After class that first day in English, Mac walked out the door behind me.

"Are you a teacher?" he asked.

"A teacher?" I laughed. Just how old did I look?

"I'm sorry, ma'am. I just thought maybe you were a teacher taking a refresher course. I didn't mean to offend you," Mac flushed.

But I was offended. I couldn't believe that I had just wasted a class period giving this fellow the hairy eyeball and he thought I was old enough to be a teacher!

"I forgive you," I lied, not bothering to cross my ankles this time. "This is my first term at Georgia. I just transferred from Duke."

"From Duke?" he inquired.

## Duke

When I graduated from Landon High in 1937, the school was considered a substandard school academically. (I've often wondered who decides these issues. Is there a committee of retired blue-haired teachers and jowl-endowed superintendents who hold covert meetings?)

In order to reach my goal as a lawyer of distinction, I needed to attend a challenging university. I chose Duke University in Durham, North

Carolina, and even obtained an academic scholarship to help defray the exorbitant expense of about $3,000 a year.

In 1937, all the women were segregated to the East Campus at Duke. I was assigned to Jarvis Dormitory. Before I left home, Daddy and I had a fireside chat.

"Sending you to a private college is more than I can afford, Rufe. If you hadn't already gotten that scholarship, I couldn't afford the tuition and fees, much less a sorority. There will be absolutely no extras, young lady." Then he added his signature quote, "Time's getting short and my money shorter."

While I promised that I would not pledge, I'm sure Daddy never understood what his decision cost me. Sororities were a tightly woven fabric worn with pride by Duke's female student body. Did Duke's sororities protect their members from cold isolation, or did Duke's sororities trap their members into the straight-jacket control of conformity? Not pledging at Duke left me feeling as obvious and unwelcome as a nudist in church—and as cold.

But my roommates at Jarvis Dormitory were more than concerned about keeping me warm. The only way I knew to deal with the other girls having so much money and me having none was to play to their benevolent nature. One night, as the girls from our floor sat around eating a pound cake my mother had sent me, they started to discuss getting their furs out of storage before winter chills arrived. I just listened a while.

"Fur coats!" I exclaimed. "Y'all mean to tell me I need a coat around here? First, I have to wear shoes, which we don't need in Jacksonville, now I need a coat?"

"Don't you have a fur, Rufe?" a tinny voice asked.

"Gosh, what do I need a fur coat in Jacksonville for? Fur would make me sweat more than a Mississippi ditch digger!"

Those girls organized faster than a Women's Mission Society. Within a week a collection had started at Jarvis Dormitory to buy me a winter coat.

"Rufe," my roommate insisted, "you better tell the girls you already have a coat, or by next week, you'll have a new one."

So my ruse was over. I thanked everyone for their offer, but assured them that I had come to Durham, not only wearing shoes, but also with a winter coat—albeit not a fur one.

But the assertion by Jacksonville's blue-hairs that Landon High was academically inferior in college preparatory proved true for me. At Landon I had excelled; at Duke I was almost expelled. I had signed up for Spanish II because I had taken Spanish I in high school, but I did so

poorly in Spanish II that I dropped the class for fear of flunking. By my
sophomore year at Duke, I had lost my academic scholarship. Daddy's
allowance of a dollar a week was insufficient to meet my needs.

So I approached the Dean about obtaining a part-time job. The Dean
sent a list of students looking for work to all the businesses in Durham.
My name was added to the list. Within the week I received a request card
in the mail.

"Please report Monday at 3:00 p.m. for modeling. Third Floor."

Modeling! Finally someone sees my inner beauty, I thought. I told all
my dorm mates that women blessed with brains and beauty, like myself,
were finally being appreciated. They all looked at me like I'd been run
over by the turnip truck.

"Rufe, you can borrow my navy wool skirt," Carolyn smiled.

"Yeah, and I'd love to fix your hair for you, okay?" another added.

"Oh, would you? I never know what to do with what little hair I
have."

So by 2:00 Monday afternoon, Jarvis Dormitory was busier than a
beauty parlor during Cotillion season. Girls were running the halls with
blouses, shoes, clips, rouge, and more red lipstick than Barnum & Bailey
ever used.

"Here, these pumps will match, I think."

"Try my pearl earrings."

"Oh, Rufe, you do look so...so...you look really nice. Honest."

I thanked my friends, took my last 50 cents and called a taxi for a ride
to downtown Durham. I found the third floor of the department store
without any problem. As I stepped off the elevator, I looked at the round
racks of men's gray and brown suits. Looking to my left I saw men's
socks, ties, and necessities. To my right was a fellow I recognized as a
student at Duke.

"'Cuse me, sir," I began. "I was supposed to report to this floor for a
modeling job at three o'clock. Do you have any idea where I'm to report
to?"

"A modeling job?"

"Well, yes, sir. I received this card last week about a modeling job
being available."

"Maybe we're working together," he said. "That's what I'm here
for—a modeling job. The manager said they needed someone to model
Hart Schaffner and Marx suits."

I flipped the card over to read the addressee again.

"Mr. Rufe Edwards," I read aloud. My face flushed, my heart kicked
into 75 rpm's, I swallowed my last bit of saliva. Coughing with my head

down, I retreated to the far corner of the elevator, then pushed the button for the main floor.

*Mister.* Why had I not seen the Mr. before? As I walked back to east campus, I blasted myself for being so vain, then blasted my mother for giving me such an ambiguous name. I had been the only girl at Landon High to receive a tie pin from Jacksonville's merchants at graduation. Rufe. What a name! The only person I ever met with a more challenging name, I married—James *Norfleet* McCombs.

By the end of my sophomore year I decided to leave Duke. Without an academic scholarship, without furs, without a passing grade in Spanish II, and without a glamorous modeling career, I felt like I might never finish college with a law degree. And that is how I found myself studying Homer's *Iliad* in Athens the summer of 1939.

### Romance in Athens

"What's your major?" Mac pushed open a door and stepped aside.

Moist heat pressed against us. The humidity wrapped my clothes around me like a warm compress. "Law. I'm headed for law school. Right now I'm studying economics."

I heard a woodpecker's rap echoing from shadows above. "What about you?"

"Business. I hope to finish up next June. Are you from Durham?"

"No. Jacksonville, sort of. That's where my folks live. My daddy works for Seaboard Railroad. We used to live in Decatur though. My mother's family's from Fayetteville, Georgia. You remember Governor Hugh Dorsey? That's Mother's cousin."

I walked backwards for two steps so I could see Mac's face when I told him my political ancestry.

"Truly?" His grin dovetailed his cheeks into his broad forehead. His brown eyes turned downward. Mac's face was bittersweet; his smile made his eyes frown. Like a classical mime, Mac could evoke laughter and tears with the same expressive gesture.

"Honest. I know not everybody likes Mr. Dorsey's politics, but I think he's a good lawyer and a decent man."

"I trust your judgment, ma'am. Perhaps you'll follow in his footsteps and be Georgia's first woman governor," Mac teased.

"Perhaps," I agreed. "But first I've got to serve my terms here in Athens."

"Athens isn't so bad. I've lived here all my life and I turned out all right, don't you think?" Mac didn't wait for a response. "At least we have a couple of places to go and watch a picture show. Would you like to go sometime? Say this Saturday? I work the switchboard here on campus every night except for Saturdays."

"Well," I said and glanced past Mac at two students loudly mocking some professor. "Let me check with my sister Liz and see what her plans are. We room together at Cobb Dorm. Can I let you know after class tomorrow?"

"Sure. But don't use your sister as an excuse; she's welcome to come along and chaperone if she likes," Mac offered. "Don't forget to read Homer's hexed Idiot tonight!"

That day Mac and I began our half-a-century romance. Mac lived in Athens with his parents on Lumpkin Street across from the university. Mac's father, William David McCombs, was a mill worker. His mother, Mittie Annie Elizabeth Senia (Smith) McCombs, was a homemaker. Both of their families were from South Carolina.

Mac was the youngest of four children. One of his brothers, William Fletcher, had drowned in the Oconee River, August 1, 1920, when Mac was only a year and half old. John David, another brother, was four years older than Mac, and Grace Vivian, their sister, was ten years older than Mac.

Like so many other families, Mac's carried a generational curse—alcoholism. Mac's father and brother suffered from it. Which is why I think Mac and Grace were so nurturing of each other throughout their years together. When they were old enough, Mac and Grace financially supported the family whenever their father lost his job or liquidated his paycheck. Mac and Grace developed their own unit within the family.

They were as close as any brother and sister I have ever met. They bonded the way veterans who've fought the same battles do. They never talked much of their personal experiences, but they remembered the locations of each other's private scars. Perhaps it was the memory of the scars that forced Mac and Grace to only speak of the treasures they found together in childhood.

Treasures like Mac's pet hen Molly. Although my daddy always thought that we were just inside the doorway of poverty, Mac's family had crossed the threshold. Puppies were too costly to feed, so Mac told me that as a toddler he found himself a friend in Molly, a red hen. Molly listened to Mac when no one else made the time to.

"Molly was a Rhode Island Red—the only one in my whole neighborhood, maybe in all of Athens. Having her was better than having a shiny red wagon," Mac's brown eyes flickered as he recalled his beloved pet. "Molly went everywhere with me. Usually because I was carrying her, but if I didn't she would follow me just like a puppy. If I was on my scooter, Molly would be just two steps behind me. And if I sat on the front stoop, Molly would jump right into my lap!" Mac's laughter was deep and mellow. "I'd just hold her right underneath my own left wing and stroke her auburn feathers."

I've always believed that a kind man is never cruel to children or animals, and Mac was the kindest man I ever met. Our daughter's childhood friends often told me that Mac was more nurturing than any of the mothers they had ever known—me included. I believe Mac developed his nurturing instinct while caring for Molly.

While growing up Mac also had a couple of pet cows, all of whom he named Betty. They were gifts from a neighboring family. After the spring birth of one calf, Mac changed the name of his calf from Betty to Rose. When Mac's father lost his job, the family became concerned about where the next meal would come from. Mr. McCombs had a solution—Rose. She was butchered and prepared for a Sunday meal.

As everyone cut into their steak, Mac exclaimed, "Poor, poor, Rose." In unison, everyone at the table groaned and pushed their plates away. No one ate dinner that night. The next day Grandpa McCombs bartered away Rose's ribs and rump to the neighbors. Mac told me he never saw any of his pet cows served on a platter again; no matter how little food they could afford to buy.

The treasured memories of childhood embraced Mac and Grace, providing them with the affection they had missed. Because of John D's alcoholism, Mac nor Grace had much to do with him during those periods of life. Maybe they both were afraid that the family curse had more control over them than they had over it. Later during our married life Mac faced the family demon without Grace. That was one battle Mac had to face and conquer all on his own.

Mac attended the University of Georgia by obtaining a loan from the Athen's Lions Club each term. Then he would work to pay it back before the next term so that he could borrow it again. His goal was to get his Business degree as quickly as possible. Mac graduated in June of 1940. And I obtained my economics degree while finishing my freshman year in law school. (At that time a student's senior year as an undergraduate could double as their freshman year in law school.)

Mac immediately found a position in Athens selling insurance. I continued with my schooling, but Mac quickly became dissatisfied with his work. One summer evening as Mac walked me home from church, he told me about his frustrations.

"Rufe, I don't think I can continue selling insurance. What good did it do me to spend all those years in college just to back a hearse up to someone's door? I don't want to do this anymore, " Mac squeezed off the end of his rolled cigarette and lit it.

"What'll you do Mac?"

Blowing a cloud of smoke away from me, he said, "There a company in Boston—Liberty Mutual Insurance. If you'd help me draft a letter of application, maybe I could get a job with them."

"Of course, I'll help, Mac. But what'll I do if they hire you?"

As we continued walking, Mac recounted how much he hated making cold calls, trying to coerce people into spending money they didn't have on insurance they didn't need. But I wasn't listening. I couldn't hear Mac's words over those screaming at me from within—*"He's going to leave you; he's going to leave you."*

Mac was the first serious boyfriend I ever had; certainly the first that had sparked rushing feelings deep inside of me. Mother had been so strict that any boys that Liz or I were interested in remained just that—an interest. Mother would let us go to church and school with males, but that was about all.

Other than Daddy, Mac was the only man I'd ever been physically close to. Oh, I had kissed a boy on the sly a time to two, okay, maybe more. But those kisses were stolen and sought more out of curiosity than commitment. It was different with Mac—with Mac, I wanted more *and* I was willing to give more.

Not that *more* then means the same as it does today. Or even that my being physically close to Mac meant then what it means today. Our physical relationship was limited by the mores of the society in which we lived, and by our own refined morality. Holding hands was acceptable, as was a discreet kiss, but Mac and I never confused hand-holding with fondling. Mac was too much of a gentleman for that, which made me love him even more.

Our physical closeness was more about the awareness of an absence of territories. We felt comfortable around each other. Sometimes I couldn't tell where my space left off and Mac's began. It was the feeling of oneness—not the act of oneness—we shared. We saved the other for marriage, which at this particular moment, looked as though it might be with someone other than Mac. Why did I agree to write his stupid letter?

We walked down to the Oconee River, the same river where Mac's brother, Fletcher, had drowned and I sat upon a boulder underneath an elm tree to write the letter that ultimately would send Mac away. I was tempted to make the letter illegible so that I could make sure Mac would stay with me in Athens. But I knew he was miserable in his current position.

"Rufe?" Mac leaned against the boulder, smashing the cigarette butt into the red clay with his right heel. "If Liberty wants me to come to Boston, will you go?"

"What are you asking me, Mac?" My finger turned white around the pen. "You want me to leave law school?"

"No, Rufe, that's not what I mean. I'd never ask you to do that. I know how hard you've worked to get into law school. I'd never compete with a girl's dream.

"I was just wondering if maybe...do you think...could you include me in your plans?" Mac's frowning crescent eyes betrayed his timid sad-happy grin.

"You want to go to law school too?" I laughed.

"Aw, Rufe. C'mon." A brilliant cardinal landed nearby. The male cardinal had spotted an earthworm that my own eyes hadn't seen until the worm was stretched between home and heaven in the cardinal's beak. "I don't think I could go off to Boston unless I know at some point in the future you would join me. I want to know if you will marry me, Rufe?"

"Today?" I teased, uncomfortable with my own feelings of longing, happiness, and surprise. Mac stared at the cardinal, avoiding my swipe.

"Mac," I slid down from the boulder, "I would be honored to marry you." Then we both watched as the cardinal flew off with the worm.

Liberty Mutual did hire Mac. He was to begin training as soon as possible in their claims department in Boston, Massachusetts, for $125 a month. Boston seemed a world away. Letting Mac leave me in Athens was harder than I had anticipated, so I made arrangements to travel with Mac by train as far as Washington. We planned on sharing a meal together in D.C., then I would head back for Athens while he traveled on to Boston. We took Southern's day coach.

When I arrived back in Athens I was summoned to the Dean's office. I had never met the Dean before so I was surprised and excited by the summons. As I sat across from the Dean in a sparsely decorated office—two pine chairs sat directly in front of Dean's pine desk and chair—I wondered if perhaps I had won some special recognition for my work as student editor of the Georgia Bar Journal.

But once the Dean addressed me, I knew right away that the kind of recognition I had earned wasn't honorable.

"Miss Edwards," Dean's lips were drawn so tightly that the corners of his mouth were white, "it has come to my attention that you were absent from your dorm room last night. Is that correct?"

"Yes, sir. My fiancée left for a job in Boston and I went as far as D.C. with him to say good-bye." My voice trembled with the emotion of having left Mac and fear of the power this man had over me.

"Miss Edwards, you understand that the university makes a commitment to the parents for the safety of our students."

Unconsciously, tapping the point of his pencil on his desk, Dean waited for a reply.

"Yes, sir." Was he worried the train would derail? Had he called my parents?

"Well, then you can see that we certainly cannot allow young women such as yourself to be traveling throughout the night with men, alone, unprotected and unchaperoned. You do understand this, don't you, Miss Edwards?" He drawled out the *Miss* for emphasis.

"Dean, sir, I was not on the train all night with a man. Mac and I took the day coach to D.C.—I returned at night, alone."

"Now, Miss Edwards, no reason to get defensive. You're not on trial. We, here, at the university are only interested in your safety. Certainly you understand that we cannot have any impropriety amongst our student body. I'm not accusing you or your fiancée of anything illicit....It's just that ... parents look at these things when choosing a university for their sons and daughters. You understand. We must maintain the highest of standards." The left corner of his lip ticked back and forth as he spoke.

"Dean, I can assure you that nothing, absolutely nothing, improper has occurred. Forgive me for any digression from university rules that may have occurred. I promise it will not happen again." I lowered my eyes.

"Fine, fine, Miss Edwards," he sighed. "Make sure that it doesn't. Otherwise you could lose your standing at Georgia."

"Yes, sir." I felt shame for acts I had not committed. Although I did understand his position, I doubted the sincerity of his personal concern for me. Anger drenched over me when I realized that just by his word alone I could have been expelled from the University of Georgia.

"Thank you for coming in, Miss Edwards. You may go now."

I left the Dean's office thankful to still be a student at Georgia, but fully aware that rules established to shield people could, in the hands of a tyrant, become swords of destruction. The Dean, his tight-lipped reprimand aside, had not been unreasonable with me, but a lesser man might have been.

## Lumpkin Law School

My accomplishments at Georgia's Lumpkin Law School filled me with self-esteem as I grew more knowledgeable of the law. As with any field, law has its specialties and I found myself especially drawn to civil law. During the three years I was at Lumpkin, I served as student editor of the Georgia Bar Journal. My work as editor increased my interest in law and its function in society.

My days consisted of rising before morning's light, I used those early soundless hours to read. Usually by eight a.m., I had breakfast and headed off for class or the library. Often I would spend the day at the office of the Georgia Bar Journal, pouring over the latest articles, or writing one myself. I was no longer anticipating the fulfillment of a vision; my dream became my reality. My passion for studying the law was so intense that my dating Mac, prior to his leaving for Boston, was limited to once during the week and just a few hours over the week-end. Sundays were reserved for church attendance, so even if Mac was with me, God was watching us.

At the end of my freshman year in law school, I decided to attempt the bar examination. In those days one did not have to finish law school to be a lawyer, one only had to pass the bar. It cost $35 in registration fees. Today $35 will buy me dinner and a movie, but in 1940, $35 was a lot of money—my parent's money. I was determined not to waste my daddy's money. Daddy was right about money being short, but it seemed to me that time was getting even shorter as I prepared for the bar exam.

Earlier that summer my parents rented me a room along Jacksonville's beach. It was just a room in the home of a widowed woman. My parent's hope was that the calm and quiet of the beach would allow me to concentrate on preparing for the bar. I stayed there for a month, often studying through the nights.

By the end of that month, I could almost recite the complete Georgia Code. God had blessed me with a remarkable memory. If a case were cited, I could recall the page number and where on the page that particular case could be found, as well as all the details regarding it. At the end of that month, I only worried about my ability to apply this new knowledge to the questions on the bar examination. It was a big enough worry to keep me awake each night and make me wish I hadn't decided to take the exam so soon.

On June 25, 1940, I arrived at the Superior Courtroom in Athens at 7:15 a.m. The test was scheduled to begin at 8:00. Early as I was, there were people who had arrived before me. The white sunlight pouring in the elongated windows made me glad I had put on the navy linen skirt and white cotton blouse; the linen and cotton would be cool—not that I was. My palms were sweating, which made it hard to wipe away the perspiration beading on my high forehead. I opened my navy clutch and searched for a handkerchief. Finding one, I wiped my forehead and looked around the room.

There were several people I knew; most were preoccupied with notes, gathering pencils, looking for a place to sit and trying to look relaxed with furrowed brows.

I nodded a hello at a guy I knew from ethics class. Frank? I think that's his name. And there's Bob. I gave him a wary smile and shoulder shrug. He mouthed back, "good luck." I smiled and pulled out a straight-back pine chair and sat down.

Then I did what I always did before any test—I prayed, quietly, of course. (Today we call these silent prayers, which may explain why prayer doesn't work as well as it used too—perhaps, even God can't hear a silent prayer!)

"Dear God," I began, "please help me on this test. Help me to remember all those laws I studied." At this point my mind was interrupted with trying to remember names....was it *Harcourt* or *Harbour* ... no ... *Hargrove*. I completely forgot that I had God on the line. "Sorry, God, I guess I'm just a bit nervous. Could You do something about that? If I don't quit sweating, I might dehydrate." I tried reason, "God, if you'll just help me to remember all that I've studied, I promise to be a good attorney. I'll stay away from tax law ... I know how You feel about tax collectors. If You'll help me, God, I promise to use my skills to go out and help others...."

Before I finished with my prayer, an older gentleman in front of the room addressed us. "Welcome to the Georgia Bar Examination. If you are here today to attempt your medical board, you are in the wrong place. But stick around, some of these people might need a doctor by the time they finish this exam." Chuckles rippled through the room; I knew he spoke the truth.

I quickly added "in Jesus name, Amen" to my prayer and looked about the room.

I knew there was well over a hundred people scattered about the room. As far as I could tell there was only one other woman besides me. I added another quickie, "Help her too, God."

I don't remember much else about the exam. It was long, grueling and tedious. My brain and body seemed transported to another dimension, one without sight, sound, emotions, or needs. I had no awareness of hunger, sweat, pain, or bladder capacity. The only thing I thought about was the answer to the question before me. And when I finished that one, there was another one equally as complicated to answer. The only concept I did grasp during that time was that of eternity. "This must be what eternity is like—it just drones on and on. How can You stand it, God? Aren't you bored?"

And I swear I thought I heard an audible reply, "No, child." God explained, "I've got just as many problems to keep me busy as you do. Now sit up straight and answer the next question." Okay, maybe the voice wasn't completely audible. But after sitting from 8:00 a.m. to 12:00 midnight, taking a test, one could certainly understand why I might have been suffering delusions.

The bar exam was as hard to pass then as I suppose it would be today. State examiners would estimate how many more lawyers the people in the State of Georgia could support and then determine how many applicants would pass. Those with only the highest scores passed. I said another prayer of mercy as I turned in my exam.

"Okay, God, I did my best. The rest is up to You."

"Oh, sure, blame Me for your failures," God retorted. Maybe. Who said that?

Although I had initially felt hopeful about the results of my exam, self-doubt eroded my confidence. On the September day the pass list came out, I waited as long as I could, until 8:30 a.m., before heading over to Judge Henry West's chambers to see if I had passed. Earlier that year Judge West had talked me into becoming a resident of Athens so that my parents wouldn't have to pay out-of-state fees for tuition. He also figured I would vote for him in his bid for Superior Court Judge.

"Rufe, good to see you this morning." Judge West rose from behind his oak desk. Motioning for me to take a seat, he asked, "What can I do for you?"

"Judge West, I was just wondering if you've received the results of the state bar yet?"

The phone rang. "Please excuse me, Rufe." He picked up the receiver. "Mornin' Jack." He cradled the phone underneath his gobbler's chin.

I stood there pretending to read the titles of the books that lined his shelves. Row after row of leather bound code books. I tried not to listen to Judge West's conversation.

I looked down and tracked a dark crevasse in the pine flooring to a corner where dust sifted over a six-inch baseboard. I looked up and out the window at white crape myrtle blossoms clustering to branches— God's embroidered lace.

Judge West shifted the phone up to his mouth, continued his conversation and motioned again for me to sit down. This time I did.

"I'm so sorry, Rufe," Judge West said as he hung up the receiver. "I hope you'll forgive me. Now what was it you needed?" he asked with a smile.

"That's okay, Judge West. I'm sorry to intrude on you so early this morning. I've just been on pins and needles wondering if you've received the list of those who have passed the bar yet?"

"It's no intrusion, Rufe. I have the list here in my drawer." Opening the right hand drawer, Judge West took out some papers and began to shuffle through them. "I'm sure it is in this mess somewhere."

Again the phone rang. "Yello. Mornin' Duane." Judge West mouthed a silent, "Sorry" to me. I wanted to jerk those papers out of his hand and tear that phone out of the wall. Did I or did I not pass? Eternity and bar exams didn't last as long as Judge West's phone conversations. I was desperate.

"I'm so sorry, Rufe." Judge West hung up the phone and immediately found the list. "Here it is, and yes, I'm happy to report that your name is on it. Congratulations!" Judge West kept me long enough to say, "Rufe, 201 applicants took the exam and only 89 passed. Only two of those 89 were women—you and Sarah Wilson of Waycross. Rufe, we're all so proud of you!"

A lawyer! I was a lawyer. I couldn't breath. Thanking Judge West I practically ran out of his office. I needed more air than was in the building. My lungs were compressed but my feet seemed weightless. Was I flying? Who cared? I passed!

As I ran from the courthouse to campus, I stopped three different people to tell them, "I passed the bar! I'm a lawyer!" Each offered me a smile. My only thought was, "I'm only 21 and I'll be a lawyer until the day I die!" I felt embraced by the arms of a loving God. I called Mac and my parents immediately.

"Oh, darling, I'm so proud of you, " Mac said. He sounded so far away.

"It's great, isn't it? Only now, I have to decide whether I should finish law school or not. I just don't know what to do, Mac."

"Sugar, you do whatever you decide. I can't wait to marry you, but I want you to do whatever you need to do so that you'll be Georgia's first woman governor!" Mac laughed.

"Oh, Mac, I have no intention of being governor and you know it! I'm just so happy to be a lawyer. I'm going to talk with Dean Hoasch and see what he thinks I should do."

"All right, doll. Just let me know when we can start that honeymoon. I hear Boston's cold in the winter. It'd sure be nice to have someone who'll keep my feet warm at night!"

The State of Georgia did not require me to obtain my L.L.B. to practice law since I had passed the bar. But Dean Hoasch gave me good advice, "Rufe, a woman is going to be very hard to place. Law firms favor men. It might help your career if you would stay on at Georgia and obtain your degree." My parents agreed. Mac spent the cold winter in Boston alone.

I took Dean Hoasch seriously when he indicated to me that finding a job as a woman lawyer would not be easy. Until that point, my gender had not been of great concern to me. The men in my law class were more than generous. They accepted me as a colleague. I never gave much thought to being the only female in my class. Mother had convinced me that doing my work well was what people would judge me by—not my gender. Women had been given the right to practice law by Georgia's Legislature in 1916, two years prior to my birth. And for most of my life doing my best at work has gotten me just what I wanted, but there were times when being a female did have its restrictions.

## Gender Matters

After I decided to stay on at Georgia and work toward my L.L.B. degree, I again applied myself diligently to my studies. Continuing as student editor of the Georgia Law Journal, there seemed to be no boundaries on what I could do. Until Professor McWhorter's Criminal Law class. Professor Bob McWhorter had been one of Georgia's exalted—a former star football player and a favorite fellow among students and faculty. One day he stopped me outside of class.

"Miss Edwards, may I see you for a moment?" He spoke with that monotone that morticians use—quiet and void of emotion.

I glanced at my classmates, Verner Chaffin and Bill Gunter. Neither indicated that they knew what Professor McWhorter wanted with me. They walked on into class.

I approached McWhorter. He smelled of tobacco and Old Spice.

"Yes, sir?"

"Miss Edwards, I'm going to have to ask you to withdraw from this class for the week." He looked down the hall away from me.

"Withdraw? Why would I withdraw from your class, professor, sir?" My mind thought back to last Friday's class. Nothing unusual had occurred. Why should he kick me out of class?

"Just temporarily, Miss Edwards." Professor McWhorter nodded at Bob Norman who was walking into class. "It's just for this week. I'll be covering a subject that I think would be far too sensitive for you."

A subject too sensitive for me? For pity's sake, I was a lawyer. What was it he didn't want me to hear? "Professor McWhorter, I assure you that any subject you cover in class will not make me the least bit uncomfortable. I appreciate your concern but I don't think it's necessary, sir." I lightly toe-kicked the baseboard.

"Miss Edwards, please don't make this more difficult. We'll be covering the issue of rape for the week. You may use this time to catch up on other work." Professor McWhorter unfolded a white linen handkerchief from his right hip pocket and blew his tunnel-wide nostrils empty.

"Professor McWhorter, I don't have any other work to catch up on. I understand your concern, but honestly, I think I can handle the class just fine."

"I'm sure you can, Miss Edwards. But regardless of whether you think you can handle it or not, Rufe, you're not to return to class this week. Are we clear on this?" McWhorter folded the handkerchief, replaced it in his hip pocket and stepped inside the doorway.

"Yes, sir. Very clear." I wanted to stay and argue, but McWhorter walked into the classroom and shut the door. As I left there, I realized that McWhorter was keeping me from the presentation on rape because he was concerned about his own sensibilities more than mine.

This was my first experience in gender bias. My classmates at Lumpkin treated me with respect and even admiration. Which is how I felt about them and still do. Fred Walker, Bates Block, Ed Kelly, Sidney Haskins, Howell Hollis, Bob Norman and Frank Edwards (no relation, but I always called him "cuz") all became outstanding Georgia lawyers. Bob Jordan and Bill Gunter became notable Georgia jurists. Another classmate, Ernest Vandiver, served as Governor.

And I will never forget David Atkinson of Savannah. David's white hot smile and disarming manners would have enabled him to sell Bibles to Buddhists. David was my first friend killed in World War II.

During the fall of 1941, I had begun to look for possible employment. Mac was working for Liberty Mutual in their Richmond, Virginia, office. I would graduate in May and knew that finding employment might be difficult. My mother's cousin, Hugh Dorsey, had appointed himself as my mentor. He felt it was his duty to make sure I found a position. As former Governor of Georgia and Superior Court Judge in Atlanta, Hugh arranged an interview for me with his brother, Cam Dorsey, at Cam's law firm. The interview was set for the first week in January.

On December 7, I was walking up the law school stairs toward the library when a group of male students broke through the landing's door like the best of Georgia's offensive lines. I either stepped or was pushed back against the stair railing.

"Hey," I shouted, "what's the matter with y'all? I didn't hear any dinner bell," I chided.

"Sorry, ma'am," came the reply from a first-year law student whose dark eyebrows ran too close together casting shadows over his eyes. With that much natural shade, he'll never need sunglasses, I thought. "The Japs have just bombed Pearl Harbor!" he shouted at me from the bottom landing.

Bombed Pearl Harbor? Where was Pearl Harbor? The Japs bombed us?

I grabbed the oak railing. War. We were going to war. My stomach constricted. Lunch had to find another place to rest, either up or down. My colon obliged. I made my way up the stairs, through one set of doors, then another. Without bothering to acclimate myself to my environment, I closed the door, sat on the toilet and sobbed.

Classmates had talked of war for sometime. Professors would debate at length the responsibility the U.S. had toward her allies in Europe. For the most part F.D.R.'s position was supported, but sometimes a voice of dissent could be heard. But once Pearl Harbor was bombed, university faculty and students spoke only in support of U.S. involvement.

By February of 1942 the university had announced plans to locate a naval preflight school on campus. These plans called for over two hundred officers to administer the school, which would include over two thousand students. Georgia's faculty and student body was changing. Many men that I knew as faculty and those I knew as classmates did not resume classes in January.

Recalling Mother's adage that, "Southerners were proud to be Americans, Jaycees, Baptists and Dawgs," I realized that this was one time when being an American took precedence over being a Dawg. I was just thankful that Mac was safely working in Richmond.

I kept my appointment with Cam Dorsey in January of 1942, but just barely. The appointment was set for 3:00 p.m. in Atlanta. I left Athens on the noon bus which broke down halfway to Atlanta. I felt like walking the remaining twenty miles myself. I had no means to call Hugh or Cam. Three o'clock came and I was still waiting for the bus to be fixed. Finally the bus was repaired and I showed up at Cam's office two hours late.

Everyone had left except Hugh and Cam, who by this time were trying to figure out what to say to my mother if I turned up dead.

"Hugh, sir, I'm so sorry," I practically wailed from the office's front entrance. "The bus broke down."

"Rufe, Rufe," Hugh ignored my outstretched hand and placed his arm around my waist for a sidesaddle hug. "We're just so glad you're okay. You're all right, aren't you?"

"Yes, sir, just fine, sir. Hello Cam, I'm sorry I've kept you waiting."

"Don't you worry about it a bit, Rufe. Can I get you something to drink?" Cam stood up from behind a mahogany desk, blew smoke over his right shoulder and pressed out his cigarette in a glass ashtray.

"I'd love a glass of water, sir, if it wouldn't be too much trouble."

"No trouble at all, Rufe. Please, won't you sit down?" He motioned towards a navy wing back. The leather sighed as it gave way to my form. Cam handed me a glass of water. "Listen, Rufe, since everyone else has already gone home, I think we can dispense with formalities. Hugh and I've already discussed what I think I can offer you at this point. It isn't much but I'm willing to offer you a job with the firm at a salary of $100 a month."

Cam took out another cigarette and lit it. I looked at Hugh who was busy clipping a hangnail. Cam continued, "You realize this is just a temporary job, while my secretary's on leave. It isn't that I don't think you're qualified, Rufe, but I would hesitate to send a woman into a courtroom, no matter who she is." Cam was talking faster than I could walk. "You understand, Rufe. The courtroom is a serious place and people would hesitate to respect a woman there."

Yeah, I thought, people like you, Cam.

"They might not treat a woman as a professional. You know how important credibility is, Rufe. That's hard for any lawyer to obtain, much less a woman lawyer."

I wished the bus had never made it to Atlanta. Hugh sat silent beside me.

"Thank you, Cam. Thank you, Hugh. I hope you'll forgive me the trouble I've put you through today." I gritted my teeth into a smile. "And Cam, I thank you for your generous offer. I'll certainly consider it." But I'll waitress at The Varsity before I accept your offer, I thought. "I hope Cousin Hugh has told you that I am considering other options." Hugh nodded. "You won't mind if I take some time to look further into those options before giving you an answer?" I countered.

"No, ma'am, not at all. I understand, Rufe. We all just want what's best for you," Cam lied, relieved that for now he wouldn't have to hire me because I was a relative and of all things, a woman.

Discouraged, but not despondent, I reported to my parents:

*January 31, 1942*
*Dearest Folks:*
*...I have so many irons in the fire now that I need a secretary to keep up with them. These are my prospects now:*
*I have sent in very good recommendations from three professors to the T.V.A.*

*Russell and George are looking for me a job in Washington.*
*Hoasch is looking for me a job in Atlanta. Shinn wrote yesterday to*
*the N.Y. publishing co. I didn't ask him to but I think he wants me to*
*go up there. Polly, his secretary, said that he sure said some*
*wonderful things. I will go if I get it, if I can't get something in*
*Washington or Atlanta at this time.*

*I have had my eye on this for a long time—I have walked a chalk*
*line for three years so I could get recommendations and I have*
*gotten some wonderful ones...I hope Dad's blood pressure is down.*
*It's enough to have to worry with getting a job saying to yourself,*
*Where will I be the best off to go the furthest, so please don't eat and*
*work so hard I have to worry about that.*

*Lots of Love,*
*Rufe*

After my meeting with Cousin Cam, Dean Hoasch's words haunted
me, "Most law firms favor men, Rufe." But now Dean Hoasch wasn't
even around to offer me encouragement—he had enlisted in the military.
Realizing that I had a war of my own to fight, I decided to call Mac.

"Hey doll," Mac's cheerfulness made me smile. "How was your
interview? Did they sign you on as partner?"

"Well, almost." I pressed the receiver closer hoping somehow to
touch Mac or feel him touch me. "Cam did offer me a job. Something
about you can dust the books for $100 a month but you'll have to stay
out of the courtroom."

Mac listened to my words and heard my frustration. "Rufe, darling,
don't you fret about getting a job. When you get to be governor, Cam
will be lobbying you for one."

"Sure, sure," I chuckled, "but it looks like the only governing job I'll
get will be as *governess* of some Senator's snotty kid."

"Aw, Rufe, you've got five more months before you even graduate.
C'mon, sugar, don't take rejection personally. It isn't meant personally,
you know. Those good ole' boys would treat any woman that way—
family or not!"

I laughed at Mac's twisted perspective. Easy for you, I thought.
You've got all the right equipment. "Mac, listen, I'm going to see about
getting a job."

"I know you will, honey."

"No, I mean I'm leaving Friday for Washington. I've sent an
application off to the Department of Agriculture. The head of the legal
department is Ashley Sellers; he used to be a law professor here at
Georgia. I've written to a friend, Mary Latimer; she works for Senator

Russsell. Mary has made arrangements for me to stay at her hotel. She's going to introduce me to Senator Russell."

Mac interrupted, "Is there time for us to get together? You know that $200 raise I told you about? I thought it was $200 a month...I was wrong. It's $200 a year. Shall I meet you?"

"Well," I hesitated, recalling the time I was reprimanded for taking the train unchaperoned. "I was thinking I might just spend Saturday with you and go on to D.C. that night."

"Saturday? This Saturday?"

"Yes, this Saturday. Do you have to work?"

"Well, sort of. I'd planned to dust some bookshelves while seducing the local librarian," Mac howled.

Just the thought of Mac with some other woman was enough to make me walk all the way to Richmond if I had to.

Fortunately, Friday's train was quicker.

My mother, Lula Claude Dorsey, upon her arrival in Atlanta at the turn-of-the-century. This may be the only picture Mother ever had made without hat and glove attire.

Don't be fooled by Schley Howard's placid pose. When provoked, Schley could hurl that chair across a courtroom, leaving behind nothing but splintered wood and ducking heads. (Courtesy of Lt. Governor Pierre Howard and family.)

After closing the boarding house, Aunt Lou devoted her attention to her grand-nieces—Liz and Rufe Edwards (seated).

Cousins (l-r) Lula Lee Duncan, Rufe, Liz, and John Duncan, Jr. We were on our way toCollege Park to visit with our cousins the nigh the Klan attacked

The Edwards family (l-r) Rufe, Claudia, Charlie, and Liz, congregate on the front porch of their Feld Avenue Decatur home after church in the Spring of 1924.

James Norfleet McCombs (Mac) gleefully holds onto Molly, his Rhode Island Red— "Having Molly was better than having a shiny red wagon," Mac claimed.

1725 Belmont Avenue, Jacksonville, Florida. After several different moves, the Edwards' finally had a place they could call home.

While we missed Minnie and our childhood in Decatur, Liz and I enjoyed time spent on the beach in Jacksonville. Notice mother's influences—we wore heels to the beach!

Rufe Dorsey Edwards takes to the streets of Washington, DC, determined as ever.

Liz (l) and Rufe Edwards (r) enjoy the soroity of sisterhood at the University of Georgia, Athens.

Mac was impeccable in his U.S. Army Airforce khakis.

The marriage of Miss Rufe Dorsey Edwards and Master Serg. James Norlfeet (Mac) McCombs, Thursday, December 23, 1944, at the New York Avenue Presbyterian Chapel, officiated by The Rev. Peter Marshall.

The only two men who captured my complete devotion—Charlie Edwards, my father, and my husband, Mac.

Lula Claude Dorsey Edwards never lost her penchant for donning a fine hat. Here she is upon her arrival at Aunt Lou's boarding house in 1900, and many years later. Notice while not wearing her gloves, she still is carrying them.

Daddy and mother sit with a picture of one of their prized possessions between them—me. I'm sure they had one of Liz around somewhere.

Daddy and mother in the garden of our Jacksonville home.

I always held Beth as if she were a Waterford Vase; I suspected she would shatter into as many pieces if I dropped her. Mac was a more confident parent than me; nurturing was his nature.

The hug any politician enjoys most comes from family. Here I receive mine from Beth, after being sworn in as Municipal Court Judge in 1975. My defeat of three male opponents solidified my spot as the first woman elected judge of a court of records without prior appointment for the State of Georgia. (Courtesy of *Columbus Ledger-Enquirer*.)

Langdon High's coveted Greely Cup precariously perched along the table's edge in much the same fashion it had been on our family's mantel the night of the accident.

Exactly half of the sixteen graduates of the Lumpkin Law Class of 1942 gathered together in 1992 to celebrate fifty years of achievements. (L-R) William R. Gignilliat Jr. (Bill), Frank H. Edwards, (I called him cuz though we were no relation; most called him Chick), Verner F. Chaffin, who returned after graduation to teach law at the University of Georgia, Edwin McDonald, and the pretty one of the boys, Rufe Dorsey Edwards McCombs, Robert C. Norman (Bob), Ernest Vandiver, former Governor of Georgia, and Fred Walker.

September 1993. Mac and I wore our Sunday best for a dinner trip aboard the New Georgia Railway. Our daughter arranged a surprise retirement party in my honor. The train took us past the Decatur Depot on College Avenue; the same place where Daddy had boarded the train to Atlanta every morning. Right past my childhood home on Feld Avenue. Nearby was the Dekalb County Courthouse where I watched Schely Howard perform his courtroom antics.

# 7

# EARLY CAREER AND LASTING COMMITMENT

## Getting the Job

I contacted Mary Latimer, a friend, who worked for Senator Richard Russell in Washington. Mary secured a room for me at the hotel where she was living and arranged for me to meet Senator Russell at 10:00 on Monday morning.

"I'm afraid I can't visit too long, Miss Edwards. I'm due at a committee meeting in just a few minutes." Senator Russell stepped out from behind his desk, his right hand outstretched. He was tall but not lanky; his rugged complexion reminded me of a country boy's face. "Mary tells me you are looking for a job?"

"Yes, sir. I'm graduating from Georgia in June. I've already passed the bar."

"Yes, so I've heard. Quite an achievement for such a young woman." Senator Russell smiled as his eyes made careful notes. "Tell me what I can do to help you, Miss Edwards."

"Well, sir, I have already sent an application to the Department of Agriculture. Mr. Sellers—I believe he heads up the legal department—used to teach law at Georgia. I'm hoping to get an interview with him."

"Ashley Sellers?" Senator Russell turned away from me and scratched out a note across the top of a newspaper. Gathering up a file, he walked toward the door, "Do you mind if we walk and visit, Miss Edwards? I must be going." I followed him. "I don't know how much help I can be, but I'd be happy to make a phone call or two on your behalf."

"Thank you, Senator." I was thankful my long legs kept my stride even with the Senator's. "I'm meeting with Senator Pepper later today." I figured I'd better keep a competitive edge going.

"You tell Claude hello for me, okay?" Senator Russell stopped, reached over and squeezed my upper arm. "I'm sure someone with your assets won't have any trouble finding a job. Especially considering the present climate in Europe."

I knew Senator Russell wasn't referring to the weather.

My meeting with Senator Pepper was just as encouraging as my meeting with Senator Russell had been. Senator Pepper also agreed to make some contacts on my behalf.

On Tuesday morning, as I prepared to leave the hotel and head over to fill out some applications with several federal departments, I received a phone call from Ashley Sellers office.

"Is this Miss Rufe Edwards?" a man's voice clipped.

"Yes, it is," I replied.

"Miss Edwards, I'm calling from Mr. Sellers office—The U.S. Department of Agriculture. Mr. Sellers has requested that you come in for a job interview. Are you available at one o'clock this afternoon?"

"One's perfect." I looked at my watch. It was only 10:30, I still had time to get some applications filled out.

"Mr. Sellers' office is located...."

"It's okay. I know how to get to Mr. Sellers'," I interrupted.

"All right. I will tell Mr. Sellers to expect you at one o'clock. Thank you."

"No, *thank you!*" I exclaimed.

I never did bother filling out any other applications. Instead I spent my time trying to decide what to wear. I had packed only two dress outfits, both suits, both wool. Because I wanted a sharp look, I chose the navy wool, straight skirt, cropped jacket, white blouse, navy pumps, pearl earrings. I could pass for a WAC, I thought. Perhaps I should join the military myself. My red lipstick smudged. This was before the days of lip liners and I had to create full lips from the two parallel lines that were supposed to be mine. I wiped my mouth and started again.

I thought about walking to the Department of Agriculture, figuring it was probably only a half mile or so from my hotel, but January's sun was deceiving. The temperature was barely above freezing. I called for a taxi.

At that time the U.S. Department of Agriculture was the largest federal building in Washington, D.C.. On the first floor alone there were some thirty-five similar halls with similar offices, small holes that serious and anxious people scurried in and out of. So in spite of my protestations earlier about knowing the way to Mr. Sellers' office, I found that I had to stop three different people before I happened upon the right hole.

"Um, is this Mr. Sellers' office?" I leaned my head but not my feet inside the doorway.

"Yes, ma'am," replied a secretary who looked like she should still be baby-sitting or better yet, needed one. Red highlights flecked her hair. Her full red lips surely never smudged—not without help.

"I'm Rufe Edwards." I stepped on inside the doorway. "I believe Mr. Sellers is expecting me." I left my navy gloves on; my palms were sweating. What if Mr. Sellers denied me? I felt my neck flush with heat. Did I look as obvious as I felt?

"Mr. Sellers is expecting you, Miss Edwards. It is "Miss" isn't it?" she inquired, a bit too curious.

"Shall I wait here?" I nodded at the chair guarding the corner. I walked over, sat down, smiled, and challenged, "It's Rufe Edwards, R-U-F-E. A family name."

"Yes, I suppose it would have to be," she retorted. "Well, then, I'll let Mr. Sellers know you are here." She stood up, head high, and pranced like a Tennessee Walker into Mr. Sellers' office. " There's a Woof Edwards here to see you, Mr. Sellers."

"Rufe, come on in. I hope your trip was a pleasant one. No delays due to snow I hope." Mr. Sellers did not ask to have me shown in—he followed his secretary out of his office and greeted me himself. His short gait was precise, heel, toe, heel, toe. Standing up, I made eye contact with Sellers without straining my neck. I was thankful for his baritone voice that slowly savored vowels as if they were expensive chocolate truffles.

"My trip was just fine, Professor Sellers." I followed him into his office. I shot off a quick smile to his secretary as I passed her desk.

"It isn't Professor any more, Rufe."

"Oh, did I call you Professor? I'm sorry. It's just that I'm so used to you being referred to as Professor Sellers, at Georgia, I mean."

"Just be glad you never had to suffer my dronings first hand, Rufe." His smile brightened the otherwise dark office: dark cherry desk, two wine-leather chairs. "Please take a seat, Rufe, and tell me how things are managing at the university without me."

"Thank you, sir." I sat on the edge of one of the leather chairs, remembering to carefully cross my ankles the way "proper young ladies sit." Who taught me that?

"I wish I could tell you everything is just fine, sir, but since Pearl Harbor was hit, nothing has seemed the same. Many of my classmates have already left school to join the service. It is frightening to see how fast things can change."

"Frightening, indeed, Rufe. We all wish things could have been resolved differently, but it looks as though many more may enlist before we're done. And while change can indeed be unsettling for us, in your case it's going to work to your advantage." Mr. Sellers leaned across his desk, played with a pen, and continued. "We expect to see many more men leaving soon, Rufe. And as they leave, jobs are going to open up. That means more opportunity for you. Now I know these are not the circumstances you would desire or design, but change is already under way, as you yourself have stated. Are you ready to step into a place of service yourself?"

"I certainly am," I replied. Did he want me to join the service? My name, Rufe, might have gotten me a job modeling men's wear, but even I didn't believe anyone would let me fly bombers.

"Well, good, then." Sellers pulled out a form from underneath a stack of papers.

"I want you to take this back into the office and fill it out. It's just some paperwork we'll need. We can give you a job in June. It only pays $300 a month, so you'll want to budget your living expenses carefully. You'll soon find out that everything costs more in Washington."

Three hundred dollars a month! Uncle Cam would have to find someone else to do his dusting for $100 a month. I was going to work for the United States Government!

"Thank you, Professor Sellers!" I forgot about my crossed ankles and jumped up, dropping my clutch purse to the floor. As I bent over to get it, I knocked my forehead against the desk. I saw red and white fireworks.

"You all right, Rufe?" Mr. Sellers came around to help me to my feet.

"I'm fine, really. You ought to see me at football games," I laughed. "Nobody will sit by me for fear I'll throw hot coffee all over them when we score." My clumsiness flashed blood like neon lights up my neck and into my cheeks.

"You sure you're okay?" Mr Sellers steadied me by holding onto my right elbow.

I rubbed my forehead and nodded.

"Well, then. Why don't you just take this form, fill it out, and leave it with my secretary. I will send you a more detailed job description before graduation. I'll also send along some reading material that pertains to the Perishable Act and the Packers and Stockyard Act. Those two Acts will be the focus of your work with us. Anything you can read on these acts, prior to your coming in June, will prove beneficial to you."

"Is there anything else I need to do, Mr. Sellers?" I took the form and walked to the door.

"Nothing I can think of right now, Rufe. My secretary has your number. If something else occurs to me before you leave town, I'll call. Okay?"

"Okay, I'll be leaving tomorrow to return to Georgia. I'll leave my number in Athens with your secretary. And Mr. Sellers, thank you for giving me a job." I heard the doorknob click as Mr. Sellers opened it.

"I'm happy that we can offer you one. I just wish I could welcome you to Washington during different times than these. Perhaps by June things will be different." Mr. Sellers' baritone voice took on a hushed tone, as if he were praying.

"Perhaps," I prayed with him. Then I shook his hand, filled out my paperwork and left. I felt like I had just eaten my first meal after a fast—restful and full. It was only January of 1942, five months before I would graduate from Georgia, and I had successfully obtained a job with the United States Department of Agriculture. Very soon I would be practicing law.

## Hurry Up and Wait

Actually it turned out to be sooner than I expected. In February I received a call.

"Rufe?" There was a quiet knock on my dorm door. I was sitting cross-legged on my bed, my neck tautly strained over a book the way newly picked daffodils pull away from the choking clutch of a child.

"Yes? Come in." I looked up to see Mrs. Clark, the dorm mother. A widowed woman, Mrs. Clark devoted her entire waking hours to her job as sentry. She guarded me and all the other virgins with a stoicism found only in those who know they've been instructed by God, Himself. Her pin curls probably have better spring to them than this mattress, I thought.

"There's a phone call for you. A Mr. Sellers from Washington. Why don't you use the line in my room?" Mrs. Clark led me down the hall and opened the door to her room. She sat in a chair, pretending to crochet, while I took the call.

"Rufe, I know this is short notice," Sellers began, "but is there a possibility that you could come to Washington before June?"

"Well, I'm not sure. Graduation isn't until June. How soon were you thinking of?" I asked, my mind creating lists of all the things I needed to get done before moving to Washington.

"I was hoping you could come next week," Mr. Sellers didn't pause for my response, which was good because I couldn't have talked anyway—my diaphragm had just deflated. "Rufe, several men in our department have recently left for Europe. We are in desperate need of additional staff. Is there any way at all you could come now? I'd be happy to talk with the faculty on your behalf."

Next week? Like a coach whose team has just had a turnover, my mind erased all previous plans, and I began marking out new plans that flashed: URGENT.

"I don't really know if I can do that, Mr. Sellers. I'd need to clear this with Dean Shinn first. If he agrees, then I could call you to work out the details."

"Fine, fine, Rufe. Do you want me to call Dean Shinn on your behalf?" Mr. Sellers' baritone voice hesitated over seldom used low notes. He seemed to be weary. Was it physical or emotional exhaustion?

"Sir, I believe I can explain this to Dean Shinn. If he has any concerns I will have him contact you. Okay?"

"Okay, Rufe. If there is anything at all he is concerned about, you have him call me immediately. Today is Monday. How 'bout I call you again on Wednesday? Do you think you might know by Wednesday?"

"Wednesday's fine, sir. I'll see what I can get done by then." I placed the receiver in its black cradle.

"Everything okay, Rufe?" Mrs. Clark stopped the rhythm of her needles.

I knew she wanted, maybe needed, me to confide in her, but I was just too overwhelmed to listen to any lectures Mrs. Clark might offer me.

"Fine," I lied. "Everything's just fine. Thank you for letting me intrude on you."

What choice did Dean Shinn really have? What could he have said that would have kept me at Georgia anyway? Our nation's people were coming from all four corners to fight the world's war. Dean Shinn could have said, "You know Rufe, the next four months at Georgia will be your most important education yet. Jobs for women lawyers are hard to obtain. Your degree will serve you better in the long run than a job with the United States Government." But he didn't.

When I went to consult Dean Shinn at his office, I felt confused myself over what would be the right choice. I was anxious to start my career, but not all that excited about starting it before I'd finished my schooling. What I really wanted to do was to stop everything that had led up to this moment, or cry because I knew I lacked the power to stop anything.

"Of course you must go, Rufe. Don't worry about your studies. You've already passed the bar. I'll make arrangements for you to take your final exams in time for graduation. There will be no academic loss due to your early leave. You'll receive your degree in June just as planned, provided you pass your exams." Dean Shinn paused, stroked his eyebrows with the tips of his fingers, then said, "We'll miss you, Rufe. You've earned the respect of everyone you've come in contact with here at Georgia—faculty and classmates."

I chewed the inside corner of my lip. Tears hid in the corners of my eyes. Emotions, not words, flooded my mouth.

"Thank you, Dean Shinn," I struggled. "I'm going to miss Georgia."

When I left Athens that Friday afternoon, many of my classmates and some of the faculty showed up at the train depot for farewells. As the train pulled away, I waved a last good-bye from my window seat. I thought about how quickly our present can change to become our past. One minute an elm shades us, the next minute the sun's white light exposes us. Pearl Harbor had left us exposed as a nation. We were seeing our present click rapidly by. None of us had time for lingering in the protective shade of the elm.

I spent the weekend in Richmond with Mac. We went for long walks and again discussed our matrimonial plans.

"Since you're taking this job, Rufe, I think you should make a commitment to stay with it at least a year." Mac added the carrots he had just chopped to a mostly vegetarian stew he was making.

"Do you want me to chop this onion?" I picked it up and began to peel. Like sunburned skin that had browned and began to peel, the outside of that onion flaked off until I reached the moist and tender inside. My nostrils burned; my eyes watered.

"Here, give me that." Mac took the onion from me.

"Are you sure you don't mind waiting, Mac?" I asked while rinsing my hands.

"Of course, I mind, sugar." Mac scooped up the minced onion and tossed it into the cast iron pot. "Look, I cry every time I think about being apart from you." He scrunched up his almond-slivered eyes until tears ran down alongside his nose.

"Yeah," I said as I wiped his face with a green plaid dish towel, "and do you chop an onion every time too?"

"Almost every time." Mac grabbed the towel from me and blew his nose.

Mac and I decided that we would wait to be married. We both wanted to work and begin our careers. I never intended to be engaged for any where near the thirteen years my parents had been. But at the same time, I had been committed to having a career long before I had been committed to becoming Mrs. James Norfleet McCombs. And Mac understood that. We agreed to wait until both of us attained some of our personal goals, a block of time that seemed longer than the 13 years my parents endured.

## Life in D.C.

It was raining that Monday I arrived in D.C. Prior to leaving Athens, I had contacted a friend who was working with the Commerce Department and she had put me in touch with a woman, Edith Kilerlane, who could get me an affordable room.

Stepping off the train my first plan was to find a phone to call Mrs. Kilerlane.

I had left Athens with $205, which in 1942 was enough to get me a boarding room and provide for my personal expenses for about two months. But I knew I had to make every effort to make it last.

As I gathered together my three pieces of white leather luggage (the set I had bought with my gift money from Mr. B.B. Williams Sr.), I heard someone call out my name.

"Rufe Edwards? Are you Rufe Edwards?"

I picked up the carrying case and looked up. A woman, fortyish, with dark brunette hair, beauty parlor styled, stood grasping an umbrella. A light rain beaded and hung from the tips of her navy umbrella.

"I'm Rufe Edwards." I picked up the biggest suitcase.

"Oh, Rufe, I'm sorry to have to call out at you like that. I hope I didn't embarrass you. I'm Edith Kilerlane. Your friend Susan works with me over at Commerce. She spoke to me about helping you find a place to live." Mrs. Kilerlane emphatically clipped her words, as though each word held rank over the previous one. She stopped abruptly and breathed purposefully into her diaphragm like an opera singer.

"Why, thank you, Mrs. Kilerlane, for coming out to meet me. I never intended for you to go through this much trouble. I had just planned to...."

"No trouble at all, Miss Edwards. I couldn't let you arrive in Washington without a proper greeting, now could I?"

She didn't wait for an answer.

"My car is parked back over here." She picked up my lighter suitcase. "You'll join my husband Ed and me for dinner, of course." It was a directive, not a question.

Edith Kilerlane took charge of situations the way a labor nurse does. She could direct people, firmly, without hesitation, but always with a touch, a hug, a pat, a physical closeness that happens when territorial boundaries aren't necessary. Edith's warmth drew people from their circle into hers. I liked her immediately. I liked her cooking too.

"Rufe, Ed, and I have caucused and have decided that although we had not planned to rent a room in our home, we both agree that renting to a fine lady like yourself would be a treat for us both. Not having had any children of our own, perhaps your youth would revive ours!" Edith said while offering me another helping of mashed potatoes.

"The only thing is," said Ed, a handsome man who looked just like the actor Authur Godfrey, "you'd have to agree to letting us call you by another name. I just can't figure out how I could possibly call you 'Woof.' Don't you have another name we could call you by?"

I not only had dinner with Ed and Edith at their expansive home in Westgate, Maryland, that first night in D.C.—I ended up living with them for the next two years. And it was for the next fifty years of intimate friendship that Ed and Edith Kilerlane always referred to me as "Dorsey", my middle name, my mother's maiden name.

After having secured a living situation so quickly upon my arrival to D.C., I was now prepared to begin my job at the United States Department of Agriculture the following morning at 8:30.

On that first day I was shown my office, a small but efficient room. Desk, phone, file case. My own secretary.

"You're not fussy are you? I've never worked for a woman before," she commented. Older than me by about ten years, she looked more like Mrs. Clark, my dorm mother, than I had wanted. Can nervousness cause a woman's hair to curl?

"Fussy? Well no more than any other attorney. And don't worry about working for a woman, as long as you type faster than a man!" I laughed.

Mr. Sellers had explained my job to me. I would be assigned cases that went first before a hearing examiner, then could be appealed to U.S. District Courts. Most of the cases involved only two federal statutes—The Perishable Act and The Packers and Stockyards Act.

My job would be to read the files and to convince the hearing examiner that any ruling the Department had made was indeed the correct ruling. The only thing that I felt uncomfortable with regarding my job was the conflict of interest—the hearing examiner was also an employee of the Department. What could be the outcome of an appeal with this kind of set up? This always seemed to me to mock the idea of a fair hearing.

There were two other women lawyers working for the Department when I began—Rozina Bullington and Helen Lutzen. We spent many lunch hours at Holgate's restaurant, which served the best seafood in town, discussing the men we worked for and with.

"Have you been summoned to meet The Prince yet?" Rozina blew over the top of a hot cup of coffee. Her black hair, loosely curled, gleamed under the lights. She must've applied a vinegar rinse to it last night, I thought.

"The Prince?" I asked stirring my iced tea.

"Bossman Wields," Helen said, unfolding a napkin, she placed it across her lap.

I admired the poinsettia red polish expertly applied to her nails. "He'll be calling on you soon, honey."

"The first thing he'll do is ask you to join him for cocktails." Rozina set the white cup back on its saucer. "He likes to spend time with all the women lawyers. Too bad his wife didn't become a lawyer—then maybe he'd spend some time with her."

"He's married?" I sipped my tea.

"Very," Helen plucked a cherry tomato from her salad.

"But he won't mention it unless you do," smiled Rozina. "Not that he looks it. None of that balding, bulging baggage. He's the cat's cream—any woman's dream." Rozina seemed to doze off.

"It's the truth, Rufe. His good looks could cure any woman's headache," Helen closed her eyes and sighed.

"Any woman's but his wife's!" Rozina laughed.

It took longer than any of us expected, but I finally did receive my call to visit the big bossman—Mr. Ben Wields. All the way up the stairs I thought about ways in which I could politely deny Mr. Wields' advances. I'd have to be demure and not threaten his manhood if I planned on keeping this job. I wasn't sure how I was going to do this—I had never before had a married man approach me with romantic, really sexual, inclinations.

Maybe I could indicate that something is physically wrong with me. No. What if he buys it and decides I'm too weak for my job? Perhaps I could casually mention Mac and our planned nuptials. Of course if this is a man who isn't the least bit bothered by his own marital state, I doubt mine will hinder his advances. Finally I decided that I would take a non-confrontational way out—I would ignore any advances, play ignorant, with only a mind for business. That way Mr. Wields would not be threatened by my rejections. Plus he would know just how valuable an employee I was—my mind focused on my work.

Mr. Wields' secretary was not at her desk. I walked over and rapped lightly on his door, hoping he wouldn't hear me so that I could quickly return to my reclusive office.

"Come in, come in," came a voice that echoed through wood and metal, like that of a high school gym coach.

"Mr. Wields?" I walked slowly across the room, unsure of whether to offer my hand. "I'm Rufe Edwards." My hands stayed at my side, sweating.

"Yes, I know," Ben Wields smiled without showing any teeth. Do snakes smile? Do they have teeth? I wondered.

"Please, have a seat Miss Edwards. I'll be with you in just a moment." Ben Wields continued flipping through some documents.

Sitting down on the edge of a Windsor-backed chair across from Wields, I watched his pen stroke the documents at various intervals. I noticed his hands were big enough to palm a Florida grapefruit and totally hide it from sight. Fingernails were manicured, healthy white and fleshy pink. His jaw flinched beneath broad cheekbones.

Long, dark lashes cast shadows across the top of his cheeks. Ben Wields was as good looking a man as God could make, considering what all God had to work with.

"Miss Edwards." Wields noticed me staring. "Are you enjoying D.C. so far?"

"Oh, yes sir, Mr. Wields," I replied. "I've not had much time for sightseeing but so far I've enjoyed myself."

"I bet you have," Wields grinned. "Do you find your office satisfactory?"

"It's great, sir," I scooted to just the very edge of my chair, keeping my feet planted on the floor. Wields leaned back in his own chair.

"It's too bad that Sellers left so quickly after you got here."

Wields was talking about Ashley Sellers who had helped me obtain my job. Shortly after I began to work for the USDA Sellers had quit and gone into private practice.

"It's too bad," I agreed. "I'm going to miss working with Prof. Sellers."

"Oh, was he your professor at Georgia?" Wields crossed one long leg over the other.

"No, no, he wasn't," I explained. "Just that I've heard him referred to that way so much that I forget sometimes." My right leg was bouncing up and down. I put my hand out to settle it.

"Well, Miss Edwards, I just wanted to take this opportunity to welcome you aboard. If there's anything at all you need, let me know and I'll make sure you get it." Ben Wields stood up.

That's it? No invitation for cocktails? I left Wields office rejected. Gosh, I thought, here's a man hotter than Georgia asphalt who takes one look at me and then pledges celibacy for life. What would I tell Helen and Rozina? Better revert back to my plan—focus on my work, play ignorant, my mind centered on business.

So that is just exactly what I did—focused my energies on my job. And because I did, my career went well. I reviewed cases that were under appeal. The purpose of the Stockyard and Packers Act was to provide an atmosphere of free market trade, to ensure weight controls were accurate, that bidding was fair, and to enforce payment. The USDA protected against fraudulent dealers and marketers.

My first job as a lawyer was not as exciting as I had planned. As I had told Mr. B.B. Williams Sr., I wanted to be a lawyer because I thought it would be fun to argue. But as Mr. Williams pointed out, there is a lot more to being a lawyer than just arguing. For this job, it was mostly review and paperwork. And throughout my career I've done more listening than arguing.

Yet, since it was 1942 my career advanced rapidly, not necessarily because I was exceptionally bright, but because so many men, attorneys included, were being drafted. I worked diligently to prove that I could do any job as well as any man. It wasn't long before I was appointed Hearings Examiner (now called administrative law judge).

My depth of experience was expanding. I was no longer sitting behind a desk doing review work. The job as Hearings Examiner required that I travel throughout the Northeast to do field work regarding cases that were pending. I enjoyed both the work and the travel. But I remained frustrated with the bureaucratic system that masked justice behind appointed judges and juries of their own choosing.

Yet, the job was still a better choice than what my family continued to offer me in Atlanta:

*Judges of The Superior Courts* Atlanta, GA.
*of the Atlanta Circuit* April 9, 1942

My dear Rufe:

I am in receipt of your letter and I assure you that I appreciate it greatly. I am delighted to know that you are pleased with your work, and particularly delighted that you secured a convenient and pleasant place to live.

I have been thinking about you a good deal and wondering as to whether or not you had forgotten your promise to write me. I concluded, however, that you, like myself, were just overwhelmed with work.

I do not know that Mr. Moore, my secretary, will leave me, but it may be that he will be drafted for the Army or it may be, if he is able to get a position to his liking, that he will feel that it is his duty to do something for his Country more than he is now doing.

Mr. Moore gets $165.00 a month. If he should leave and you want his job during his absence I would be most happy to give it to you. I feel, if for any reason he should come back and is able to resume his old position, that I ought to give him the job back.

If I live and nothing happens I will hold this position until the first of January, 1945. I will be up for re-election in 1944. If you should take this position and anything happens to me or I should be defeated, then you probably would be a statesman without a job.

This is a matter for your consideration and determination. So far as I am concerned if Mr. Moore does leave me nothing would please me better, it if suits you, to have you take his place.

...I send you my very best wishes and congratulations on obtaining the position and upon winning your first case. If you change your address be sure to let me know and keep in touch

with me, even if you decide not to accept the position if the
vacancy occurs. With sincere good wishes and love, as ever,
    Your cousin,
    Hugh Manson

My own notation across the top of this letter reads:

*Of course, I cannot afford to consider this.*

## 1942

Mac was also doing lots of traveling. He would often catch the
train from Richmond to visit me in D.C. over the weekends. Edith
wanted Mac to use the other spare bedroom when he came on these
visits, but she worried about what people might think. So Mac would
get a room in Washington. Ed and Edith enjoyed Mac's company;
many of our weekends were spent with the Kilerlane's—enjoying
dinners, walks, political discussions, and personal stories.

Mac was also enjoying his job with Liberty Mutual in Richmond,
but in June of 1942, I received a disturbing call from Mac.

"Rufe, honey." Mac began, his voice as slow and thick as sorghum.

"Mac?" I was surprised to be hearing from him. It was only
Tuesday. "Is somethin' the matter? Are you okay?" My first thought
was regarding Mac's health, then I began to shuffle through family
members who might not be okay. "It's not your mother is it, Mac?"
She had a variety of aliments that came up from time to time.

"No, Rufe. I mean, yes, I'm okay. Mother's fine." Mac took a
breath, "But something is the matter, sugar—the army's drafted me,
Rufe."

I felt that same sudden need to breathe—the way I had when as a
child I'd asked Mother why she kept me from having a relationship
with her father. We were in a car back then and I had wanted to roll
down the window and be hit in the face until air was forced back into
my lungs. When Mother recounted her molestation by her father, I'd
regretted ever having asked my question. Now here I was—years
later—regretting questions and their answers and trying to breathe
again.

"The army?" I stammered. Tears fell as my fears took form.
"When darling?"

"Rufe, honey, please, don't cry," Mac pleaded, fighting back tears
of his own.

"I leave this Friday to report for basic training in Biloxi. Pray I don't have to stay there too long. With those swamp monkeys, the heat, and bugs, I'd be better off in Europe."

"That's not funny, Mac," I scolded. "I'll pray for you, but it will be for reasons other than spending a summer in Mississippi."

"Well," Mac retorted, "I know we'll win this war if the army keeps training everybody in Biloxi, 'cause I imagine fighting Hitler couldn't be much worse than fighting Mississippi mosquitoes!"

Of course Mac was wrong. Headlines thick with black type confronted Americans daily:

**"Stalin Warns Nips Against Any Back-Stabbing"**

**"Hitler Masses Planes Off Africa"**

**"Allied Fliers Wreak Havoc On Rommel"**

In 1942, Americans were just beginning to understand the devastation occurring in Europe. *Life* magazine brought home the realities by publishing, page after page, the names of the known dead. Students from across the nation began one of the first recycling programs, collecting tons and tons of scrap metal to be melted down and reused. Auxiliary groups would set aside times to roll bandages or can sugar. Men were gone, women were working, and children were coping.

Mac survived basic training in Biloxi and obtained rank as a Private. After that he was transferred to Fort Logan, Colorado. There for less than a year, Mac was transferred once more, this time to Indianapolis. By the time Mac arrived in Indiana, he had been promoted to Master Sergeant.

I began to think that Mac's job was very much like the office manager job he had held in Richmond. Because of his job in the Troop Carrier Command, Mac knew the General; knew him so well in fact that whenever this General came to Washington, he requested that Mac accompany him.

Some of our friends who had family overseas resented Mac's frequent trips into D.C.. Mac and I were both young and in love, so while we were initially embarrassed over Mac's good fortune, we were also quite thankful for it. By then, it seemed certain that Mac was going to serve all of his time stateside—which is what happened. Youthful passion often rationalizes away shame.

## Married in the Chapel

Mac and I felt the instability that dominated our existence due to World War II, which heightened our desire to be together. We decided to move ahead with our wedding plans.

Since arriving in Washington I like so many others sought out fellowship at New York Avenue Presbyterian Church. Known in history as being the place where Lincoln worshipped, it became even more prominent in the forties because of a simple Scotsman—Peter Marshall.

Looking back over my life, I am amazed at how many times my life paralleled the lives of others—people like Catherine Marshall. Peter Marshall had immigrated from Scotland and eventually ended up in Decatur, Georgia, where he studied at Columbia Seminary. Years later he met Catherine Marshall at a prohibition rally in Georgia. Catherine was a student at Agnes Scott College, the same campus in Decatur where my family had taken our Sunday walks from our home on Feld Avenue.

New York Presbyterian Church had become my home church after I relocated to Washington. I had heard much about Dr. Marshall when I was at law school and he was serving in Atlanta as pastor of Westminster Presbyterian Church. Mr. Marshall's ability to relate scriptures in a practical yet entertaining fashion caused rapid growth at the congregations he served. New York Avenue was no different. I, too, stood in lines for a seat.

In September of 1943, Mac and I went to see Dr. Marshall to ask him to officiate at our wedding planned for Thursday, December 23, 1943. Dr. Marshall's greatest concern was that we did not marry because of the influences of a war-time climate. After talking with us, Dr. Marshall agreed to perform our ceremony.

"I don't believe your marriage is being dictated by our present circumstances, but that yours will be a marriage that lasts a lifetime." Dr. Marshall's Scottish accent hovered over "r's". His golden hair rippled across his crown like mature wheat across a broad landscape. He had contoured cheekbones, thick neck, and a muscular build that reminded me of Georgia's best dawgs.

"Almost one in every six marriages in our country ends in divorce," he continued, "but I know that young people like yourselves will work to make your marriage succeed. This means sacrifices from both of you. Marriage runs best when it is a union—not the coming together of two independent states with negotiations in process. To be successful marriage will require you both to be of one heart and one mind," he admonished us.

At the time I wasn't quite sure how Mac and I were going to be a union since we weren't even living in the same state as each other, but Dr. Marshall was correct in that we were of the same heart and mind—we both couldn't wait to be married. Our desire to be joined together physically as one was multiplied exponentially everytime we kissed goodnight.

Mac sent me this letter only a few days before our wedding:

Athens, Georgia 19th December 1943

My darling Rufe:

Darling it was so wonderful to talk with you last night. You sounded as though you were in the next room...Darling this is going to be the best Xmas ever. Darling, I'll have you and that means more than anything else.

I told Mother last night that I was going to leave Athens today for Washington and she almost had a fit. I suppose I will leave here Tuesday as scheduled. Will leave on the 3:50 train and will arrive there much earlier. If I should come on the 9:50 it would be 4 p.m. the following day before I arrived... I just wish there was some way that you could go back with me for a few days but if you can't at this time hope that you can come out to Indianapolis in the near future. I would love for you to meet the people at the field and for them to meet you—my wife....I can hardly wait for the time when I'll arrive there...I love you. Will see you on Wednesday.

Your hubby on Thursday,
Norfleet

Mac (Norfleet) ended up arriving late in Washington, not because he took the 9:50 train but because of bad weather. He ended up arriving in Washington after midnight on Wednesday. My parents who had arrived by train earlier that week from Jacksonville, ended up not making the wedding at all. Mother fell ill with influenza and was told by a Washington physician to return home to Jacksonville as soon as she could, so that she could be treated by her own physician.

Influenza in the 1940's could be a very threatening illness. Tuberculosis was widespread at that time; even Dr. Marshall's wife,

Catherine, was fighting her own battle with it. Having traveled by train from Jacksonville, Mother risked exposure to the bacteria. I am sure the Washington doctor was concerned that Mother's influenza could be the onset of something even more disturbing. The afternoon of my wedding an ambulance took Mother to the train, where she traveled by private car arranged by the president of the railroad—arranged I'm sure because he was concerned about the risk Mother brought to other passengers.

Mac's own parents had not traveled to Washington for the wedding. His mother had been ill for some time, and as I mentioned earlier, Mac's father spent much time indulging other pleasures. Grace, Mac's sister, would have come to the wedding if it had not been at Christmas time and if their mother had not been ill. So our wedding party consisted of Ed and Edith Kilerlane.

My sister, Liz, was not in attendance. To an outsider it may seem strange that I would not have my only sibling as an attendant in such an important event. And even those who have known me for years have expressed surprise when, during other significant moments of my life Liz has rarely been involved. I always wanted Liz to be involved and I believe she always wanted to be involved. There is never a simple answer to the complexities of people and their relationships with one another.

During her teen years, Liz was diagnosed with scolosis, curvature of the spine. It is hard to understand in our medically advanced technological time the existence of a society whose medical care was based largely on myths. But prior to our technological age, treatment of physical aliments, such as scolosis, depended more upon folklore than it did the local pharmacy. Liz had been told that it was doubtful that she could ever have children due to her scolosis—so Liz never married, although she was courted by many.

A natural beauty throughout her life, people were often attracted to her. But Liz did not seek out, nor desire attention. We were always very different in that regard. I spent my life seeking recognition in a variety of arenas, and Liz sought to avoid even the slightest attention. My wedding would have drawn attention to her and Liz has never placed herself in any situation that would cast a spotlight upon her. But as I said these are simple answers that wrap up our relationship without revealing all that's in the box.

Since my father was not available to give me away at my wedding, Ed Kilerlane obliged himself to service by giving me away. My gown was a creamy satin with leg-o'mutton sleeves and a Juliet veil with matching lace. It cost me $100 which was probably more than the cost of the rest of my wardrobe combined. There were no attendants. A few days after the ceremony Edith Kilerlane wrote a letter to my parents:

Dear Mr. and Mrs. Edwards:

This is just a note to tell you about the wedding. I am not a good one to be reporting as I was just slightly less nervous than Rufe and Mac. We were all just terribly worried about you Mrs. Edwards that neither Rufe nor I dared to speak of you for fear of having us both in tears.

Rufe, Ed and I reached the church just about 5:45 p.m. and I went up to Dr. Marshall's study with them. Mac was already there looking very nervous and groom like. It seems that Dr. Marshall had availed himself of the opportunity of stressing upon him the solemnity of the occasion, the seriousness of marriage, etc., and poor Mac looked pretty desperate by the time we got there.

Dr. Marshall then proceeded to give Rufe, Ed and Mac instructions regarding the ceremony. He made it so clear that the wedding went off without even the least little hitch.

At six o'clock we went down from the study into a good sized reception room and I hastily arranged Rufe's veil, straightened her skirt and hastened to my seat. Dr. Marshall entered from the front of the chapel which was very attractive. There were draperies behind where he stood and rugs on the floors and aisles, which added to the attractiveness of the setting. White flowers and candles filled the altar and the organist played very beautiful music.

Mac came next from the front just as Rufe and Ed started down the aisle. Rufe looked beautiful and hid her nervousness. Both of their voices were very steady. The service was very impressive and rather long for a wedding. Afterwards Rufe and Mac, Mr. and Mrs., went down the aisle to the wedding march...

I hope you will accept this epistle in the spirit in which it is written. I am sure if it were someone in my family I would want the details...I do hope that we will hear that you are improving fast Mrs. Edwards.

With love to you all,
Edith

Edith's account was an accurate one. Mac was so uptight his uniform didn't need starch. When we arrived at Dr. Marshall's study Mac, his forehead shining like his military issue shoes, turned to Dr. Marshall and asked, "What happens if I don't come out to meet you at the right time, Dr. Marshall?"

"No need to worry, Mac," Dr. Marshall let loose a bold and hearty laugh, "If you don't come out, I'll come in and get you—there's room at the altar for any who are lost!"

After the ceremony we stopped to change clothes at the new apartment I had leased earlier in the fall. Mac only had a few days of leave so we arranged to spend the first night of our honeymoon at the opulent Shoreham.

I was stunned by the magnificent Shoreham. Opened in 1930, The Shoreham had cost $4 million to build. Its furnishings combined Renaissance with Art Deco design. The 10,000 lights that illuminated The Shoreham's rooms made me feel like I was surrounded by angels from heaven. I searched the corridors for the special ramp and elevator that was rumored to have been installed to accommodate F.D.R. when he had held office. I wondered if it was true that this was the place where Harry Truman held private poker games?

The other rumors I heard were that during World War II The Shoreham had turned its own riding stables into a chicken ranch where broilers were raised and they had purchased the entire stock of a Scottish distillery to keep customers satisfied. Everyone knew The Shoreham was headquarters during the war for visiting Heads of States. As the war continued, The Shoreham seemed like an elegant peacock strutting through the chicken yard—a thing of beauty in a place of mire.

Over the years The Omni Shoreham's Blue Room has featured some of the most notable figures in the entertainment world—Lena Horne, Mel Torme, Tony Bennett, Frankie Avalon, Frank Sinatra, Eartha Kitt, Marlene Dietrich. On December 23rd, 1943, Mac and I danced to the pulsation's of Benny Goodman's big band. Like tall pines in a gentle wind we swayed to the whispering melodies of Kaye Kaiser. Our time at The Shoreham may have been short but the memories we made there have lasted a lifetime.

We married on Thursday, by Sunday Mac had returned to Indianapolis and I was home alone in my apartment. Mac never did end up living with me in that apartment because I soon sought and received a transfer to Indianapolis. I was still with the USDA but now I was with Mac as well.

Adjusting to Indianapolis was harder than I had expected it to be. I missed the prestige the D.C. office had given me. And I missed my friends—Ed, Edith, Rozina and Helen. What I needed was time to develop some lasting friendships in Indianapolis.

Unfortunately, that time never came.

# 8

# ARBITRATING LIFE

## Halting Hitler and the Pig Farmer

Indiana's terrain seemed like a saucer, flat with a slight concave. Sometimes I thought I could see the very edges of where Indiana ended and the mounds of Kentucky Bluegrass began. I left behind the white pristine buildings of D.C. for the tarnished pewter-colored buildings of Indianapolis.

Our main source of heat—coal—powdered doorknobs, windowsills, mailboxes, dashboards—anything not in motion with a fine charcoal residue. Throughout downtown Indianapolis smoke lingered heavily like sarcasm during a holiday meal. Its weight made breathing difficult for me. Nosebleeds became an everyday occurrence.

I developed a minor, but persistent, cough. And the whole time I lived in Indianapolis I felt like I'd washed in another person's bath water.

Our living situation made me feel as dirty in the inside as I did on the outside. Apartments were as scarce as peace of mind during the war. Rents were frozen so we could have afforded a really nice place— if we could have found one. As it was, we only found an apartment because Mac had a friend who worked in real estate.

We scrubbed for three days before we got the dirt off the windows and walls. Landlords at this time were under no obligation to repaint prior to new tenants moving in. Actually we were lucky there was even one layer of paint on the walls. I think those walls were made from old newspapers and cheesecloth. What we couldn't read through the paint, we heard through the walls.

"Mac, I swear all that moaning sounds like an animal caught in a trap."

"Should I go buy a hunting license tomorrow?"

"Yeah? Just try it, you might find yourself on the other end of a gun barrel. Now give me that pillow." I grabbed Mac's pillow out from under his head and buried it over my own.

The apartment we rented was located in the core of Indianapolis' oldest trade center. Business went on day and night. Those girls must've loved their work because they rarely took a break from it. Like ants advancing toward the queen's colony, soldiers lined the hallways and stairwell of our apartment complex.

"I hardly got any sleep at all last night, Mac."

"Yeah, well from the sounds of it neither did anyone else."

"I went next door to Mrs. Walters' place when I got home tonight and tried to explain to her that if the tenants banded together and collectively complained to the landlord, perhaps we could change the way business is done around here."

"You want some more tea?" Mac poured himself another glass.

"No, thanks. Don't you want to know what Mrs. Walters said?"

"Sure I do, sugar."

"Mrs. Walters said she had no idea what I was talking about. Said that I should just be thankful to have a place to live—she certainly is. Then she said her phone was ringing, which it wasn't 'cause I didn't hear it. She shut the door in my face."

"I'm sorry, Rufe. I wish I could have found us a better place. I'll call the real estate office again tomorrow and see if something else is available."

But we never found another apartment. Since we were members of the Indianapolis Athletic club, we spent much of our free time swimming, dining and meeting busy couples like ourselves. My job required me to do a good bit of traveling. More and more packers were being shut down due to violations with the Packers Act.

"Rufe, it's almost impossible to find bacon in the store any more. If y'all don't lighten up on those regulations, you're going to put the pig farmers out of business."

"I'm surprised you haven't bought them all out yourself, Mac. I think I saw four packages of bacon in the ice box this morning. Who's going to eat all that bacon?"

"We are, honey. I found it at the corner market yesterday so I bought all they had. You never know when government officials are going to make bacon illegal!"

On May 8, 1945, a little over a year after we moved to Indiana, President Truman announced Victory in Europe for allied forces. Someone at the office pulled out the brandy. We were all so busy celebrating we almost didn't hear the phone. It was Mac, calling me from a phone at Stout Field.

"Darling, did you hear the news?"

"You bought us a house?"

"Very funny, Rufe. The Allied forces have been successful. We've stopped Hitler!" Mac spoke with speed and excitement like a boy before his first kiss.

"You're too late, Mac, I already heard. Isn't it great? Our boys can come home!"

"Bet you didn't know they're not the only ones who get to go home. The army announced today that even though we are still at war with Japan, any service personnel with family problems can put in for a discharge. My paperwork's already started. I've explained that since Dad's heart attack he hasn't worked and Mother needs us closer by. I don't think I'll have any difficulty obtaining a discharge."

"What'll we do if you get the discharge, Mac?"

"Don't worry, hon. I've already called Liberty Mutual and told them the same thing I've told the army, and they've agreed to give me a job in their Atlanta office. We can go home, if you want to, I mean. What do you think? Would you mind leaving your job here?"

"Mac, I don't know if I could bring myself to leave this sooty saucer. You know the girls next door told me that if you ever left me I could join their work force. I know as hard as they work, they've got to be making better money than us."

"It won't do you any good now, Rufe. Supply and demand dictates the market and I suspect that now the war is over the demand will diminish. Most of the soldier boys will be going home to old girlfriends. You sure you don't want to go back to Georgia with me? I promise no more loud moaning at night."

"Don't make promises you can't keep, Mac," I laughed. "I'll call Atlanta tomorrow and see if they have an opening. Just remember you can't afford to leave me yet."

"Okay, okay. Under the advice of my attorney, I'll not vacate the premises until you're ready!"

## Next Train to Georgia

It didn't take me long to get ready. With just one phone call to D.C., I landed a job in the legal department of the USDA in Atlanta. Our furniture was to be sent via the Army Air Force to Atlanta. On the day we left Indianapolis, the Army Air Force movers were to meet us at our apartment by 10:00 a.m., but by 3:30 p.m. they still had not arrived and we were due to catch the 4:00 train. I took one last look around the apartment, checked the closets for stowaways, and looked out the window for a moving van coming from either direction.

"Mac, we can't keep waiting. We'll miss the train."

Mac looked longingly at the boxes stacked against the dining room wall. He's probably wondering whether he should take me or his precious cookbooks and mixing bowls, I thought. Mac's love of cuisine cooking was just beginning to bud. For a minute I was afraid that he cherished his new mistress more than his old bride. He looked at his watch.

"We've gotta get going. I guess we'll just leave a note on the door telling the movers where to ship our stuff. No guarantees though. What'd you think?"

I thought that if I had to spend one more night in Indianapolis I might just suffocate from coal dust or anxiety; I wanted to leave. Mac wrote a note, tacked it to the front door, which he left open, and we both prayed that our meager household would find its way to Atlanta. Then we caught the next train to Georgia.

When we arrived in Atlanta, we took up temporary residence at the Atlanta Athletic Club. We were told that it would be all right for us to stay there for as long as it took us to find an apartment. At first I worried about the expense, but Liberty Mutual offered to pick up the tab. A generous, but perhaps not too wise, offer on their behalf.

Atlanta's Athletic Club offered all the amenities a person could desire, in one of the most elegant surroundings to be found anywhere. Built on the site of the old Lyric Theater at Carnegie Way and Cone Street, the Club was eleven stories tall. We both admired the tiled swimming pool, squash courts, handball courts, basketball courts, wrestling, boxing, billiard and bridge rooms. There were places we could eat, places to get haircuts, and we even enjoyed a rooftop garden. Plus, the Club was conveniently located to both our jobs. Why in creation would we look for another place to live?

The only drawback to living at the Club was a nearby fire station. It seemed as though Sherman was setting fire to Atlanta every night. Trucks would roar past our window; their screaming alarms piercing through the densest of pillows. I could've slathered Mac in mustard spice and thrown him over an open barbecue pit, and he probably still wouldn't have woken up. But I rarely slept after those sirens pierced my dreams.

We finally found an apartment at Little Five Points. In my mother's youth, Pitt's Drugstore at Five Points was a place to gather for a milkshake and a visit. But when we found our apartment in the fall of 1945, Five Points reflected the changes that were occurring throughout Atlanta. Instead of seeing people leisurely strolling Decatur and Edgewood Avenues, horses and buggies sashaying along, Five Points was dominated by traffic lights and honking horns as people hurried about getting somewhere in life. Visiting became a pastime we could ill afford in a city where there was money to be made.

And Mac and I were anxious to make as much as we could. The transition to new jobs and city life was easy. We both enjoyed our work. I, in particular, was enjoying being back near my old hometown of Decatur. Plus, I had the added advantage of being able to work with Linton West who I had worked with in D.C.. Linton was now the Managing Attorney of the Atlanta USDA office. My life, my marriage, and my work seemed charmed by a Deity whose sole pleasure was blessing me.

## Charmed Life Ends

"Hey, Mac, guess who called, cuugghh, me today?"

"Rufe, what's the matter? Don't you know choking on your own words is very bad for attorneys?"

"It wasn't my words, it's that tuna casserole you made. Looks like my stomach liked it even less than my taste buds." Grabbing for a nearby glass of water, I tried to stop my coughing.

"Are you okay?" Mac reached over from where he sat at the table and patted my back gently.

"I'm fine, dear. I think I must be run down; I've been feeling so tired lately. I'm probably just coming down with the flu. I think I'm going to go on to bed." Tightly closing my mouth I tried to swallow the next round of coughs.

"I don't know Rufe, it seems to be that you've had this cough for months now. Remember you thought it was allergies to the coal dust in Indianapolis? I think you ought to see a doctor." Mac cleared the rose-patterned plates from the table.

"Really, I'm fine, Mac. Just worn out tonight. Wake me up at six in the morning. Okay?" As I passed him, Mac leaned over and kissed my cheek.

"Hey, wait a minute, honey, you never told me who called today."

"Cousin Hugh did. He wants me to meet him for lunch tomorrow."
"Wants to check out the female competition, does he?"
"I'm no competition, Mac. Besides he's paying, so I'm going."
Ever since we had returned to Atlanta, I had experienced an overwhelming tiredness. It seemed as if the mineral rich blood, that normally warmed and energized me, had been replaced with a watery kool-aid substitute. It kept my veins filled, but did very little else. I had a persistent cough, accompanied by chills and a fever. And, as my mother used to say, I had reached the point where I was sick and tired of being sick and tired.

At first I had attributed my tiredness to the move and adapting to a new work environment, but underneath all that rationalization was buried fear. I knew I had not felt well for a long, long time. While in Indianapolis I had blamed the coal dust for my constant nosebleeds, but they had not stopped since we returned to Atlanta.

My cough had intensified as my energy level diminished. I could not tell Mac what I was afraid to tell myself. I suspected that this ebbing away of my energy force was not due to an allergies, or sinus problems, as my doctor in Indianapolis had diagnosed. My denial stopped that next day.

"Hugh Dorsey, please, this is Rufe McCombs calling."
"Just one moment, I'll see if he's in, Mrs. McCombs," came the reply of Hugh's secretary. It was a male's voice. Hushed and reverent, he had the kind of voice that uses the same tone to welcome newborns and dismiss the departing.

I glanced at my watch, 11:35. I hoped Hugh had not left his office yet.

"Rufe, what's up? I was just about to leave."
"Hugh, I'm afraid I can't meet you for lunch today."
"Why's that Rufe? Off to investigate a hot tip on a chicken choker?"
"No, Hugh, I'm just not feeling too good. I'm going to go on home and get some rest."
"I'm sorry to hear that, Rufe. I was really looking forward to our visit. Is there anything I can do for you?"
"Thanks Hugh, but I don't believe there is. Don't think you'll get out of buying me lunch though; I'm going to call you as soon as I feel better."

What Hugh didn't know, what no one knew, was that I canceled that lunch because I knew that I would not be able to walk the ten blocks to the courthouse.

I wasn't sure that I was even going to make it back home. I called my doctor.

"The earliest appointment Dr. Warmack has available is next Wednesday at 10:00. Do you want me to schedule you for then?"

"Yes, ma'am, I do. And you'll call me if anything opens up between now and then?"

"Yes, ma'am, I will."

I continued to work that week in spite of constant coughing, fever, and chills. On a crisp, golden day in October of 1945, I saw Dr. Warmack.

"Rufe, from what you tell me, I think you just have the flu bug that's going around. Why don't you take a couple days off work and get some rest? Take a couple of aspirin for your fever. You'll be better in a week." And with those instructions, Dr. Warmack took his pen, scribbled some notes, and handed me a bill.

"I want to see you back in two weeks if you're not better. This bug could turn into pneumonia. Go ahead and schedule the appointment; if you're better just call and cancel."

By the first week in November, I was back. The flu must have turned into pneumonia because by then I was coughing up blood. This time Dr. Warmack scheduled an x-ray. That was on a Friday. Shortly after 8:00 a.m. on Saturday morning the phone rang.

"I've got it, Rufe," Mac called to me from the kitchen. I could smell the brewing coffee from my bedside—it nauseated me. Taking off my slippers, I tucked my feet back into the still warm blankets and covered my head. I was freezing. Seeking to warm myself with my own body heat, I curled into a fetal position. I heard Mac hang up the phone and head back down the hallway. I sensed him standing in the doorway.

"Who was it?"

"Dr. Warmack." Mac walked over and sat on the edge of the bed. I peeked out from under the ivory spread. Gently brushing my eyebrows with his fingers, Mac said, "He wanted our address. He's coming out."

"Why would he be cocuughoming out?" I sputtered.

"He said he needed to talk with us, Rufe. I think you'd better get dressed." Mac stood and opened my closet door. "You want the blue robe or the pink one?"

Mac answered the door when Dr. Warmack arrived and led him into the living room, where I was nestled into a corner of the couch. Wearing my pink robe, which I hoped put some color into my cheeks, I attempted to move.

"Don't get up, Rufe." Dr. Warmack's usually broad smile was tautly closed.

"Won't you have a seat?" Mac stood behind Dr. Warmack, waiting for him to be seated first.

"Thank you, Mac, but I won't be staying long." I noticed Dr. Warmack's forehead and eyebrows were knitted in tension. "Mac, Rufe," Warmack turned so that he could face Mac standing, as well as me sitting, "the x-rays we took yesterday have come back. They're not good. It's tuberculosis. You're in the advanced stages of tuberculosis, Rufe. You'll need to be tested, Mac. We need to get Rufe some help as soon as possible. I've already made arrangements for her to be admitted to Alto today."

Tuberculosis? I wanted to throw up. My stomach contracted around the remains of the dry toast I had eaten earlier. Tuberculosis. Didn't people die from tuberculosis? My hands were sweating.

"What's Alto?" Mac sat down on the arm of the camel-colored wing back that Dr. Warmack had refused.

I thought about all those years I had just spent getting through school. I can't be sick. I looked at Mac. Would he wait for me to get better? How could I fulfill my role as his wife? Mac picked up the chair pillow and held it tightly, as if it were a float and he was in the midst of a storm at sea. I tasted saltwater as tears caverned somewhere in the depths of my throat.

"Alto is the State Sanitarium for tuberculosis, Mac. It's in the mountains at Alto, just north of here." Dr. Warmack nervously shuffled his ample weight from one foot to another and back again.

"Don't you worry, Rufe. We're making great progress in the treatment of TB. We're going to do everything we can to get you better, but you understand that we have to isolate you, for your own protection, as well as everyone else's." Dr. Warmack took out a balled up hanky from the right pocket of his brown flecked tweed jacket, wiped at his brow that had relaxed a bit and said, "Mac, I've some papers for you to sign. You'll need to pack some things. Do you think you could drive Rufe up this morning?"

I caught Mac's eyes, tears puddled there. Fear froze my oxygen-depleted blood. No warmth flowed to my feet or hands—they shook in a violent chill. I doubled over trying to find the center of my body's warmth and realizing my body had no warmth of its own, I began to weep. The hot tears felt good.

Grabbing an afghan from the back of the couch, Mac wrapped me up and held me as I cried. Dr. Warmack shuffled his weight again.

"It's all right, everything's going to be okay, honey," Mac rocked me gently against his chest, but tears fell from Mac's eyes too. At that moment we both knew that life wasn't okay and chances were good that our lives might never be okay again.

We did not own a car, so Mac borrowed one to make the 100 mile excursion to Alto. The drive up was quiet as we both grieved over open wounds. The silence was like a dose of mineral oil, heavy but beneficial. As oaks and pines blurred by, so did questions of how long and how bad would this disease be? Would the white steeple we just passed be the last I'd ever see?

The glass of the car's window magnified the sun's rays—the heat felt good. We passed a church graveyard where brightly-colored flowers were strewn about like so many children's unmatched socks. Colors stood out vividly from the earth's red clay and each alabaster headstone. It must be cold underneath all that moist dirt, I thought. Goose bumps formed over every pore of my body. I hated being cold.

## Bargaining

At the time I arrived in Alto, in November of 1945, there were only about 500 beds available for treatment of tuberculosis. Fate often wraps bitter fruit in sweetness—so it was with Alto. My own beloved cousin, Hugh Dorsey, had, while serving as Governor of Georgia, authorized the Board of Health to update the facilities at Alto. Sales tax on tobacco were earmarked for improvements. The older buildings housed the coloreds; the newer ones were reserved for whites.

Mac pulled the borrowed Fairlane up to the front entrance. Massive oaks positioned themselves intermittently, like protective guards, throughout the grounds. Hill tops hovered about in every direction, rounded in softness by forests of pines. Elongated windows invited in sunshine, but they were closed to the cold, sharp mountain air.

Mac walked around in front of the car to my side of the door. A colored man, dressed in whites, came through the double-door entrance pushing a gurney. Mac opened my door.

"Macccuughh," I could hardly speak without coughing, "I can walk."

"I think you'd better just let the man take you, honey." Mac scooped me up and gingerly placed me on the gurney. The colored man tucked the sheets and blankets around me. He smiled, his teeth were as white as his slacks, but he did not make eye contact. Someone had probably told him years ago not to look a white person directly in the eyes, especially a white woman's eyes.

"Thanks," I sputtered, touching his hand for a moment.

"Don't chew be talkin', Ma'am. You needs to be savin' every breath."

"He's right, Rufe. You do everything you're told, even if it means you have to be quiet." Mac, walking at the foot end of the gurney, opened the door. Before I was pushed over the threshold, I breathed in as deeply as I could. I was worried this might be my last chance to breathe fresh air. It sent me into a fit of coughing spasms.

"Good girl," Mac bent over and held me close to his chest, rubbing my back. "See, you're already learning to swallow your words and we haven't even been here ten minutes!"

Patients at Alto were placed in wards, unless they were in critical condition, in which case, they were put into private rooms. So that others would not be subjected to watching their comrades die, I suspected.

I was admitted to a ward. The ward was nothing more than an expansive hallway, separated by heavy doors from the next hallway or ward. Twin-sized, iron beds, lined both sides of the ward. Most of them were full.

"Rufe, I'm going back to the car and get your things. The nurse is coming for you in just a moment to take you to x-ray. I'll be waiting here for you when you get back."

Even though I knew he would return, my heart felt betrayed the minute Mac left me alone in that ward. I was angry because he could just turn and walk out the door.

I resented Mac's well-being and the freedom that went along with it. Sure, I thought, just leave me the first chance you get. I'd leave too if I could. The place smelled of stale urine and dying breath. Four people coughed up sputum the first minute after Mac left. Several more did before the nurse arrived.

"Mrs. McCombs?" The nurse squatted down beside the gurney to make eye-contact. "My name is Margaret. I'm your nurse. Otis, here, is going to take you to x-ray. Okay?"

I looked into Margaret's green eyes, admiring a face that was as flawlessly sculptured as the most expensive ivory and thought, What choice do I have, Margaret?

I nodded a silent, and reluctant agreement.

As Otis wheeled me deep into the belly of Alto, I realized that Otis, here, was probably going to become my most constant companion. All righty, I thought, it's just me and Otis, here, from now on out.

Otis was a square man—fingers, shoulders, chin, and forehead were all chiseled in angular squares of one form or another, like a statue of some Civil War hero that I used to see during my summer visits with Granma Patsy in Tennessee. Otis had plenty of hair, salted with gray, but shaved close like a marine barber's. He'd be handsome if he wasn't so dark, I thought.

"Don't you be frett'n, Mrs. McCom's. Most folks comes to Alto gets better. It takes sum folks awhile, but theys shore 'nuff better whens they leave. You goin be better 'fore you knows it."

By the time we passed the sign that said "X-ray Department" I'd figured out that Otis liked to talk. That was okay with me since I didn't really feel up to it, and wasn't sure when I might. Other than the hushed murmurs of the staff, there was very little talking at Alto. Lots of coughing, but not much debate or exchange between patients. Otis' rambling kept my mind employed.

When he wasn't talking, Otis was humming or whistling. Church songs—*"The River Jordan" "At the Cross" "Power in the Blood."* If I could get a hold of somebody's powerful blood I might could get outta here. Wonder if Jesus could just heal my bad blood or do I still only need His? *Dear Jesus, Are you listening? Let's make a bargain.*

Otis didn't seem to have anything else to do all day but take care of me. He helped me get situated in X-ray. He waited outside the door for the technician to call him. He came back in, lifted me off the slab of cold table, placed me back on the gurney, and was wheeling me out of the room when the technician stopped him.

"Otis, Mrs. McCombs will need to be moved to a private room. Check with Nurse Preston, see where she wants Mrs. McCombs moved to."

"Yes, sir."

Otis looked at me for the first time that day. Maybe he saw the fear in my eyes, or maybe he saw an Angel of Death nearby, whatever he saw Otis never said, he just started singing. Not humming, Not whistling. But singing—*"There is Power, Power, Soul-Saving Power in the Precious Blood of the Lamb."* And I kept praying—employing all my bargaining skills, pleading before God, the Ultimate Judge, trying to help Him understand why this should not be happening to me.

It wasn't the first case I'd ever lost, but it certainly was the most costly one.

"Three to five years" is how long the doctors told Mac I would be confined—if I pulled through. Mac made me promise to do everything just exactly the way I was told. No problem there. I was as concerned as anybody about my own physical condition.

In 1945, there was no pharmaceutical answer to tuberculosis. Streptomycin was not used in Georgia until 1947, and even then was limited in use by its prohibitive cost, and eventually by its side affect—deafness. So the only treatment for myself, or others like me, was isolation, confinement, complete bed rest, and artificial pneumothorax.

Twice a week I was taken to a room where a Pulmonalogist and an x-ray tech would work together to insert a needle into an area of my lungs. This needle was used to collapse the lung in areas of infection as determined by the x-ray. Thereby allowing that area of the lung to receive needed rest. It was the standard treatment for patients with the more advanced stages of tuberculosis, of which I was one.

My doctors also told me that if I would lie as still as possible, my recovery would progress faster. The idea was to slow down my metabolism as much as possible, thus decreasing the drain upon my respiratory system. So I laid in bed day after day, refusing to turn over at night, or even blink more than I needed.

Mac would visit me as often as he could. We were both relieved to find out he had tested negative. My own exposure had been traced back to a co-worker at the D.C. office. An attorney whose office was next to mine. He, too, had been put into isolation, but had left, and returned to work prior to clearance on his sputums. He died shortly after I left D.C.—I had been infected since then.

Liberty Mutual gave Mac a company car and assigned him to the North Georgia region. (I had taken medical leave from my job with the USDA) This arrangement allowed Mac to visit me on Sundays, maybe once during the week if he was on assignment in the area, and on holidays.

# Happy Holidays

My first Christmas at Alto, I was still in a private room. Mac had told me the previous Sunday that he would be back up Christmas Day. With little else to occupy my mind, thinking about Mac consumed me like a hormonal thirteen-year-old who has just discovered that one true love. I daydreamed about the plans we'd made, the plans we'd accomplished, and worried about our plans now left undone.

"I hope I isn't bothering you, Mrs. McCom's."

Without moving my head, I tracked the voice to the doorway, Otis, here.

"C'm in, Otis." I tried to smile.

"I jus' stopped by to wish chew a Merry Christmas. Snow is a blowin' out there. Most snow I ever did see. I's goin' on home 'fore it gets worse. Anythin' I can get chew 'fore I's go?"

Slowly I shook my head, no. "M'ry Christm's, Otis."

By midnight on Christmas Eve, Alto had lost all electricity and heat. Every meal on Christmas Day was a cold one. Feeling sorry for myself, I contemplated crying, but figured it would use up energy that my body needed to heal itself. I knew Mac would have heard the radio reports on the weather condition, which meant this would be our first Christmas apart. He had planned to drive up Christmas Eve, stay at a motel about 30 miles from Alto, and spend Christmas Day with me. I silently cursed the snow that I could neither see nor touch—the snow kept me from seeing or touching the only Christmas gift I wanted— Mac.

At 5:00 p.m. someone knocked softly on my door. Probably another cold turkey sandwich, I thought, a little mayo slapped on white bread; seems everything around this place is white. The snow, the bread, the shoes, the clothes, the sheets, even my pallid skin.

"Merry Christmas, honey."

Lifting my head, I saw Mac standing in the doorway, holding a two-foot tree in one hand and a red foil bag in the other. His brown overcoat was wet, as were his gray slacks all the way to his knees. I knew his socks and shoes must be too. His grin was bright enough to lead wise men.

"Mac! What are...how did? Mac! I can't believe you're here!"

"You didn't think I was going to decorate this big tree by myself, did you?"

Mac walked over and placed the two-foot tree on the bedside table. It looked like a Christmas tree for leprechauns. Taking off his overcoat he leaned over and kissed my forehead. His lips were cold, but the smell of his tobacco and Old Spice warmed me from the inside out. Mac looked so handsome, I longed to have him closer. How does he do it? How long can he wait for me to be the wife he needs? I want to be at home, in our bed, taking care of him, instead of him taking care of me.

"Listen, honey, if my being here upsets you, the nurse will make me leave. She'll probably think I bought you the wrong gift." Wiping the tears from my face, Mac added, "Your folks called this week.

They are awfully worried about you. I told them how good you're being, how careful you are to follow every instruction. Your mother said she'd try to come up soon."

Pulling out a few silver bulbs from the bag, Mac began to decorate the little tree. "Oh, yeah, this is for you." Mac handed me a chocolate bar he'd pulled from the bottom of his sack. "Although you're sweet enough without it. Merry Christmas, Darling."

"Merry Christmas, Santa," I cried. "Having you *and* chocolate—how is it you know what every girl dreams for?"

"Trust me, I have my sources."

"Well, she'd better be a fat old grandma!"

That first Christmas at Alto has become one of the most tender of my memories. Mac had taken the company car on Christmas Eve and driven to the motel. When he awoke the next morning to snow and closed roads, he decided that he would walk to Alto. So he did, carrying our tree all the way. This was the first of many times that Mac made me feel so special, so loved, so cherished. Healing can come through medicine, but sometimes just basking in another person's love is all the healing one needs.

By Christmas of 1946, I was home in Atlanta, with my family and Mac's. Everyone showed up to welcome me home from Alto. I had worked diligently to do everything the doctors instructed; I believe I put more work into getting well than any job I have ever done. I was rewarded by being moved from a private room, to a ward and then home for two weeks at Christmas. The doctors allowed me to leave for a short visit because I was better, but also because Alto was closing.

And as happy as I was to be home, I felt guilty. Guilty about getting better when so many others were dying. I had a husband who loved me, family who cared for me and a God who watched over me. Did God love the other patients less? Why did God spare me when so many others, seemingly less ill, died? What would be the price I would have to pay for this redemption?

And what about Otis? He would be out a job once Alto closed. As would many other employees. There was no balance to life—mine, or anyone else's. Hospitals, which had been used by the Federal government during the war, were being claimed for public use since the hostilities abroad had diminished. Alto was overcrowded. An effort was made to secure a military hospital, Battey General, in Rome, Georgia, for expansion. Battey was given back to the State and I was relocated there in 1947.

Leaving Alto, Otis and the other patients was difficult for me. I knew these friendships were the kind born of trauma—intense for only a season in life. We poured our energies into encouraging one another, each aware of our own mortality. Would anyone on the outside every understand? I doubted it. Prior to my transfer, I had thought Battey was a state of mind, not a state hospital. Come to find out, sometimes they are the same thing.

## Healing Body and Soul

Prior to my release from Battey in late 1947, I took to heart the bargaining I had made with God that first night at Alto. Taking out pen and paper I wrote to every person in my life who I thought I might have offended at one time or another.

There was the time when as a new attorney in D.C. I had failed to send Mother a Mother's Day gift. Realizing my mistake, I rushed to get a card in the mail. Mother had told me later how hurt she was that I was so insensitive.

"But Mother," I defended, "I *did* send you a card."

"That card you sent me bothered me more than if you'd just plain forgot."

"Why in the world would a card bother you?" I cried.

"Because, Rufe, the card said, 'You've been just like a mother to me!' Well, I should hope to shout I've been like a mother to you!"

I knew that Mother was not the only person I had ignored while pursuing my own professional interests. So I wrote Mac, my sister, my father, and others asking their forgiveness and promising them that I would attempt to never again put my career before them. This was part of the bargain I had made that first night at Alto.

Remembering the story of Jephthah from my bible school days, I knew God took the vows of man seriously. Jephthah, an Israelite, had promised God that if He would provide victory over the Ammonites, then Jephthah would offer as a burnt sacrifice the first thing crossing over the threshold of his door upon his victorious return. I'm sure Jephthah was thinking it would be the family dog. Turns out it was his only child, his daughter. Jephthah kept his vow.

I certainly intended to keep mine. The 18 months that I had spent in confinement had forced me to reevaluate my life's priorities. I wasn't sure how much time God was going to allot me, but I figured He would eventually ask me to account for every moment of it. Having grown up in the church I had always believed God existed because I was told to. Now I believed in God's existence because I had personally spent time in His abiding presence over the past eighteen months. My faith in God was now my own.

But at first, I found it to be a fickle faith. Shortly after I was released from Battey, I began dealing with another kind of sickness—an emotional one. Tuberculosis had left me relatively unscathed physically. My retina had detached from my right eye, the same eye that caught the rock Frannie threw, but at that time there was nothing to be done for it. So other than a certain amount of blindness, my body was free from the ravages of tuberculosis.

"Rufe, I cannot believe how clear your x-rays are," commented Dr. Hobby, my Pulmonalogist, a year after my release from Battey. "There's not even a trace of a scar from your TB! Amazing! What a fortunate young woman you are!"

"Yes, I am."

"Have you returned to work?"

"No, sir. When I was released from Battey, I was told not to work for at least a year. The USDA wrote me a couple of months back and said I needed to let them know when I'd be back at work or they'd have to release me from employment."

"It'd be okay if you returned, Rufe." Dr. Hobby's elongated fingers held a stethoscope to my chest. "Your lungs are strong as a skunk's scent."

"Gee, thanks, doc. I hope my breath isn't."

"Better than most," he laughed.

"I'm just not ready to return to work yet."

"That's okay, Rufe. I'm not suggesting that you do. I'm just telling you that there's no medical reason why you can't at this point."

"I told them to hire someone else to replace me."

Dr. Hobby leaned back, crossed his arms, hugged himself and looked at me as if I were some new strain of deadly bacteria.

"You did? I'd been happy to extend your medical leave, Rufe. There's no need for you to quit."

My cheeks flushed red. I began to count the green asbestos tiles on the floor beneath my feet. Four squares, all those right angles, so simplistic. Why isn't life?

I can't seem to get anything squared away.

"Thanks, I appreciate the offer. It's just that I'm not sure I want to work any more."

Dr. Hobby was wrong, TB had left a scar, not one visible to anyone else, but one that I felt everyday. My lungs might have been clear, but my mind was not. That first year after I returned home from Battey, I began to experience an emotion I had never dealt with before. Fear. It was a comprehensive fear that undermined everything I did. All that confidence that had come to me so naturally before was gone. I believed that God had healed me, but I also knew that all healing is just temporary.

I was afraid that the same thing would happen again. I was afraid to go back to work. I was afraid to not get 10 hours of sleep and a nap during the middle of the day.

I was afraid to lift anything over two pounds. Pursuing the law had become unimportant to me compared to my staying well—which consumed my every thought.

As I look back on it now, I know that I needed help to put this illness behind me. However, I did not seek the help that I needed. During that time anyone who sought professional mental health was considered crazy.

I had been instructed to have an x-ray every six months, but the fear was so bad I insisted on having one every two months. When the USDA asked me to return to work, I didn't even consider it. I wrote back to them and asked them to terminate me immediately. There was no way I was going to compromise my health just for a job.

Mac was very patient with my fears. He did not press me when I told him I was not returning to work. Demanding nothing of me, Mac looked for ways to be of comfort and support. Of course, Mac was pretty busy with his own job at the time.

Liberty had him traveling several days a week. It was during these trips of Mac's that my fears became even more pronounced. I would envision Mac coming home to find me lying dead, my hand reaching for the phone. Every headache, every cough, every pain, sharp or dull, had its claws of death choking breath from me.

One Sunday, as Mac and I sat on the first row of the balcony at North Avenue Presbyterian Church in Atlanta, my fears reached their highest pinnacle. I began to feel as though I was falling. My head began to spin. My heart was racing. Perspiration blanketed my body like fresh morning dew. I grabbed hold of the rail in front of us with such a grip that Mac turned to look.

"Rufe, what's the matter?"

I didn't answer. The chandelier was spinning like a music box ballerina. I watched it twirl.

"Honey, are you okay?"

My eyes began to roll back into my head. Mac quickly put his arm around my back, under my arms, picking me up as he stood.

"Stand up, Rufe." Mac's normally gently voice was terse, "I'm taking you home."

It was after this incident that we both knew that I was sick again. Tuberculosis slowed me down, but fear had paralyzed me. With Mac's help, I began another healing process. I realize now that I was battling depression, but at that time I did not have a framework for my illness. I just knew that I needed to redirect my mental state.

So when thoughts of death, or illness arose, I purposed to deal with them.

I began memorizing anything that would help me control my own thinking pattern—poetry, scripture, literature. Determined to control my fears, I would meditate on those things: *"For God has not given us the Spirit of Fear, but of Love, of Power, and of Sound Mind...But sweet are the fruits of adversity...Whatsoever things are good, lovely, pure, think upon these."*

This inner healing took as much time to be effective as did the physical healing of TB. The healing required consistent effort on my behalf, but eventually the effort began to work, which, in turn, made me confident that I could. In 1950, I opened my own law practice.

## From Patient to Practice to Parent

By current standards, my practice was not anything to brag about. My gender, while not keeping me from pursuing law, did inhibit me from pursuing high-profile cases. During that time, about the only law cases entrusted to women were divorce cases (of which there weren't many) title searching deeds, and drafting wills. Basically, I'd spent all that time in law school learning how to fill out the right forms. I might as well have worked for an insurance company or for Mac.

During this time, Liberty Mutual promoted Mac to supervisor. Our lives took on a routine that lulled us into a sense of security. My health was restored. For the next several years, we worked hard and lived well. Just the two of us.

But by 1957, Mac and I decided that we didn't want our lives to revolve around the two of us. We wanted a child. Many of our friends were older couples, with no children. Mac and I found their conversations mostly centered upon themselves and their health problems. Hypochondriacs, we thought. I'd already lived with that disease and certainly didn't want it again.

In June of 1957, I paid a visit to Dr. Warmack.

"Did you bring in a morning sample, Rufe?"

"It's behind you on the counter, doc. You don't think that x-ray your partner did last week will cause any problems do you?"

"I don't think so. But why didn't you tell him you could be pregnant?"

"I told him I'd been gaining weight. That I felt uncomfortable. As old as I am, I figured I was having bad gas. But your partner thought I might have a tumor. The x-ray was his idea, not mine," I protested.

"Doesn't look much like a tumor to me, Rufe. Let me listen to those lungs of yours before you go. I'll call you tomorrow and let you know how the hunt goes."

"The hunt?"

"Yeah, you know—how many rabbits die."

Dr. Warmack never told me how many died, but I know at least one did.

"Rufe, the test was positive. You're pregnant."

I couldn't believe it! I was almost thirty-nine years old and pregnant for the first time! I rubbed my hand over my uterus trying to feel a two-month old life.

"I'm scheduling you a check-up with Dr. Hobby on Friday, Rufe."

"Okay," I replied. Then thought again, "Why?"

"I'll need his signature, as well as another doctor's, before I terminate the pregnancy."

"Terminate the pregnancy?"

"Rufe, you can't possibly be thinking of carrying this baby to term!" Dr. Warmack was almost shouting at me.

"Of course, I will. Mac and I planned this baby. We want this baby."

"With your medical history, Rufe, carrying this baby to term could jeopardize your well-being. I recommend an abortion."

"You can make the appointment with Dr. Hobby. But I don't care if you both agree, I'm not aborting my baby," I stated through gritted teeth.

Dr. Hobby found my lungs to be clear, as usual, and refuted Dr. Warmack's advised abortion. He felt there was no reason for me not to go ahead with the pregnancy.

"I wouldn't consider terminating this pregnancy, Rufe. There's just no reason for it. Your lungs are clear; you're quite capable of having a healthy pregnancy. I don't believe you could find three doctors who'd verify the need for an abortion."

Finally, Mac and I felt free to rejoice in our new upcoming role as parents. Just as with every new role in my life I wanted to prepare as much as possible for this job, so I signed up for parenting classes at the local YWCA. This was before Lamaze or Bradley methods were offered, so I had no idea what the class taught. The first night there I was kicked out of class.

"Excuse me, Mrs.," a tall woman, whose brunette hair was pulled straight back into a bun, spoke, "Can I help you?"

"Yes, ma'am, I'm looking for the Parenting Class. They told me at the desk it would be in this room." I took a look around the room at the girls sitting on folded chairs, most had ponytails and long bangs. I looked around the room, searching for future mothers. One girl, nearest the door, smiled at me. Her belly resting on her thighs.

I realized these girls, young enough to still need mothers of their own, would soon be mothers themselves. I felt old enough to be a grandmother.

Apparently, I wasn't smart enough to be one, though. During class that night, I soaked the doll I was given to bathe and then twisted the doll's head around in an effort to get out all the excess water.

"You do that to a real baby, Mrs. McCombs, and you'll be arrested!" our instructor laughed, taking the doll from me. I was so embarrassed by her remarks, I never returned for another class.

But ready or not, Grace Elizabeth McCombs, was born January 6, 1958. From that moment on, no job held as much honor or prestige or significance as that of being the best parents we could be to our daughter, our only child, Beth.

And the only thing I've learned from 38 years of parenting is that everyone knows how to raise everyone else's child, but no one is ever sure how to raise their own!

# 9

# GEORGIA LEGAL SERVICES

## The Beginnings

"Martelle, I'm thinking about opening my own law office."

"Might as well do it out of your home, Rufe."

"Why's that?"

"'Cause I don't think you'll be able to afford the overhead for your own office. Unless you plan on setting up one of those offices like they have in White County, where everyone does business."

"What kind of office is that, Martelle?"

"A privy in the backyard. Overhead is low, business stinks, flies are bad, but seems the office is always occupied."

"Very funny."

Martelle Layfield had a runner's body, tall and lean, but it was his runner's mentality that I noticed most. He never did anything slowly, methodically. He did everything as if he was struggling to set record time in the 50 yard dash. I bet even his pulse kept a double-time beat.

"Honestly, Rufe. I don't think you can make a go of it as a woman attorney in town. Not on your own. Columbus is just not ready. Beverly Kiel practices in juvenile court, but she practically grew up herself in Joe Ray's law firm."

Martelle, a partner with one of the most notable law firms in town, Grogan, Jones, and Layfield, had been my neighbor for several years. And even though he was young enough to be my own son, I was always seeking Martelle's advice. Martelle was a very successful attorney, who often used his abilities to benefit the city of Columbus. Martelle was one of the visionaries behind the consolidated municipality of Columbus.

Layfield's office was located on Broadway, downtown Columbus. His clientele list included big businesses, like the newspaper, The

Columbus-Ledger, the Medical Center, and the airport. Raised in Columbus, Martelle had come back to his hometown after obtaining a law degree from Mercer. Familiar with the community, he felt it was an honor to be involved in most of the civic organizations in town. Of course, Martelle was savvy enough to understand the financial benefits of networking prior to the term being coined. His mind never rested.

"Aw, c'mon, Rufe. You know this town as well as I do. There is no way a woman, even an intelligent woman like yourself, could obtain enough business in Columbus to run her own office. Who's going to refer people to you? You don't play golf, smoke cigars, or drink enough to get in on any of the real money deals in town. You can't advertise. I doubt many women will come to you; they're not going to want you to know their business. Specifically not who they, or their husbands, have been sleeping with!"

"What am I supposed to do, Martelle? I'm ready to go back to work. Beth's busy with school and Mac's busier than ever with his job. If I stay home any longer Mac's liable to demand that I learn to cook."

"That's not likely, Rufe. Mac would have to find you a recipe book written in Latin first, wouldn't he? With footnoted cross-references, of course."

"Were you always so quick-witted, Martelle?"

"Quick-witted? No. I've almost always been out-witted!"

I just shook my head. I trusted Martelle Layfield, if he thought it would be futile of me to open my own office, I knew he was probably right. It was July, 1969. I was fifty-years old, too old to be hired by any law firm in town. Staying home to take care of a family that wasn't home seemed a waste. I wanted to contribute more than just a clean house to my community. I wanted to do what I had always longed to do—practice law, again.

"Martelle, if I don't open my own office, I'll never work. No one's going to hire me at my age." Nervous, I picked at my navy skirt for lint that wasn't there. Maybe Martelle was afraid of the competition between us, I thought. No, not at all. How can I be considered competition? I'm a woman. Columbus attorneys aren't threatened by a woman, particularly an old one. Most of them treat me like they would their own mothers. They refer to me as "ma'am" and grin at me like a two-year old in search of approval.

Martelle jumped up. "You know Rufe, I was reading about something the other day. Hold on just a minute." Martelle's long legs took him across the room in less than four strides. "I think it's in this one." Martelle shuffled through a file. "Got it." He read to me from across the room. "Says that in August of '68, at a Board of Governors of the Bar, the Young Lawyers obtained permission to prepare an application for funding of a legal services program."

"Did they get any money?"

"No. By the time they got around to applying for the funding through the Office of Economic Opportunity (OEO) the funds were no longer available."

"Gee, thanks, Martelle, for this economic lesson, but..."

"Wait just a minute, Rufe. I'm not finished. The OEO didn't come up with the dollars, but this article says that earlier this year the Health, Education and Welfare (HEW) drafted regulation that requires the inclusion of legal services in every state's service plan. What that means is that legal services are going to be available to welfare recipients through funds provided by HEW."

"So?"

"So, Rufe, a proposal is already being drafted calling for the creation of a non-profit corporation, Georgia Legal Services Program, to be presented to the Board of Governors at their next meeting in August. If the Board agrees to incorporate the program, Columbus would need somebody to run the office here."

"Oh, I get it, Martelle. You want to relegate the care of the poor and homeless to the old and feeble."

"Now look who's trying to be funny. Tell me how such a feeble mind guides such a sharp tongue?"

"Perhaps one acts independent of the other one, Martelle."

"That might be true for other people, but not for you. You're far too discerning a woman, Rufe. I happen to know you've never had to feast on wasted words. Why don't we wait and see what happens at the August meeting? If the proposal is successful we could have the funding we need to create an office in Columbus." Martelle's fingers scratched at his dark sideburns. "Why don't you think about it for a few weeks, Rufe? By the time the meeting occurs, you should have some idea if you'd be interested or not."

"Okay. Thank you, sir, for your advice, for taking time from you busy schedule and all that." I rose to leave.

"No need to thank me, Rufe." Martelle waved a hand through empty space. "Just pay the bill as you leave," he laughed.

The proposal to create the non-profit, Georgia Legal Services, met with sharp criticism at the August meeting of the Board of Governors. It was withdrawn with the intent to resubmit it at a later date. But by that time, I had decided that opening an office to serve indigent clients was something I really wanted to do—with or without the funding—I knew I had Martelle's support.

Together we plotted. One of the Catholic Churches in town ran an outreach ministry from an old one story home downtown. They agreed to give us a room, for an office, rent free. Martelle put together a Board of Directors, comprised of all white males, mostly attorneys.

The Directors were in full support of providing legal services for the indigent client. The consensus among the attorneys in Columbus was that these clients needed help, had a right to legal help, but these same attorneys didn't want clients who were unable to pay. Nor did these attorneys want to establish an office that would compete in their financial arena. If money could be made off a case, they wanted it. My framework was very clear. Columbus' Legal Aid Society was established to provide clients who could not afford legal counsel with those services.

## The Clients

By October of 1969, I was in business. I had phone, a desk and two chairs, a file cabinet, and lots of determination. What I lacked was a secretary, a paycheck, and common sense. But most of my clients were so thankful to have my help that they were willing to overlook my faults.

Our first clients came to us via referral. If a client showed up in someone's office without a penny in their loafers, they were sent to us. Attorneys and bankers have a sixth sense that most other people don't—it is the ability to track the scent of money. I remember one client that got by the scent hounds.

This man came into my office suffering a disability from a series of heart attacks.

"Good afternoon, sir." I rose from my desk, immediately noticing his shuffled walk and jaundiced skin tone.

"Ma'am." His brown eyes greeted mine just briefly, then he lowered his head, as if he were suddenly embarrassed. Was he disappointed I wasn't a man? This man looked as though he'd just climbed five flights of stairs, his shoulders were stooped around his narrow chest. His breathing was deliberate. His fingertips were a coffee-stained brown.

A recovering smoker.

"What can I help you with?"

"I'm not sure you can help me, ma'am. See I've had three of these heart attacks, looks like the doctors can't help me much more. I've not been able to work since the last one. My doctor declared me disabled." His voice faltered over the last word. "I guess that means I'm not going back to work. My doctor says I'm entitled to benefits through my Social Security, but every time I try I'm turned down. I'm thinking all this work trying to fight Social Security's probably going to cause me another attack."

"Have you been to see any other attorney in town?"

"Yes, ma'am. I've seen two different ones. They take a look at my papers here, then they send me to someone else's office."

"So neither of the two attorneys you've seen have been able to help you?"

"No, ma'am. And I sure hate to bother you, but my doctor keeps telling me that I should be getting some sort of disability."

"Can I see those?" I nodded at the rubber-banded papers he was clutching. As he handed them to me, I began to review the facts in my mind. A man with three heart attacks and a doctor's signature should be able to receive medical disability. And if he could receive disability, any lawyer who took the case would be entitled to collect a fee for the work involved. Which meant if there was money to be made, it wasn't a case for Legal Aid. I would have to refer him again.

So I did. Three times I referred him to three different attorneys in town. Everyone of them sent him back to me. Finally, I decided that I would represent this client. Our first hearing was before the Social Security Board. After Social Security examiners heard the case, they turned us down. But I wasn't finished. I took the case to Federal Court, where Judge Bob Elliot remanded it back for a hearing before the Social Security Board for another review. But Judge Elliot made it clear to me that if I failed to get the help I needed there to bring it back to his court— Judge Elliot was determined that my client was going to receive a fair hearing.

The Social Security examiner must have taken Judge Elliot's remand seriously because on our next attempt they decided to give this client his disability. By the time a decision was made in his favor, my client's disability had gone on for so many years that Social Security ended up cutting their largest check ever for a disability claim. Legal Aid did not receive any of the money, nor did I, but if one of the lawyers that I had referred this client to, or that he had sought out himself, had been willing to represent this client, that lawyer would have taken in fees of approximately $18-19,000, a significant amount in those days. The case was written up in the law journals for its unusually successful settlement.

Many of the clientele serviced at Legal Aid were those who were in arrears. Given our current national debt, being in arrears doesn't seem that daunting of a problem, but our clients were often unemployed, living from domestic job to domestic job, or from laborer job to laborer job, and most often lacking in formal education. These clients would purchase items they could not afford with money they didn't have. Many clients signed documents they didn't understand; many signed documents that demanded exorbitant interest fees.

Several different companies were violating Georgia's Industrial Loan law, lending money to individuals, who were likely to be a debt risk, and then overcharging the amount of interest collectible under law. When these cases came in, I would draft a letter informing the said company that they were violating Georgia law, that they had so much to time to refund all of the overcharged interest and to write up a new contract for my client or I would pursue the case under the Industrial Loan Act.

Most often the company would send the refund check directly to our office and we would notify clients that we had a check waiting for them. I remember one such couple who had bought a washer and dryer and was charged fraudulent interest fees by the lending agent. They were a very old, very poor, white couple. By the time they shuffled into seats in my office fire ants could have built Manhattan.

"How're you all today?" I began.

"Fine, fine, Mrs. McCombs." Taking a handkerchief from the pocket of his suit jacket the old man wiped his forehead, upper lip and beneath his eyes. His brown jacket, dark enough to hide any stains, lumped around his body like quilts on an unmade bed. "It's a scorcher today, hot enough to fry bread without the skillet."

"Can I get you all some ice water?" I offered.

"Thank you for the offer, but I believe we've imposed upon you enough already," shaking blue-tinged curls about her face, the willowed woman sat clicking and unclicking a small red satin change purse.

"It's no trouble," I stood up. It was hot, my nylon slip was damp and sticking to my thighs.

"Please, ma'am, don't bother." The old man began to stand himself. "We appreciate your offer, but Mother here is right, we've already imposed on you enough. Your waiting room is already so crowded I bet dust can't find a place to settle."

I handed the fellow his check. "This is the refund check the lending agent sent back for the overcharges. I need you to sign these papers, this one is the new contract they drafted with amendments for the reduced amount of interest. I don't believe you'll have any more trouble with them, but if you should, feel free to call me."

Click. Click. I looked at the old woman. She smiled.

"Before you go, I do have to ask you for a dollar for registration fees. I hate to ask you, but it's our new policy. It helps us pay for all the paperwork involved."

The clicking stopped, both of them looked at me like I'd just asked for the deed to their home, if they had one. Rising, the old woman shoved the change purse deep into the pocket of her green-flowered shift. Folding up the refund after checking its three-digit amount, the man solemnly placed it within the folds of his wallet, from which he had taken a dollar bill. The slow way in which he handed the dollar over made me wonder whether it was the last dollar he had, or the first he'd ever made. I felt guilty.

After thanking me again, they both left. On the way out he turned to his wife and said, "Well, Mother, I believe that was the best lawyer I could get for a dollar."

Before I had felt guilty about asking clients for the one dollar fee, but now I felt like marked-down merchandise at a blue-light special. I half-expected my receptionist, Deena Nelson, to yell out, "Sale in Aisle Three. Hurry." Instead she just sent in the next client. I refused to ask him, or anyone ever again, for the dollar fee.

## The Staff

In October of 1969, the Board of Governors agreed to participate in the HEW's plan to provide services to clients in need. By March of 1970, Georgia Indigent Legal Services, GILS, was incorporated, which provided the Columbus' office with some funding. Deena Nelson was only twenty-three when she applied for the job of receptionist.

A young mother, Deena had been working at Kinnett's Dairy prior to joining our small staff. With her stylishly cropped hair, full lips, high cheekbones, dark, intense eyes, Deena looked as if she were one of the queens etched by ancient Egyptians. I soon found out Deena possessed many of the qualities a queen would need. Organized, punctual, determined, and ambitious, Deena continues to work with Columbus' Legal Aid as a paralegal. She has lasted longer than any of us attorneys.

Besides Deena, we had a couple of attorneys on staff. These attorneys were usually recent graduates from law school and typically stayed about a year, long enough to find a job in town that would cover their dry cleaning bill. Working for Legal Aid was definitely an entry-level position.

We also employed a pool of secretaries. Mary Taylor was one of the women in the secretarial pool. I will never forget the day Mary showed up to interview for the job. She wore white gloves. I remember wondering if she wore them while typing. She didn't, but even if she had, she still could have typed better than me.

## The Haunted House

As we enlarged, Martelle found us a new office on Second Avenue—an old two-story Victorian, owned by an attorney Rick Fry. Legal Aid rented the downstairs and Fry had his office upstairs. It was my practice to be the first one at the office, and often the last one to leave. This meant that my normal schedule ran from 7:30 a.m. until 6:30 p.m..

This was a work habit that evolved during our first year, when we served clients without scheduled appointments on a first-come, first-serve basis. I would stay until every client had been seen before going home, and then return early the next day so that I could finish up the previous day's paperwork. I found that even after we began to schedule clients, I still needed that respite in the mornings to organize myself.

One summer morning as I sat at my desk, which faced the front windows of the old house, I looked up from my papers and saw Mr. Fry pull his car up to the curb. Glancing at the clock atop my desk, I noted the time, 7:40, and wondered aloud, "What's he doing here so early?" I was miffed that Fry was about to interrupt my quiet sanctum; he usually didn't get to the office before 9:00 a.m..

After parking his car, Fry reached over the back seat and picked up something I could not see. I heard the car door slam and Fry bound up the wooden porch. Intent on my work, I hoped he would not stop to chat. The unlocked front door rattled as Fry shoved it open. Ordinarily, walking from the front door to the stairs that led upstairs would take a person about ten steps, Fry bounded there in two. The stairwell upward was a steep flight of approximately fifteen stairs. He must've taken them five at a time: I only heard Fry's shoes on three of those steps.

At the time I didn't think much of this, other than noting that he seemed to be in an awful big hurry. Then came a sound that even to this day thunders in my brain. Crack! Thud! It sounded as if lightning had bolted above my head, knocking flat whatever it hit. But I knew it wasn't lightning; it was a gunshot.

I jumped. Shivers ran to my fingertips. I think even my wig hairs were standing on end. My heavens, I thought, has someone shot Mr. Fry? A burglar? I looked around the room for a weapon. What I wanted most was a shield. I listened. I heard the bluejay's melody outside my window, but nothing upstairs. If a burglar had shot Mr. Fry, the intruder made no effort to scurry away. Was he lying in wait for me? His gun aimed at the foot of the stairwell?

I was never more aware of my own animalistic nature than in those next few moments. Drawn to the source of horror, I headed for the stairwell. I had to see what happened, even if it meant facing down a gun barrel.

Opening my office door, I called out, "Mr. Fry? You all right, Mr. Fry?" That ought to forewarn anybody who might be present that now would be a good time to get out. I waited. The clock on Deena's desk was ticking. My palms were sweating.

I rubbed them down my hips, like a gunslinger getting ready for the big draw. I took a deep breath and let it out. Then slowly I walked toward the stairwell.

When I reached it, I grabbed hold of the curved oak rail with both hands. They were still sweaty. God, I wanted to just go home and start this day over! I looked up. No gun barrel. My heart skipped to a double-time rhythm.

I knew Fry was at the top of those stairs. I once heard a preacher say that we might live in a crowd, but we face God and eternity alone. How I would have loved to be in a crowd at that moment! It was then that I realized we face more than just eternity alone, we face reality alone too.

I never made it to the top of the steps. I saw Fry as soon as I reached the middle of the stairwell. The bottoms of his shoes were visible from where I stood, as were his brains, splattered like sponge-painting, on the wall behind him. I turned and ran back down to my desk. My heart was racing. I could hear my own pulse. I felt nauseous. Picking up the receiver, I dialed the police station.

"This is Rufe McCombs at Legal Aid. Send someone quickly, Mr. Fry has been shot." Excited with fright, I spoke with rapid-fire authority.

"Ma'am, would you please repeat your name?" came the dispatcher's reply.

"Rufe McCombs. I'm at the Legal Aid office on Second Avenue. Mr. Rick Fry owns this house. I think he's dead. Upstairs. I believe he shot himself. Please send someone over."

"Are you all right, ma'am?"

"I'm fine," I said, although, I wasn't. I don't think the dispatcher believed me anyways.

"I'll send someone out right away," she reassured me.

It wasn't quick enough for me, I dialed another number. The main fire station was located directly across the street from our offices.

"This is Rufe McCombs at the Legal Aid office. Mr. Fry, who owns this building, apparently just shot himself. Could you send over a couple of your men?"

I didn't say why I really wanted them to send someone over. How do you tell a stranger you'd rather be with them than alone?

"Rufe McCombs at the Legal Aid office across the street?"

"Yes, sir."

"Did you call the police, ma'am?"

"Yes, sir."

"Someone over there got shot?"

"Yes, sir."

"Are they still firing?"

"Still firing?"

"Ma'am, is anyone there still armed?"

Did this idiot think I'd take the time to call him while someone randomly unloaded lead above my head?

"Sir, I already told you that I think Mr. Fry shot himself, looks like he had a fairly steady hand. There's nobody else firing off guns over here."

"So you're okay?"

Why did everyone keep asking me that question? Obviously I was more okay than Rick Fry, but not okay enough to stomach a bowl of Brunswick stew.

"I'm a little shaken up. I'd appreciate it if you'd send somebody over."

"Yes, ma'am, I reckon you are. We'll be right over."

Although I'd seen his brains clinging to the wall like cottage cheese on a plate, no one had yet confirmed that Fry was dead. I knew I wasn't going back up to check his pulse. Maybe one of the firemen would. The police still hadn't arrived. I figured I'd better call an ambulance, just in case.

As I placed the black receiver back into its cradle, I heard sirens. I looked out the window, hoping to see a police car. Instead I saw the hook and ladder red fire engines across the way pull out of their garage. The trucks headed around the block, with the sirens going full blast, then pulled up in front of Legal Aid. Five men dressed in yellow regalia trounced up the porch; the only thing missing was the Dalmatian. The sirens were on, blasting screeches and red lights throughout the neighborhood, which was now wide-awake thanks to the parade of trucks around the block. Why in the world did they need their engines, when they could have just walked across the street?

A couple of the firemen went upstairs. The police arrived, as did the ambulance. The firemen were the first to confirm that Fry was indeed dead. He had put a revolver in his mouth and pulled the trigger. Lt. John Wood, the officer in charge, questioned me. Lt. Wood and I knew each other well enough, his son Jerry had been courting our Beth. While conducting the investigation, Lt. Wood scared me, "Please don't leave town, Mrs. McCombs, in case we need to get in touch with you. We need you to be available for any further questions we might have."

It was no longer a matter of a courtesy interview. I was forbidden to go anywhere that would remove me from the watchful eye of Columbus' Police department. Was I a suspect? I had been the only other person in the building. Did they think I shot Fry?

By the time the police left with Fry's body, several of the office staff had arrived for the day. It was obvious that there was no way we were going to be able to see clients. Deena started calling people to cancel appointments and generally informing them of the morning's tragedy. I sent the rest of the staff away for the day, but stayed at the office myself.

Emotionally numb, I tried to focus on the piles of paperwork stacked around me. As I read through a file, my mind replayed the morning's events. Should I have come out of my office and greeted Rick? What would he have done? Was he so distraught that he would have shot me first? Perhaps I could have said something that would have stopped him. Why didn't I come out of my office?

By noon the upstairs had warmed up considerably. Deena was still at her desk. Walking over to her, I inquired, "That smell is bad, huh?"

"Yes, ma'am, it's strong."

"This heat's making it worse."

"I could open some windows if you think it'd help."

"You can open them if you like, Deena, but I guess I'm going to have to find someone to clean that room up." We looked at each other awkwardly, like parents deciding who's turn to change the diaper.

"I could call someone," Deena offered.

"Yeah? Where do you look in the yellow pages? Hydro-blast your wasted matter?" I smiled wryly. "Thanks anyway, but I think I'll just run down to the Employment office. There's bound to be some laborers there who need a job for the day." I didn't tell her, but I think Deena knew I was more than anxious to get some fresh air.

I was right, within minutes of arriving at the Employment office I had four men in the car with me, ready to earn a day's wages—until I stopped at the first traffic light.

"What kind of work you got for us, ma'am?" The oldest of the four men called to me from the back seat of the Oldsmobile. "Grant and me, we's done lots of jobs together. Last week we put a new roof on the Piggly Wiggly. That was one sorry job, carrying them shingles up that ladder. Shore enough was hot, huh, Grant?"

"This is an indoor job," I replied, looking into the rear-view mirror at his wide brown eyes. I hoped I sounded calm. "Shouldn't be too hot, although it is an upstairs room." I looked at the still red light. "The job might be hard though. A man shot himself in the office this morning. I need for y'all to clean up the room." The light turned green.

I heard a car door slam. Looking into the mirror again, I saw the tailends of all four men running down the street. I would have laughed if I hadn't felt so grief-stricken.

"Deena," I called out as I walked through the front door, "you'd best get on the phone and call Striffler-Hamby Mortuary."

"Are all the laborers already busy for the day?" Deena picked up the receiver, ready to dial.

"Yeah, they were all laying tracks today. Ask someone at Hamby's if they know of someone we can get to clean up this place." Shutting my office door behind me, I went directly over to the window and opened it.

Rich Fry's suicide haunted me for many years. Actually, I think it might haunt just more than me. When Legal Aid moved out of that house on Second Avenue, the Jaycee's bought the house. Deena tells me that they didn't do any renovations to it. The Jaycee's use it to host a haunted house there every Halloween.

# The Publicity

My tenure at Legal Aid was rarely a high profile job. In fact, many of Columbus' residents didn't even know Legal Aid existed. Attorneys were restricted from self-promoting or advertising by law, so all referrals came by word-of-mouth. When I look back on the work I did for Legal Aid and how it has paid off over the years, it doesn't bother me that I didn't initially draw a salary.

Today, I realize that I never could have commercially produced the name recognition and reputation that Legal Aid provided me. My work there remains the most cost-effective advertising I've ever done. People remember names they see in print, especially if that name happens to be in the police log, or the obit section. So far I've avoided those two, but my name has made headlines ever since I started working with Legal Aid.

And that's not because the contacts I made at Legal Aid were the recognized pillars of Columbus' society. If one could afford legal help, one went elsewhere. But between late 1969 to 1975, the years I worked for Legal Aid, I saw thousands of clients; people who would remember me when I chose to pursue a political career. And these clients had friends, who sometimes *were* the recognized pillars of Columbus' society.

One such friend was Elena Amos, wife of John Amos, founder/owner of AFLAC, American Family Life Company. Elena, a Cuban native, often makes headlines herself because of her passionate concern and involvement on behalf of many politically repressed Cubans.

While I was at Legal Aid, Elena referred one of her friends to me for legal advice. It was not a complicated case; it did not involve anything of a political nature, but Elena never forgot that I helped. To my knowledge, John Amos, never supported my political career financially, or any other way, but Elena did whenever the opportunity arose, sometimes handing me a campaign contribution and whispering, "Don't say anything to John about this."

But not all my contacts with Columbus' society women were as positive as my relationship with Elena. One Columbus woman, owner of a Collection Service in town, was making large profits through means of extortion. Under her direction, the agency used several different forms of intimidation to coerce clients into paying illegal fees.

Clients would receive angry letters, phone calls, and even personal visits. Down South, we're fairly friendly, so unexpected house calls are not unusual. But in this case, the owner of the Collection Service took the old adage "drop by" too seriously. She, or one of her employees, would show up any time, day or night, to collect. And if she couldn't find a client at home, she would go to their place of business, or stalk them alongside the roads, waiting for the opportunity to run them down.

When her agency received a collection or report of a NSF check they would dictate the following type of letter to a client:

Dear Mr. Posey:
We have in our possession a $50 check that you endorsed to the Uneeda Eye Clinic. This check was returned for non-sufficient funds. You have until Friday, 1:00 p.m., to have $150 in our office or we will prosecute you.
Sincerely,
A. G. Collection Services

These clients came to Legal Aid afraid they were on their way to jail. So many clients came in with letters from this particular agency that I decided we should use some intimidation of our own. I wanted to shut them down.

I called in a friend of mine, Harry Pettigrew, an Atlanta lawyer, to help me on the case. Harry had never been to Columbus before, but I have never forgotten the observations Harry made during his visit.

"Rufe, Columbus is a very strange town. It appears to me that there are particular women who can do just about anything and get away with it. Are most of them Society Saints? Apparently these matrons can do no wrong in the eyes of this community."

Harry had an acute awareness for the obvious. He understood that women have always played powerful roles in the development of community politics, even before holding elected positions. I wasn't sure how much political power the owner of this agency had in Columbus, but angry over her bully tactics, I was determined to challenge her image, the source of her political power.

So I did something so unusual it had only been attempted once before, I filed racketeering charges against her. The Ricco Act, designed to prevent the continued transgression of extortion, made the headlines during the Nixon Administration when Bebe Rebozo, a mob affiliate, came under investigation by the Justice Department. Rebozo was never prosecuted, but headlines declared great concern about Rebozo's ties to Nixon and their combined real estate dealings that had occurred in Florida during the fifties.

At the time I began exploring the possibility of using the Ricco Act to prosecute this one-town agency, there were no other tried cases to use as a source of referral or definition of the law. Currently, The Ricco Act is used in both State and Federal Courts, but in 1973, racketeering charges were a Federal offense that were only tried in Federal Court.

What Pettigrew and I had to do was find clients who were willing to say that this Collection agency was using intimidation as a means of extortion; which proved to be easy, since this agency apparently recruited its employees from the Wednesday Night Wrestling matches at the Coliseum.

These wrestlers suffered from chronic buffness that depleted their oxygen supply. A lack of oxygen in grown men apparently results in a constant state of aggression. Our clients were anxious to testify; but that anxiety worked both ways—our clients were scared to testify and scared not to testify. Either way they felt threatened. Winning this case was really important to them.

Pettigrew took most of the depositions. I did a lot of the research and paper trail, which turned out to be longer than I expected. In the course of pursuing the racketeering charge, I found that many of the original contracts signed by Legal Aid clients violated the Truth and Lending law. Several of the businesses in town that offered credit to their customers, failed to disclose to those same customers the amount of interest they would be paying for that credit. One of these businesses, Skinner's Furniture, was owned by my next-door neighbor, Mr. Darnell.

Darnell called me at home.

"Rufe, just how is it that you are going to go through with this case against A.G. Collection? Don't you understand that I have a signed contract with your clients? We agreed to allow them to purchase that couch and they agreed to pay for it. Don't you think they ought to pay for the merchandise?"

"Mr. Darnell, those contracts are in violation with the Truth in Lending Law. Did you ever tell my clients exactly how much that couch is going to cost?"

And Mr. Darnell wasn't the only one who called me at home to get me to drop the case. The owner of the agency called me as well.

"Mrs. McCombs," she began with sugar-cane sweetness." I hope I'm not disturbing your dinner."

"Not at all," I replied, while tuna-fish casserole congealed on my plate.

"This business regarding the agency is getting out-of-hand."

Out of your hands, I thought.

"Isn't there some way we could work this out between us? All these legal fees are going to put me out-of-business."

Exactly the point.

"I'd help you if I could," I replied, meaning it, but understanding that this woman needed a different kind of professional help than I was qualified to give. "There's really nothing I can do at this point. I suggest if you have any further questions, you need to contact your lawyer."

Click. She hung up on me.

Norwood Pierce was her lawyer, and he gave her good advice, which to her credit, she took. Instead of going before a jury trial, she agreed to allow Judge Elliot of Federal Court to hear the case and write an order. Norwood advised her to face Elliot and to do whatever Judge Elliot required. Pettigrew and I had the depositions of eight clients. Judge Elliot reviewed the case, ruled the client's contracts void, and the agency closed.

And again my name made print, for setting legal precedence on behalf of Legal Aid. Headlines declared me a heroine for the agency's victims; praising me for having the foresight to pursue this case under the Ricco Act.

But I've often wondered if Pettigrew's remarks about the way Columbus esteems certain women as having an ability to do no wrong, thus granting those women immense power, was epitomized later by my own political achievements.

Or, perhaps, some of the credit needs to be given to Judge Elliot. It was because of the quality of jurist Bob Elliot is that I had the confidence my clients would receive a fair hearing before his court.

Yet, today, I suppose the woman I prosecuted, could claim the sweetest victory—her husband currently holds a elected position, and I do not. Talk about injustice. If you live long enough you begin to regret it.

## Death—Life's Motivator

But in truth, I am very appreciative that I've lived this long. There were days I didn't think I'd live to see seventy, much less eighty. Spending that year and half in the sanitarium with tuberculosis magnified my mortality. During the fall of 1972, my physical limitations became an issue once again.

Actually, sickness and death stalked my life during the early seventies. Tucked in cotton sheets behind the doors of a private room at the Medical Center, Mother became death's first victim. Lula Claude Dorsey Edwards lived to be ninety, before suffering a stroke that led to kidney failure and her passing on March 21, 1971.

In December of that same year, Daddy was admitted to St. Francis. He had been diagnosed with colon cancer, which necessitated a colostomy—partial removal of his colon. Daddy made it through the surgery, but a bleeding ulcer attacked him and he, too, became death's prey on January 3, 1972.

Gorged and gloated, but not yet satiated, death crouched in a corner and waited for me. I turned fifty-four that August, and as was my usual practice, I scheduled a yearly check-up with my physician, Dr. Bruce Newsome. Since I had returned to work, these check-ups kept getting pushed further away from my August birthdate. I was beginning to practice selective recall. Other than eating the frosting, I had no use for birthdays, much less physicals.

So it was October before I scheduled my annual visit. But that particular Friday the office was so busy, I kept telling myself that I was going to call and postpone my appointment, or perhaps cancel it, which is what I really wanted to do. However, something within kept yanking at me, until I felt that canceling this appointment would be paramount to murdering somebody. And maybe that somebody was me.

So even with the office full of people, I left Legal Aid at 10:30 a.m., assuring Deena that I would return by 1:00 p.m.. After having my weight registered, my pressure gauged, my privates scraped, and my blood drawn up, Dr. Newsome sent me away, indebted to him for at least fifty bucks.

The next day, Newsome called me at home.

"'Mornin', Rufe, hope I didn't wake you."

"No, no, not at all." Holding up my wrist, I glanced at my Timex, 9:00. "It's late for tee-off though, isn't it, doc?"

"Too much exercise too early is bad for the heart, Rufe. My blood doesn't begin to percolate until after ten. Tee-off's at one today. But speaking of blood, Rufe. I got the results back on yours last night and I need you to come in for some more tests."

I turned around and watched Mac throw a load of wash in the dryer. I motioned to him to open up the dryer door; I couldn't hear over the noise. "Pardon me, doc. The dryer was going and I missed what you said."

"Rufe, your white blood count was considerably high. We need to schedule you for some more tests. Can you come back in on Monday?"

That same voice that had nagged at me to keep the appointment, now screamed at me from within, "Told you so! Told you so!" My mind hit replay. "High Blood Count. High Blood Count." Sweat beaded over my pores. Stomach juices began carving a hole. "C-A-N-C-E-R, cancer, cancer, cancer," the voice was chanting now.

"What time on Monday?"

"How 'bout ten, is ten good?"

"As good as any, I guess."

"Okay, I'll see you on Monday. Plan on staying the morning, Rufe."

"Sure, doc. See you Monday."

On Monday, Dr. Newsome found a lesion in my rectum. He scheduled a hospital visit for further tests, all the while trying to reassure me.

"I don't think it's cancer, Rufe."

But I knew better than to believe him; I didn't think he believed himself. Daddy had been diagnosed with colon cancer less than a year ago, and he was dead. Most people think of death as cold, but I felt the bated breath of death behind me; it felt hot, like a passionate lover, one who easily betrays. The hunt was on; I felt death chasing me.

I checked into St. Francis Hospital in Columbus the next day for test. I took with me a stack of files to prepare a brief for Appellate Court that following week. But Newsome kept me busy with one exam after another.

Finally, he conceded, "It looks suspicious, Rufe. We're going to do some further exploration."

And in an ironic mimic of the drama of a courtroom where the suspicious suddenly become guilty as hell, Dr. Newsome scraped the lining of my colon, where sure enough, cancer cells were propagating. Death was licking his lips.

"Rufe," Dr. Newsome lowered his eyelids, avoiding eye contact, and my pain, or his, "I recommend that you undergo radical surgery to remove your large intestine and rectum; they are both infected. I know this is difficult." He lifted his gaze momentarily, then looked away. "But I don't see any other way, Rufe. I'm scheduling you for surgery on Thursday, okay?"

"No, doc, not Thursday, that's my parlor day. I couldn't possibly cancel a hair appointment just for radical surgery. You'll just have to wait."

Dr. Newsome's gray eyes searched my face, and my hair. Was I kidding? He wasn't sure. I think he was stumped by the fact that I already wore a wig, what did I need a parlor day for?

"Tell you what, Rufe. You just send your hair on over to the parlor, and I'll see you in pre-op, Thursday morning. Think of how much time that'll save you," he laughed.

Yeah, time, I thought, my eyes taut with held-back tears. How much do I really have?

By the time the cancer was found I had already undergone three different minor surgical procedures (if there is such a thing), so facing another surgery just seemed like one more process I would have to go through, before either I died or got better.

I hoped for the latter; I feared the other.

But this surgery was hardly like the others. Radical is just another word for revolutionary which is another word for extremist. Which is what the surgery turned out to be—extreme in every way, particularly the pain.

Having undergone the procedure of having my lungs artificially collapsed with a needle several times a week while I was being treated for tuberculosis, I was on fairly familiar terms with pain. But this time pain demanded more attention.

When I woke up after surgery in the Intensive Care Unit, I was very, very ill. I remember that Mac was there. His presence was soothing, although I can't recall anything he said or did during that time. Under the influence of anesthesia, I only recall that I have never been in as much pain as I was for the next several days. My stay in Intensive Care lasted about two weeks. Other than the pain, the thing that frustrated me most was that blasted nurse call, it was never within reach; a cow bell would have been more effective.

During that time, I really needed the help of a nurse. Mac who was at the hospital each morning, noon, and evening, finally arranged for me to have a private nurse and I was transferred to a private room. Then the healing process began to speed up rapidly. By the end of the next week, Dr. Newsome released me for home care, with the strict instructions that I was not to return to work for another two weeks, at least.

I had never been able to complete the brief I had taken to the initial hospital visit, so I began to work on it shortly after returning home. I stayed home the required two weeks, then I took a blanket and pillow and returned to work. My intention was to rest during the early afternoon. But once I was at the office and faced with a lobby full of clients, I just could not rest. Despite admonitions from Mac and Dr. Newsome, work began to consume me once more.

And actually, I believe work helped me to heal. Perhaps because the intensity of which I approached my work, my job seemed more powerful than death's appetite. That's a delusion that many workaholics suffer, but as far as delusions go, it appears to have been an effective one. The more I worked, the more quickly my body recovered.

But the surgery was, and has been, a terrible handicap for me. Mac, as always, was there for me. He did not seem repulsed by me. I feared at that time, just as I had during my years in the Sanitarium, that Mac would no longer find me sexually attractive and would seek the company of other women. But to my knowledge, he never did.

In fact, he seemed to grow closer to me, always seeking ways to express his pride in me, his love for me, and his desire to meet any of my needs. Mac really sought to make life better for me.

And Beth did the same. Only fifteen-years old at the time of my surgery, Beth, along with her Daddy, sought to serve me. Each took every opportunity available to ask, "What can I do for you?" Their nurturing restored an inner healing in me, as well as an outer one. I am positive that I would have dealt with a lot more scars, both mental and physical, if it had not been for Mac, Beth, and my work.

Yet, the cancer cast a shadow over my life. Not only the changes it made in my daily routine, but the reality that I had no control over it; I didn't know what caused it; I didn't know how to cure it; I wasn't sure it was gone. In the beginning, I grieved the loss of part of my body, and abhorred the thought that I was now unlike everyone else.

Never was this more pronounced than when we went swimming as a family one Saturday, the summer following my surgery. Beth motioned for her daddy to come away from where I was lounging poolside.

"What was that all about?" I inquired when Mac returned.

He smiled. "Beth was all worked up about how it was you could swim with a ...you know... She was pretty distraught."

"What'd you tell her?"

"I told her to ask you, of course." Mac nodded towards Beth. "You better go talk to her."

"Gee thanks." I got up and walked over to steps where Beth sat splashing her feet.

"Beth," I stretched out beside her, "your daddy says you're worried about something."

Scooting down the steps until only her head was above the water, Beth asked, "How can you do this, Mother?"

"Do what?"

"Get in the water."

"Why shouldn't I be able to get in the water, Beth?" I walked down the steps and joined Beth in the water.

"Well, what about your..you know? Can you get it wet?"

"Listen, Beth, I think I'm in a much better position to go swimming than you are."

"How's that?"

"I don't wear the bag swimming, Beth, but I do put a clean Band-aid over my opening and you don't, so I guess that makes me more sanitary than you, or anyone else, in this pool!"

But the surgery has oftentimes made me feel unsure and insecure. Which is why I moved out of our bedroom after my surgery. At the time, I told Mac it was because I didn't want to disturb him during the night. Mac believed that for awhile, until I didn't return to the bedroom. Then Mac figured out the real source of my discomfort—shame.

How could anyone want to be intimate with a woman in my condition? Mac forced me to talk about my insecurity, assuring me that he loved me and that he was still attracted to me. But he didn't demand anything from me. He waited until I grew comfortable with my own body, or what was left of it. Then we resumed the intimate part of our relationship. And between swimming with Beth and sleeping with Mac, I have used up more Band-Aids than 225 primary schools!

The first five years following surgery the thought of the cancer returning never left my subconscious. Now that it's been over twenty years, I feel a lot more confident about claiming victory over death, but as a doctor friend of mine once told me, all healing is just temporary.

When I allow myself to wonder why I ever entered the political realm I always come back to these same three events—the suicide of Rick Fry, the victories I had in Elliot's courtroom (particularly, over the corrupted collection agency) and my own encounter with death—each event challenged me to evaluate where I was in my life, and what it was that I wanted to accomplish before my life was over.

Rick's death disturbed me. I wanted, still want, to somehow affirm his value as a person, and perhaps to have healed him from despair.

After the experience with Rick, I never again wanted to let another person go through my life without somehow finding a way to connect with them, to affirm them, to be a source of help for them, if I could.

And my dealings with the collection agency magnified for me the potential I possessed to really be of help to others. That's when I began to mull over Pettigrew's assessment of the power of certain women in Columbus' society. I believed Harry was right, that Columbus has held up certain women beyond reproach. And I began to suspect that I was one of those women. If Harry's speculation proved correct, then I would be able to use my position in the community not only for my benefit; I could use that position to be of help to many people who might not otherwise have representation in the community; people like the clients I served everyday at Legal Aid.

And as every Bible preacher knows, there is nothing that motivates people like an encounter with death, especially their own, and I was no different. By 1974, I had successfully recovered from my surgery and received blood clearance; the cancer was in remission.

Was God giving me more time for a purpose? If so, I wanted to use that time as purposefully as possible.

My own wearisome death watch over, I vowed that not only would I thank God for the extra time allotted me, but that I would strive to make God thankful too.

# 10

# THE JUDGESHIP

## Nilan's Job

Late in 1974, I heard that Municipal Court Judge John Nilan was ill. Approximately 20,000 cases were tried annually in Columbus' Municipal Court. Judge Nilan handled preliminary hearings on criminal cases involving state violations brought by the Sheriff's office, as well as deciding upon civil matters in small claims up to a $5,000 maximum. Over 65% of all our Legal Aid cases were heard in Nilan's Municipal limited jurisdiction court.

Months later, when it became apparent that Judge Nilan's cancer was terminal, several people, including Court Clerk Rob Welch (the same court clerk that I later discovered stealing from Municipal Court) approached me about running for Nilan's unexpired term.

"Mrs. McCombs, Rob Welch is on line two, can you take the call?" Deena asked.

"Which line?"

"Line two."

"All righty." Pressing down line two, I greeted Welch, "Hey Rob, how are you?"

"That depends, Rufe."

"Depends on what?"

"It depends on how this phone call goes." "What's the matter Rob? You got a caseload of Girl Scout cookies to sell? I'll take two boxes, but that's all!"

"Well you're right about this being a sales pitch, Rufe, but not for cookies." Rob took a breath before continuing. "I suppose you've heard that Nilan's not coming back."

"I'd heard that he was very ill and that it was unlikely he'd be back. Is there something I can do to help?"

"Well, yeah, Rufe, there is, sort of. Several of us over here at Municipal have discussed the possibility of you running for Nilan's position." Welch's voice was booming with eagerness, "We need someone who we think we can work with, Rufe. We think you're that person. Would you consider it?"

Rob Welch was not the first, nor the last, to approach me regarding the possibility of running for Judge Nilan's position. And I told him what I told everyone at that point, "I'll give it some consideration."

Having lived in Columbus only fifteen years at that point, I had strong reservations about setting myself up for what I feared would be a total defeat. Columbus, like most Southern cities, had been settled for decades. During the 1820's Columbus was a main trading post for settlers. The Creek Nation occupied territory west of the Chattahoochee, while settlers claimed territory on the east bank. By 1859 there already were eight cotton brokers and six banking agents doing business in Columbus.

Compared to the hundred and fifty plus years that Columbus had been established, I figured my five years of service at Legal Aid was probably as noticeable as moss growing around the roots of a sprawling live oak. On the other hand, Legal Aid was the perfect venue for a grassroots campaign to sprout from, since so much of my work had been in Municipal Court.

Prior to Nilan's death on Thursday, August 7, 1975, his courtroom sat empty. Nilan had thought that he would return to the courtroom, so his cases were rescheduled for a different time. Whenever a judgeship vacancy occurs, the governor has the right to appoint someone to fill the vacancy until an election is held. But in Nilan's case, he never stepped down, so the vacancy wasn't official until his passing.

If Governor Busbee had appointed someone prior to Nilan's passing, it would have been as if Busbee were handing Nilan a death sentence. No one was willing to make that determination. I certainly had no morbid intentions of giving serious thought to the position until the vacancy was official. But once the vacancy was announced, August 8, 1975, I considered my options by doing as I always did—consulting Mac and Beth.

"What would the two of you think about me running for Judge Nilan's Municipal Court position?" Tucking my chin down, I looked out over the rim of my glasses at Mac sitting at the glass and wrought iron breakfast table and at Beth absorbed behind a t.v. tray loaded with nail polish, emery boards, cotton balls and remover. I wanted to see if either of them would flinch at the thought. Beth's nail file paused mid-air, she looked over at me, then at her Daddy. She was smiling. Mac was the first to speak.

"Well, I have just one question before I answer you."

"Sir?" I was ready for any questions he might ask.

"Is this a paid position or another one of those volunteer jobs?" Mac grinned that pie-eating grin that he always got whenever he out-witted me, or anyone else, which was most of the time.

"It's a paid position." I laughed along with Mac and Beth. "But don't get to thinking I'll make enough money for you to retire. I'm not going to work all day so that you can chase golf balls on the fairways and flirt pool side with women half my age!"

"Oh, sugar, you know me better than that," Mac retorted.

"Cat got your tongue?" I looked over at Beth. She was painting her nails a glittering lime green.

"It'd be groovy to have you be a judge. You oughta do it. Daddy and I could campaign for you. If we got some buttons or flyers, I could go over to Columbus Square and hand them out everyday after school."

"I'm only taking you to Columbus Square if you promise to leave your Kiralfy's charge card at home!" Mac retorted.

## The Campaign

On Wednesday, August 13, 1975, I turned in my resignation as head of Legal Aid, paid my fees and became the first candidate to qualify for the Municipal Court Judgeship. Because the 1915 state law creating the office of Municipal Court Judge provided that an election must be held within 35 days of a vacancy, the Columbus Council scheduled a special election for Thursday, September 11, 1975.

I made headlines in the evening paper—First Candidate Formally Files For Judgeship. (*Columbus Enquirer*, Wednesday, August 13, 1975) Pledging a door-to-door campaign for the office, I was quoted as having earmarked "$3,000 of my own money for the race" which I thought at the time to be a sizable amount of money. Actually, it was a sizable amount when one considers that the salary that went with the judgeship was only $16,500 a year.

But the salary was not important to me, nor obviously to the other three candidates who entered the race. State Court solicitor

Thomas W. Hughey was the second qualifier, followed by former City
Court Judge E.C. Britton and attorney William Ford Pearce Jr..

We each sought the judgeship for our own personal reasons.
Hughey sought the post for promotional reasons, "I have ambitions. I
want to get ahead, and this will probably be the only opportunity I
have...It offers a little more money and is a prestigious job,' Hughey
admitted."(*Columbus Enquirer,* August 12, 1975)

Britton claimed that he was not seeking a promotion or to further
his political career, but "...for the simple reason that I feel I can be of
service to the people of this community." Pearce, at 34, the youngest
among us, claimed youthful enthusiasm and "the reputation for
having a little common sense and for being honest and trustworthy."
(*Columbus Enquirer,* August 12, 1975)

My own reasons for seeking the judgeship were directly related to
the bated breath of death I had experienced throughout the previous
year. If Death was going to come knocking at my door, I intended to
be too busy to greet the ghoulish guest. Behaviorist might say I am a
classic case of a workaholic; that I use work to escape my own
mortality. Any such assumption is correct. I did it in 1974 and I still
do it today. Given my current schedule, Death is going to have to
make an appointment well in advance if he wants to pay me a visit.

Feeling like I had nothing to risk, I entered the campaign:

"The person who gets elected should be the most qualified and I
believe that I am. I have presented more cases before the Municipal
Court this past year than any other candidate" (*Columbus Enquirer,*
September 5, 1975). Due to number and quality of candidates and the
relatively short campaign period, the race was intense.

The League of Women Voters sponsored a public forum to
familiarize the community with all the candidates. While most of the
questions addressed that evening concerned general information—
Why do you feel you are best qualified for this position? If elected,
what changes do you plan to implement? In retrospect, I realize some
of the questions were the very ones many of us who had worked with
Legal Aid debated daily:

*What kind of sentences do you favor for crimes not against
persons?*

*It's been said that the wealthy have an advantage in our court
system. Do you feel that this is true, and if so, what do you think can
be done to equalize this advantage?*

With thick dark brows furrowed, Britton stated, "I do not believe
that the wealthy receive an advantage in our Court system." Wide-
eyed Hughey, perspiration gleaming from his retreating hairline,

concurred, "I would think that this is not true today. I have found public defenders, well qualified, who in many cases served well without charge to indigents."

Attorney Pearce chimed in, "The Columbus Legal Aid Society Inc. should be commended for its work in this area. As Judge it would be my duty, just as the jury swears, to serve without favor of affection to either party" (*Columbus Enquirer,* September 7, 1975).

And me? What did I say? I cocked my head a little to my right, hoped that my wig wasn't askew and that the audience was focusing on my good eye, then I said what I had said so many time before to Deena, Martelle, or any of the others that I worked with at Legal Aid:

> "I think the wealthy have a better chance of winning cases in our court system today because they are more educated, understand the law better and are able to hire the better lawyer. I feel this is true because I have seen the poor discriminated against in our court system. I feel that I can equalize the advantage the wealthy have by seeing that a poor man can receive the same justice as a wealthy man. I will do this by seeing that he gets his day in court and asking any questions that the court might need to know to render a fair and impartial judgment." (*Columbus Enquirer*, September 7, 1975)

The next day news reported:

> "Former Legal Aid head Mrs. Rufe McCombs had complained bonds are often set too high for lower-income defendants, forcing them to spend time in jail—perhaps on minor charges of which they may later be found innocent."(*Columbus Enquirer*, September 8, 1975)

The *Enquirer* also claimed that:

> "Britton said three times he did not believe someone who had committed a crime should be given special treatments simply because of their income.
>
> 'I believe everyone should be fed out of the same spoon. I wouldn't be lenient to someone who had committed a heinous crime just because he is poor. I wouldn't be lenient on

someone who has committed a heinous crime just because he is rich.'" (*Columbus Enquirer*, September 8, 1975)

Reviewing these comments, I realize that Britton's statements reveal exactly what I meant when I said that the system favored the wealthy. Britton stated he wouldn't be "... lenient on someone who has committed a *heinous crime....*" Wasn't that, isn't that, the problem? For the rich to be convicted, a *heinous* crime has to be committed. And if they are rich enough to buy the right lawyer, conviction is rare. Whereas, the poor seem to get even poorer representation.

But while I was taking the high road, traveling the speaking circuit, Mac and Beth were making U-turns (hard to do in a car without power steering or power brakes) on every dead-end or cul-de-sac in Columbus, handing out flyers door-to-door.

"Hey," Beth would hand a 3x5, *Elect Rufe E. McCombs Judge of Municipal Court* flyer, to anyone who answered the doorbell. "I hope y'all will vote for my Momma," she'd shout from the middle of the front lawn as she headed to the next house.

*Elect Rufe E. McCombs* stickers covered the back of Mac's white car like burrs on a barn cat's behind. I'm sure our neighbors wished we had a garage, not just a carport, to hide that unsightly car.

## Ignorance of the Law

But fortunately not everyone in Columbus recognized the driver of that old car as my husband. One morning as I was working on some files at Legal Aid I received a call from the Columbus Postmaster.

"Mrs. McCombs, I'm sorry to disturb you at work, but I thought I'd best contact you before the police do."

"It's no bother. What's the matter?"

"Ma'am, I know you haven't had anything to do with this, you're not the kind of person that would, but some old man and a young girl are going all over town in a white Falcon Coupe stuffing your literature into mailboxes, which as you know, is against the law. Several people have reported that the car has your bumper stickers all over it."

Of course, I knew who that old man was, but I did not dare tell the postmaster.

"Is that so?" I feigned surprise. "Don't you worry about this. I'll find out who it is and make sure that they stop immediately. I sure do appreciate your calling me; thank you."

When Mac picked me up at work that evening I lit into him, "Are you trying to get me elected or arrested?"

"What are you so fired up about?" Mac's brown eyes grew wide with interest.

"I got a call from the postmaster today. Said that some old man and young girl were going around town stuffing my literature into people's mailboxes. He said he knew I didn't have anything to do with it, but that it was a federal offense and that since it *was* my literature they were stuffing into people's boxes, I certainly should find out who is doing this and put a stop to it before we all get arrested!"

I took a deep breath and looked across the seat at Mac. The light turned red at the five point intersection at Wynnton Road. Mac pulled the Falcon up behind a green Malibu. I scooted down into the seat hoping no one I knew would recognize me in the old man's Falcon.

"You mean to tell me that the postmaster called me an *old* man?" Mac looked over at me.

"That's exactly what he said, 'an old man with a young girl,'" I smiled. "But are you going to sit here and tell me that you didn't know putting those flyers into people's mailboxes is illegal?"

"Well, let me ask you something, hon."

"Yes?"

"Did you?"

"Did I what?"

"You knew Beth and I were putting those flyers in the mail boxes; did you know it was against the law?"

"No, I surely did not," I replied sheepishly, embarrassed to admit even to Mac that I had not associated the distribution of those flyers in that manner as a federal offense.

"Ignorance of the law is not the same as innocence, sweetie," Mac mocked me.

The light turned green. Cautiously, Mac stepped on the gas and explained, "Listen hon, initially, Beth and I weren't putting those flyers in the mailboxes; we were putting them between the flags and the boxes, but the flyers were being blown away every time a car went by. So we thought that putting the flyer in the mailbox was a better idea. We never thought about it being against the law. Technically, we weren't tampering with the mail; we were just making deliveries." Mac grinned. I didn't. "I'm sorry, honey. I never meant to get you into trouble. I suppose we're bound to get into trouble for one thing or another—which scandal do you prefer—littering or mail tampering?"

"If you don't mind," I retorted, reaching over and rubbing the back of Mac's neck, "I'd like to avoid a scandal altogether. Do you think y'all could find a way to get me elected without getting me arrested?"

"My, my, you're asking an awful lot from us." Checking his graying temples in the rearview mirror, Mac asked again, "Did the postmaster really call me 'an old man with a young girl?'"

"Mac, are you listening to me? I want your help, but breaking the law isn't going to help..."

"I hear you, sweetie. I said I was sorry. It won't happen again."

"Mac?"

"Yes?"

"You are, you know."

"I am what?"

"Old."

"Apparently so. But, hey, at least I still have all my own hair—that's more than you can say!" Mac tugged at my wig and laughed.

## Numbers Count

And according to the *Enquirer*, Mac wasn't the only person whose age was an issue. On election day, headlines read: "Judgeship Hopeful Britton Says He's 70, Not 64 or 65" (*Columbus Enquirer*, September 11, 1975).

The story clarified that Britton was 70 years old, not the 64 or 65 previously reported. Britton initially told the Enquirer, the day before qualifying for the race, that he was only 65. Then on the Friday prior to the election, Britton claimed he was 64 and would turn 65 on November 18, 1975.

Asked to explain the reported age discrepancies, Britton reasoned: "I don't know why my age has gotten to be so important."

The *Enquirer* reported that Britton was "nervous and frustrated" but had no intentions of misleading anyone:

> "I don't feel older than 55. I just don't feel it (age,sic.) is an issue. I don't feel old. I run my bird dogs. I just don't feel my age," Britton defended the confusion. (*Columbus Enquirer*, September 11, 1975)

At the time of the election, I don't even recall being aware of the age debate surrounding Britton. But looking back on it, I can see why Britton felt that his age should not be an issue. I have felt that same frustration for several years now; ever since 1993 when I was benched from my Superior Court seat due to a controversial discrimination suit.

But in 1975, at age 56, I was the youngest female candidate running for Judge of Municipal Court. Okay, okay, so I was the only female candidate. Which is probably why most people didn't believe I stood a chance against Britton and Hughey. I was not too threatened by Pearce, since he was so young, but I distinctly recall being told by several people that there was no way I could win; and even those that did support me, like Martelle Layfield, didn't believe I could win without a run-off.

"Why, Rufe, it's a great idea," Martelle commented when I told him that I was going to run. But as the campaign progressed, Martelle cautioned me, "Rufe, with four people in this race, you just cannot avoid a run-off. You need over 50% of the votes to avoid a run-off. It just can't happen. I suspect Hughey will draw at least 40% of the votes, that leaves 60% to be split between the rest of you. You need to aim at getting the majority of that split and not worry about the run-off until then."

## I Can Help

Martelle wasn't the only person whose advice I sought. There was a young attorney, Larry Taylor, who served on the board for Legal Aid, who I respected as an attorney and as one of the most thoughtful people I had ever met. Larry's mother, Mary, was the white-gloved woman who worked in Legal Aid's secretarial pool.

I asked Larry what he thought.

"I don't know, Rufe. I just don't think Columbus is ready for a woman judge yet. But I'll be glad to help you if I can. I guess it won't hurt to try."

And Larry wasn't the only person who offered help. After my announcement came out in the paper, I received a call from a woman who I had never met, Jean Cantrell.

"Mrs. McCombs, I read in the paper about your decision to run for Municipal Court. I just want you to know that if there is anything at all I can do to help, I will." Without taking a breath this energetic woman continued, "Do you have an office for your headquarters?"

I didn't. My boss in Atlanta had informed me I could continue to use my Legal Aid office if I needed to; he even said I could have my job back after I lost the race. The idea of keeping my office was appealing to me, as was having my job back if I needed it. However, I knew that a lot of people did not support Legal Aid, so I thought it best to distance myself as far as possible from a physical identification with Legal Aid. Thus far, we had been running the campaign from our home in Columbus.

"An office?" I inquired. "No, no office. We pretty much have everything spread out here at home."

"Well, I don't know if you'd be interested in it or not, but I have a place down on Hamilton Road that you could use for your campaign headquarters. I mean it's nothing special, but it's yours rent free if you'd like. Who's organizing your fund-raisers?"

"Fund-raisers?" I hadn't even thought of those. When I announced my candidacy I had just planned on using up the $3,000 I had set aside for the campaign. I had never considered any fund-raisers. But with all the professionally designed posters, yard signs, bulletin boards, bumper stickers, and flyers, dollars were dwindling away.

"I could help you plan some, you know, yard sales, bazaars, those kind of things. I've worked on this kind of thing before; I think I could be a great help to you."

She was. Jean Cantrell worked tirelessly for my campaign. Organizing all the things she had indicated she would—bazaars, yard sales, making poster after poster, assuming the responsibility of treasurer, and establishing campaign headquarters in a nice office next to an old ceramic shop of hers on Hamilton Road.

Two other people who were of great service to me during the campaign were William and Cricket Crittenden. William, a kitchen supervisor for St. Francis Hospital, had suffered a heart attack that year and was recuperating. Cricket, a former teacher at Carver Elementary, had taken a year off from teaching to care for her ailing mother and her recovering husband. Cricket maintained that the illnesses gave them both more free time than they would have had otherwise; so they volunteered their time towards my campaign.

"You're a smart woman, Rufe, but you don't know anything about black people and their habits," Cricket chastised me after rescuing me from one potentially embarrassing situation.

A man, I'll call Mr. Neer, called me about an idea he had to help me solicit the black vote.

"I have an idea that can get you a lot of votes," Neer assured me.

"What's that?" I asked, sticking a pen behind my right ear.

"What I'll do is I'll go to the black nightclubs for you on the busy nights, buy everyone a drink, and tell them to vote for you."

"Well..." I didn't even consider the first idea before Neer jumped on another.

"Tell you what, I'll take you with me. We'll just go around to all the nightclubs; I'll buy all the drinks; you can do all the talking. You can tell them to vote for you."

"How much is all this going to cost me?" I was fairly certain that although Neer was offering to buy all the drinks that it would be my pocketbook paying for them.

"Oh, probably $300 should get us started. Let's try that and see how well it goes." Like any good salesman, Neer knew when to act assured and when to act nonchalant.

"Okay, I guess that's all right," I agreed. "When can we go?"

"How 'bout Wednesday night? I'll take you down to the 103 Drive-in. It's a busy place, lots of people there you can talk to."

We agreed to meet on Wednesday night. Wednesday afternoon, Cricket and I took a break from some paperwork we had underway at the campaign office and I told her of my evening plans with Neer.

"Mr. Neer called me the other day and told me if I would go along with him to these nightclubs that I could get a lot of black people to vote for me. I'm going to meet him down at the 103 Drive-in at 7:30 tonight."

"Hell no, you're not!" Cricket's brown eyes lit up like a firefly's butt. "I could just see you in the morning paper coming out of that place—103 ain't nothing but a honky-tonk, Rufe. Nobody who goes to that place votes. Neer's just going to take your money to drink and have himself a good time laughing at you making a fool outta your white self. He's just trying to get money and a laugh outta you."

"Listen, Cricket," I was beginning to see how stupid this idea was, "I won't go if you don't think I should. I'll call Neer right now and tell him thanks, but no thanks."

"Here," Cricket handed me the receiver, "what's his number? I'll dial it."

I could not have run the campaign successfully if not for people like the Crittendons and others who gave of themselves. From the very first, my campaign was a grassroots job. With very little money and even less time, we covered much ground, most of it by foot, but by the time of the election, it was still anyone's guess as to whether the hard work would pay off or not.

## The Election

I had my doubts, but on Tuesday, September 9, two days before the election, both the *Columbus Enquirer*, our morning paper, and the *Columbus Ledger*, our afternoon paper, endorsed me as their choice for Municipal Court Judge. Because this was a special election brought about by Judge Nilan's demise, the judgeship was spotlighted in a fashion that had never occurred before. The race was receiving a fair amount of publicity.

The *Enquirer* endorsed me because of my experiences with Legal Aid:

"As a result of handling many Legal Aid cases in the court, Mrs. McCombs has probably the most thorough knowledge of Municipal Court of any of the candidates." (*Columbus Enquirer*, September 9, 1975)

The *Ledger* described Municipal Court as a "consumer-oriented court or the people's court." Thus, they supported me:

"...because of the nature of the court, it is important that the judge posses a certain sensitivity to the people's problems which come before the court. We believe Mrs. Rufe McCombs has those qualifications to bring a sense of fairness and compassion to this important judicial post."

But the *Ledger* did add a disclaimer:

"It is not a question of having a woman judge. Rather, it is one of having a person on the bench who has those qualities to assure even-handed justice in Municipal Court" (*Columbus Ledger*, September 9, 1975).

I never could tell from this remark if they considered my femininity a handicap or an asset. Perhaps the remark was not a disclaimer, perhaps it was just an observation. After all, no woman had ever been elected to any office in Muscogee County before.

So in spite of the endorsements from both the Ledger and the Enquirer, by Thursday, September 11, election day, I did not feel as if I had much of a chance of obtaining enough votes for even a run-off.

Like most of Georgia's Septembers, that Thursday was clear and warm, lacking the seeping sultriness of August. September in Georgia doesn't begin with leaves changing or brisk mornings; temperatures still reach the 90's, but the air is almost always sweeter to breathe; the heavy scent of magnolias recedes and the delicate scent of honeysuckle lingers.

I tried to keep busy. Breakfast with Mac. A trip to the polls. Mac and Beth were poll attendants. Beth was downtown at the Government Center and Mac was at Hamilton Road. Rumor had it that votes were being bought. Many people who came to vote could not read. Volunteers from the V.F.W., A.A.U.W. and other civic organizations would read the ballots for those who needed help. Beth told me later that sometimes people would come in and say, "I want to vote for that lady with the funny name."

Back at home, I answered the ringing phone, "Thank you, I appreciate your support." When not on the phone, I tried reading: briefs, journals, mail, the paper, but nothing kept my mind occupied like the election.

Can I gather enough votes for a run-off? Is it possible that Britton won't take the whole 40%? What if he only takes 30%? That will leave 70% for the rest of us to split. How close will the three of us come? If I lose, I hope it's by a lot. I'll take any chance at winning I can get; but if I have to lose, I hope it's a total defeat, not a near miss. I couldn't stand to lose by some ridiculous calculations—Britton 38 %, Hughey 32%, McCombs 29% and Pearce 1%. No, thank you. With a scenario like that, I'd rather be Pearce. At least then I would know I didn't stand a chance.

The polls were open until 7 p.m.. It was after eight o'clock when Mac, Beth and I climbed into the car on our way to campaign headquarters to await the election results. My stomach felt double-knotted.

"Mac, can't I just go to bed and wake up when this is all over with?" I pleaded as Mac backed our car out of the driveway.

"Aww, Momma," Beth moaned from the back seat, "don't be so negative."

"Out of the mouth of babes," Mac chimed in. Leaning over the wheel a bit, Mac switched on the radio. "I bet some of the early results are in already."

"That was Johnny Rivers singing *Stagger Lee*. We'll be back with more of your favorites after this election day report. Stay tuned to WRBL..."

"Turn it up, Daddy," Beth insisted. "I can't hear it."

I turned the black knob to my right, "How's that?" I looked back at Beth.

"Shhh," Mac hissed. "They're going to give out some of the results."

"Early results in from Bibb City have McCombs trailing behind Britton, Hughey, and Pearce. So far McCombs, the only woman candidate running for Municipal Court has only fourteen of the counted precinct votes..."

I switched the radio off. Fourteen votes? How could I only have fourteen votes? Only fourteen people in all of Bibb City voted for me?

"Take me back home," I instructed Mac.

"Now you know I can't do that, Rufe. Jean's already called; all those people who've worked so hard are waiting for you to make an appearance. You have to show up."

"Oh, yes, we can. Go back home," I whined. "What I can't do is go and look at all those people who've worked so hard for me and tell them that I'm such a loser that I can't even carry Bibb City. Good Granny, Mac, Bibb City is where a significant portion of my Legal Aid clients live. If my clients didn't vote for me, nobody did! I was a fool to think anyone would..." Tears welled up, my voice broke, I swallowed my words and my pride.

The rest of the drive to the campaign office was quiet. Mac alternately whistled or hummed. Beth tapped her nails on her purse, but no one spoke. I tried to think of what I could say to everyone that would express my appreciation but not reveal my tender emotions. It would be so unprofessional to cry. I'd never seen a man cry when he lost and I certainly wasn't going to either. I'd have to save the slobbering for a midnight shower. Dang, I hated to lose. Fourteen votes—what a total embarrassment!

When we arrived at campaign headquarters very few people were there—Jean, Cricket, William and one or two others. William had made enough food to feed all the Methodists and Baptists in town. There was macaroni salad, potato salad, three-bean salad, baking powder biscuits, cornbread, sliced bread, barbecue ribs, barbecue pork, barbecue beans, pound cake, carrot cake and caramel cake.

"William," I gazed over the tables of food, "I might go home a loser tonight, but thanks to you, I'll be the best fed loser in town."

William, whose heart matched his appetite, waved me away from the table with a large serving spoon, "You just go on now, Rufe. There ain't going to be any leftovers here this evening by the time we get done serving everybody and celebrating your victory."

"Why, I know we look like we eat all the time," I protested "but William, even with your help I can't eat all this! You got enough food here to feed all of Alabama for a year." I looked around the near empty room, *Elect Rufe E. McCombs Judge of Municipal Court* posters looked back at me. "The first returns said I didn't get but fourteen votes from Bibb City," I lamented. "I'm in last place, William."

"Don't you be worrying about those first returns," William stuck a ladle into a big pot of Brunswick stew. "You can't tell nothing from those early returns. You just wait."

"William's right," Cricket added, "but I can't believe that any of us voted for you as judge after you agreed to go honkey-tonking with Neer. All of us know you don't practice good judgment!" Cricket and the others laughed so hard they didn't have any cheek strength left. I laughed along with them. It was more fun than crying.

"Here, sweetie, you better eat something now," Mac brought me a plate of food and a glass of sweet tea. "You'll be too busy to eat once you get the job." I gave him a wry grin, but I couldn't help but think of how much I loved him. Mac just gave and gave and gave, never asking anything of me other than the day Beth was born.

"Would you be willing to put your career on hold for just a while?" Mac had asked me the day Beth was born. Unwrapping the pink thermal blanket, Mac counted Beth's toes for the twentieth time that morning. I think feet fetishes are developed in those early hours after birth when people become mesmerized by the toes of newborns.

We agreed that day I would not return to work until Beth was out of elementary school. Neither Mac nor I wanted someone else bringing up our daughter. We knew she would be our only child. I have never regretted that decision, and Mac always gave me a place of honor because of my sacrifice. So when I was ready to work again, Mac supported me in every way imaginable.

Looking over at Mac and Beth, I realized how fortunate I really was, win or lose. Mac sat at a nearby table, eating a piece of caramel cake and drinking a cup of steaming black coffee. Beth, her long chestnut brown hair almost touching the hip-fit of her bell-bottom jeans, was carrying a pitcher of tea, refilling people's glasses. They had both worked so hard, been so faithful, believed so much in me, I wanted to win if for no other reason than to make them as proud of me as I was of them.

Beth, only 17 at the time, had taken it upon herself to help in my campaign. She had found a man who painted "Jesus Loves You" signs in his carport out on St. Mary's Road. Beth took this man eight 8 x 4 plywood boards and had him paint them red, white and blue—ELECT RUFE MCCOMBS MUNICIPAL COURT JUDGE. Then she had him help her tie those eight signs on to the top of her new Satellite Sebring and with a one-handed death grip she clutched them to the driver's side as she drove them home. When Beth arrived home her insurance-minded Daddy had a royal hissy fit!

"Are you crazy?" Mac screamed at Beth. "YOU DON'T DRIVE DOWN THE ROAD HANGING OUT THE WINDOW! YOU COULD'VE BEEN KILLED!"

Beth didn't respond. Mac's tirade continued. "What kind of idiot ties plywood on to the roof of a new car?" Mac didn't wait for an answer. Hopping into his own car, Mac went over to the sign man's house to inform him that he had just endangered the life of our only child.

But before Mac could speak, the sign man said, "I know your wife's going to win, sir. Your daughter has such faith in her mother and in God. You'll see, this faith will see her through anything. Your wife is going to be a winner; I just know it!"

I couldn't stand losing when I knew how much people like the sign man and my daughter believed in me. I wanted to bring honor to Mac and Beth because of their devotion. "Please, Lord," I prayed silently, "don't let me be a disappointment to them. Help me find some way to make them proud of me."

## The Results

And so God did. William was right—we couldn't tell anything from those early returns. As a lavender dusk gave way to a velvet night, the votes cast in my favor began to outnumber the stars, or so it seemed.

By 9:00 p.m., campaign headquarters looked and sounded like a Baptist Homecoming. People formed lines to pile plates full of the food that William had fixed. These people greeted each other boisterously with slaps, hugs, and shoulder-wrenching handshakes. Overhearing their comments made me grin.

*"Hey, Buddy, what is this, your fourth trip to the table? Save some for the rest of us, okay?"*

*"Why, Mary, I don't believe I've seen you since last year. Remember? Wasn't it at that production down at Springer Opera House?"*

*"Looky there. Is that Miles pulling up in that new Lincoln? Last I heard his business wasn't doing so good—must've picked up. That or somebody died and left him some money."*

And in between their private conversations, these people were coming up to Mac and me, hugging us, slapping us, shaking our hands, reaffirming their allegiance to me.

*"I told the boys downtown that if any woman could do this, Mrs. McCombs, you would be that woman."*

*"I never doubted that you'd win."*

*"Columbus couldn't have chosen a finer woman."*

About halfway through the election returns the newspaper hounds sniffed out the party. When two-thirds of the precinct votes had been counted, the radio blared in the background, "McCombs ahead at this point. She could win without a run-off."

Mac's co-workers showed up. Local attorneys came. Martelle Layfield made an appearance. By 11:00 p.m. all the predictions were that I had won the race without a run-off. But I still felt unsure, right up until midnight when one-by-one Britton, Hughey and Pearce all conceded, only then did I allow myself to believe it.

Of the 33 election precincts and mounds of absentee votes, the only precinct I *did not* carry was Bibb City. Once two-thirds of the precinct votes had been counted, I went over the 50% margin. The vote never changed from that moment on. I took in over 9,000 votes, Hughey finished second with over 3,500 votes, Britton finished third with over 3,000 votes and Pearce last with about 2,400 votes.

"I kind of feel like ol' Bear Bryant," Pearce said. "I don't feel like shaking hands after it's over with" (*Columbus Enquirer,* September 12, 1975).

"I accepted Mrs. McCombs as my strongest opponent," Britton stated. "She'll make a good judge, I think. She had a lot of support."(*Columbus Enquirer*, September 12, 1975)

"It looks like she ran a good, hard race," Hughey congratulated. "She was a lady all the way through. I respect her as a lady and as a running opponent." (*Columbus Enquirer*, September 12, 1975)

But the words that meant the most to me came from Judge Nilan's widow, Mrs. Leonora Woodall Nilan, when told of the election results she stated, "I think she's the greatest" (*Columbus Enquirer*, September 12, 1975).

On Friday, September 12, 1975, the morning paper headlines announced:

*McCombs wins Judgeship—Voters Choose Woman*

To this day, the race for Municipal Court Judge, remains the hardest race I ever ran, and the sweetest victory. I think in part because none of us expected a win without a run-off. The local media acknowledged that by winning the race I became the first elected woman official in Muscogee County:

> "A judge...a lady judge on the bench of Municipal Court in Columbus. It's a first in our city. To the best of our investigative ability, we could not find record of any other lady elected to that particular post.
> Rufe McCombs campaigned against three men. All of them good men and good candidates. Her margin of victory was high. Does this say that women are about to invade our courts? We doubt that. Though we're sure we'll begin to see more ladies in higher positions of government, including our courtrooms. It won't be so much an invasion; but rather a recognition that there are women in our communities who are entirely capable of dispensing justice or administering the affairs of state. They will not be elected just because they are women. They will be elected on their credentials...in the same way that their male counterparts are elected. And that, from our viewpoint, is good.
> Judge McCombs is well respected in the legal profession. We are confident that she will bring wisdom, compassion and even justice to our Municipal Court" (G. Gingell, Viewpoint, The Lady Judge, WRBL, October 1, 1975).

What many did not know was that the only other woman serving in a court of record in Georgia, Dorothy Robinson, a State Court Judge, had initially been appointed to that position in 1972, prior to being elected to that same position in November of 1974. So when I was elected to Municipal Court in 1975, I was the first woman in the state to win a judgeship position solely by a vote of the people, without prior appointment.

Of course, because I never sought the position based upon a feminist platform, I never knew this myself until now. And while I believe that some people may have voted for me just because I was a woman, I don't believe that is why the majority of people voted for me. I believe Muscogee County voters elected me because of my record. I think they knew I would always try to be fair and that I would always work hard.

I did not then, and I do not now, believe in legislating affirmative action. I know that opportunities arose for me because of World War II. The job in D.C. came about because so many men were going off to war; but it was always up to me to position myself for those opportunities. Mother had told both Liz and me that women would have more career opportunities during our lifetime, than during hers. She was right, but it was up to us to be prepared.

Prior to my working with Legal Aid, I probably could not have found a job with any established Columbus Law firm, not only because of my gender, but because of my age as well. Have I been discriminated against because of my gender? Yes, remember McWhorter closed me out of the class discussion on rape. And my own cousin felt I could only serve as a clerk. Yet, I still do not support the legislation of affirmative action.

Why? Because I believe that if a person works hard at improving themselves and the business that they work for, others will notice. When an employee gives of him/herself to their job, employers notice. And a reputable employer does not care about gender as much as they care about running a successful business. The employee who works hard to make that business successful will achieve recognition and, most likely, advancement.

Hiring someone on the basis of gender, regardless of performance or ability, seems like a bad business practice to me. Enforcing a federal policy that requires the private sector to implement such bad practices has dulled our economic edge.

Never have I wanted or sought a position based upon my gender. I wanted to be an attorney because law interested me. I wanted to be a judge because it allowed me to delve deeper into law. Never did I want the voters to elect me to any position because I was a woman, but because I was a hard worker. Less than six weeks after being elected I gave wrote this update for the paper:

> "...Because of the backlog of untried cases, the last two weeks have been very busy. We scheduled 81 cases for these two weeks; however, it is doubtful that we will have to try over 30 of these 81 cases. As Judge Nilan so often said, 'The jury has a settling effect on the parties.'
>
> As far as being a woman, I do not believe that it will make any difference at all. I believe that compassion is part of the law, but I also believe that the law that is on the books must be upheld and anyone who is in violation of the law should be held accountable....
>
> ...It is much too early to tell the type of Judge I will be able to be, but it is not too early to say that I am enjoying the

work. I plan to work very hard at the job and if dedication and a desire to do a good job are the essential elements, I feel we will soon have a very smooth-running, efficient court." (*Columbus Enquirer*, October 30, 1975).

The following summer, when I ran unopposed for a full-term in Municipal Court, I provided some examples of my work ethic:

"...to handle the backlog that had built up during Judge Nilan's illness and after his death. We went night and day up until 10 o'clock some nights. We set jury trial cases at 5 p.m. until we caught up" (*Chattahoochee Magazine*, July 18, 1976).

In reference to the issue of gender, I stated:

"A couple of people told me recently they thought I'd won because it was the right time for a woman to be elected in Columbus. I told them I'd much rather feel I got elected because I was qualified...I'm just good and qualified for what I have been elected to do, nothing more. My womanhood was never an issue in the campaign" (*Chattahoochee Magazine*, July 18, 1976).

I guess the question of how I defeated three very qualified men for Muscogee County's Municipal Judgeship in the election of 1975 will always been open for debate. I don't mind. I'm just thankful that the voters chose me. I hope I have never given them any reason to regret their choice.

# 11

# LIVING THE DREAM

## Seeking Superior Court

From 1975-1978 I served in Columbus' Municipal Court. Since the majority of my Legal Aid cases had been heard in Municipal Court, slipping into a new role as jurist was as easy as putting on a robe. A very distinguished robe. But I did make some alterations—like running court late into the night, or on Saturdays, to eradicate the backlog.

Isn't it humiliating to admit that perhaps the most significant contribution I made to Municipal Court was a clerical decision? I established a system of mailing the attorneys copies of the docket, the jury list, and case notes from the previous month's memorandum decisions from Municipal Court. Several firms wrote letters of appreciation, all declaring what a help this service was to them:

1/19/76

Dear Judge McCombs:

On behalf of the firm, thank you for sending us the case notes which we received together with the January dockets. Publication of decision such as those set forth in your case notes will be of great benefit to those of us who practice in your Court.

Very truly,
J. Barrington Vaught

3/16/76

Dear Judge McCombs:

Please accept my sincere thanks for the compilation of
Municipal Court case notes. The preparation and distribution
of these case notes is a very fine service to the legal
community. Having these notes is the equivalent of several
law courses, in my opinion. I will make good use of them.

Thanks again,
Hal Shortnary

3/15/76

Dear Judge McCombs:

I was surprised and delighted this morning to receive in the
mail not only a copy of the docket, which heretofore I have
had to obtain myself, but a copy of the jury list and
memorandum decisions recently made by your Court. I
heartily endorse this idea and would like to take this
opportunity to thank you very much for providing the
attorneys with these.

I was especially pleased to receive the case notes since these
notes are of great benefit in areas of the law that are changing
dramatically. Thank you once again for the Court's efforts
along these lines and I sincerely hope that the Court will
continue this policy.

Best personal regards,
William E. Hawkins Jr.

Enacting a policy of sending attorneys Municipal Court case notes
brought unexpected accolades from my colleagues. Distributing these
case notes just seemed like a common courtesy. Again, I realize,
details define our lives, so I wrote back:

3/16/76

Dear Bill:

Thank you for taking the time to write us a letter concerning our case notes and mailing the docket. It is gratifying to know that our efforts to be a good public servant are appreciated. We have sent out case notes to all the attorneys that were listed on the docket for the last three months. If for any reason you did not receive our case notes for December and January, we will be so happy to furnish you a copy of these for your file. Like the case notes which you received this month, they are memorandum decisions made by this Court in December and January.

With my thanks, may I take this opportunity to send every good wish to you in your practice of law from the Ralston Center.

Sincerely,
Rufe. E. McCombs

State Court solicitor, Thomas Hughey, was correct in his assessment that Municipal Court was a promotion, a prestigious job worth pursuing, but as far as jurist jobs go, many still consider Municipal Court an entry level position. One particular attorney never failed to greet me without displaying his obvious disdain: "G'mornin' Judge. How're things in Monkey-Simple Court?"

I never could determine if this particular attorney's dislike was for the position held, or for the person holding it. Did he think Municipal Court beneath his abilities? Did he think I was less skilled than he? Perhaps it was a mixture of both. However, I do think he needed to enroll in a manners course at Mabel Bailey's Charm School. Poor Mabel would've had her work cut out for her! Perhaps, never having been appointed to any position has made me appreciate my role as a public servant. I assumed that getting elected was a vote of the community's confidence in me. No matter what court I served in, I was always obliged to the public.

It was an honor to serve in any court, but, of course, like most successful people, I was ambitious. When the opportunity to advance through the courts presented itself, I lobbied for that promotion. In April of 1978, Superior Court Judge Alvan Davis resigned mid-term, creating a vacancy which would be filled by appointment. At age 59, I fretted that if I wanted to scale the career ladder I best do it quickly before I lost my footing. So I announced during a press interview my desire to be considered for the position. The *Columbus Enquirer* reported as follows:

"Judge Rufe McCombs said she will actively seek Judge J. Alvan Davis' Muscogee County Superior Court post. The 59-year old Columbus Municipal Court Judge said she will fill out the necessary questionnaire and return it to the Judicial Nominating Commission...Mrs. McCombs said she will not campaign for the Superior Court post.

'I will be unable to contribute my own time for seeking this appointment,' she said. 'I cannot and will not neglect the position to which I was elected by the people...However, I am appreciative of the efforts of others and, if appointed by the Governor as a Superior Court Judge, will be honored to accept.'" (*Columbus Enquirer*, April 11, 1978).

State Court Judge Kenneth Followill and State Representative Albert Thompson were the other two nominees considered for the position. Fifty-eight-year old Albert Thompson had credentials from having served thirteen years in Georgia's legislature. Thompson, a black man, successfully defeated a white man, Dr. I. A. Maxwell Jr., in a bid for State Representative in 1965. Thus, Thompson became the first black Georgia State Representative from Muscogee County in this century. Thompson was also one of the first blacks to hold committee chairmanships in Georgia's House when he served as Chairman of the House Special Judiciary Committee.

Prior to his election to the Legislature, Thompson served as the only black attorney in Muscogee County. The absence of blacks in the legal field was evident throughout the courtroom; Albert Thompson worked as an attorney for 15 years before he ever tried a case before black jurors.

However, minority status didn't carry much influence in Georgia during 1978, so Thompson didn't receive the appointment and neither did I—Governor Busbee appointed forty-two-year old State Court Judge Kenneth Followill to the Superior Court seat. Followill was young, white, and male. Yet, I maintain, Busbee's decision was a sequential one; Judge Followill had served in State Court; he had earned the appointment.

## Settling for State Court

However sequential Busbee's decision was, I found myself needing a change as desperately as an ICU nurse who has just attended to a gunshot victim. On Wednesday, May 17, 1978, the day Followill was sworn into Superior Court, I announced my candidacy for Followill's former State Court seat. At that time, this was the only State Court position in Muscogee County. Albert Thompson stated that he, too, was considering running.

When Albert did not run, I won the State Court judgeship in an unopposed special election, June 20, 1978. Running unopposed is the cheapest and easiest way to win a race; I wish I could have run all the races by myself. While the democratic process is expensive, I believe other forms of government are far more costly in due time. The only real drawback to winning by default is the victory party consists of T.V. dinners instead of William Crittenden's seven-course meals.

Followill's move to Superior Court had created some backlog in State Court. My first week in State Court we disposed of 236 criminal cases, mostly through guilty pleas.

I have always believed that part of my job as a judge was not only to get a defendant a fair trial but also an expedient one. In Municipal Court the backlog had been so overwhelming I sometimes held court until 10:00 p.m. during the week and on Saturdays, if necessary.

I was willing to do that in State Court. To expedite matters and update the civil docket, I scheduled 36 cases a week for the first few weeks.

I took to State Court like kudzu to a billboard. Starting at the bottom I found my way all over that place. In no time at all, I knew the reporters, the attorneys, the clerks, the other judges—all men— and the law. On occasion I was treated by certain attorneys as if I didn't belong on the playing field. Some of the same attorneys who had set the guidelines for me as Director of Legal Aid were now trying cases in my court. Sometimes they failed to recognize our playing field had changed.

I am sure my age played a large factor in the amount of respect people afforded me as a judge. Most people I worked with, both men and women, seemed to view me the way children do their parents, or any other elder, as an asexual being.

Overall, I think this elder stereotype worked to my advantage because people just assumed my age made me wise. (This deception has failed to prove beneficial to most Presidential hopefuls, however.)

Of course, the downside to all of this is that never once in all my years on the bench did any attorney try to seduce me. It would not have worked, but it would have been flattering to see one try! Well, perhaps not flattering. Maybe more amusingly pathetic.

But I have known other women judges who have defined their professional relationship with male attorneys in a much broader fashion. And while it is true that these women tend to be a lot better looking than me, I still choose to believe it was my age that frightened those would-be seducers away. Or perhaps, it was that wig.

Despite my age and accompanying wisdom, some of my peers still treated me with disregard. The newspaper often chose to use my marital status as my title instead of my position, referring to me as "Mrs. McCombs" instead of "Judge McCombs." This may not have necessarily been a manner of disrespect because such titles were the custom of the day; however, I know full well that they never would have referred to Judge Followill as "Mr. Followill." Sexism endures in subtle ways.

## It's True ... Honest!

Young attorneys were the worst about displaying their stereotyping assumptions. Sauntering into the courtroom, they would flash me one of their prom-night grins, confident that their boyish manners would entirely disarm an old lady like me. Sometimes I would envision their cartoonish thoughts, "Here grandma, let me help you."

Assuming I was too old to hear well, some of these fellows actually raised their voices when addressing me. In reality, those boyish behaviors earned more than one of them a contempt of court charge, especially when they back-talked me or argued with each other. Just ask Willy More.

A dark-haired high-priced attorney, Willy wore shoes that cost more than my car and suits that cost more than my education. Next to Willy More all the other attorneys in my courtroom looked like yesterday's leftovers. And Willy More talked as smart as he dressed, but within a few days of trial, Mr. More began to try my nerves.

This was a personal injury case in which Mr. More represented the plaintiff. During trial Mr. More had this annoying habit of walking over to the jury and murmuring before them. I did not know if Mr. More was making asides regarding his client, the defendant, or me. Several times I called him to the bench and asked him to refrain from mumbling to the jury.

"If you have something to say Mr. More, you need to speak up so that we all can hear you," I instructed.

But Mr. More ignored my counsel. After yet another instance, I called him to the bench.

"Mr. More, I have repeatedly asked you over the past several days to refrain from making asides to the jury that others in the courtroom cannot hear...."

"Your Honor, I was not...."

"Yes, you were, Mr. More. If you insist on being argumentative with the Court then I'm goin...."

"Argumentative? I hardly think I'm being argu...."

"Enough of that, Mr. More." I picked up my gavel. "I'm sick of your arguing with me, of your obvious disrespect for the Court, and your snide remarks to the jury. I charge you with contempt of court. Bailiff?"

Willy lost his arrogant stance in my courtroom; even $500 suits hang funny on men with slooping shoulders. When the trial threatened to tarry through the Thanksgiving Holiday, Willy worried whether turkey was served well-done in jail. After More sat a few hours in jail, I called him back up to the bench.

"Mr. More," I leaned over to see him better but Willy was avoiding eye contact, "I'm not going to leave you in jail tonight because tomorrow's Thanksgiving. But if you ever come into my courtroom and argue with me or others the way you have during this trial I'll not hesitate to sentence you to the maximum twenty days in jail for contempt of court!"

Willy More is an Atlanta attorney today. He still looks and smells as good as Sunday pot roast and he can steam up a room as fast as one. Willy came to see me shortly before I retired. Finally looking me in the eyes, he thanked me.

"I appreciate having had the opportunity to work with you, Judge," Willy confided. "I always found you to be a fair and reasonable jurist."

And merciful, I thought.

State Court allowed me to cultivate long-term working relationships with others. During my tenure in Municipal Court I had a variety of court reporters who worked with me; Raymond Campbell was one of them. Raymond is a man of ample appetites. He enjoys fine foods, fine clothes, and fine people. Raymond's laughter could topple boats at sea while his embracing nature would be sure to carry the survivors ashore.

I believe Raymond only worked once or twice for me in Municipal, but when I was elected to State Court the reporter that came with the job expressed a lack of interest in working with me, mostly by failing to show up. When I realized the first court reporter was lacking a working constitution, I asked Irene Conner, my secretary, to find me a good reporter; one who would at least present face. Irene suggested Raymond and like any successful boss, I always took my secretary's advice. I asked Raymond to take over as my court reporter. Raymond accepted the offer and served as a reporter in my court until my retirement. When I retired Raymond commented that he was always amazed that I had remembered him from Municipal Court.

Irene Conner was with me from the earliest stages of my judgeships. I had a secretary before Irene, but that particular secretary had a dehydration disorder—she could never get enough to drink. My first contact with Irene had been through the clerk's office where Irene worked at the time. I had always found the attractive brunette to be efficient, but not disturbingly so. I have always suspected that people who were too efficient, too cheery, were probably automated workers developed by the Japanese to undermine the morale of American workers. Irene has frightened me on several different occasions by her efficiency and cheerfulness, but if she's automated, her parts are lasting longer and looking better than my real ones!

Irene and Raymond and I became so close over the years that if one of us was hit, we'd all three fall down. Many of our days in court were routine and about as entertaining as the drone of the National Emergency Broadcast Test. (Which explains why I've had to admonish jurors for falling asleep) But there were times in court when I thought I would burst a seam laughing.

I realize that the dress code for society has changed since I was a child. Mother's routine of putting on a hat and gloves every time she went anywhere would be considered outrageous even for today's charm school graduates. So I am really not surprised when people come to the courts wearing cut-off's and Big Johnson T-shirts. I don't like it, but I'm just used to it. However, the day a woman came into court wearing a blue terry cloth robe and pink slippers, I noticed.

"Bailiff," I tried to get the bailiff's attention without arousing anyone else's.

"Yes, your honor?" The bailiff turned to me.

"Could you step up to the bench, please?" The woman had taken a seat on the second row. Her hair was covered with a shower cap. When the bailiff approached me, his back was turned to the woman.

"Sir," I smiled, "I believe there's someone in this room who wants my job."

"Excuse me, your honor?" The bailiff was confused. With good reason.

"There's a woman in this courtroom, I believe, she wants my job," I insisted. At that point, the bailiff was probably wondering if he ought not let some of the others present know that I was delusional.

"What makes you think that, your honor?" The bailiff probably suspected that my lunch beverage was a mite stronger than Colombian coffee.

"Well, turn around and look at the second row," I instructed. He did. "See that woman there with the shower cap on?"

"Yes," he replied, a bit startled himself.

"That woman's got a robe on. Nobody has permission to be in this courtroom wearing a robe except me. She's after my job!" I whispered, loudly. "Get her out of here before someone gives it to her," I laughed.

Raymond and Irene have often commented that the poor woman probably could have done as good a job on the bench as some jurists—though they have never ventured to say she could have done a better job than me—at least not within earshot. Irene did question whether the woman drank her lunch.

Once I had a case before me that required the testimony of an elderly Chinese fellow. This man shuffled forward to take his oath but paused and addressed me first.

"In China we take a special oath," he said. "Is it possible to have that oath given to me now?"

"What is your oath?" I inquired. This man was sincere in his desire to honor his country's oath and I was momentarily intrigued by his honor to his native customs.

"First, I will need a chicken. Then I cut off the head of the chicken and if...."

"Sir," I cut him off, "we have no chickens in our courts and I'm not going to get you one. But tell me, sir, are you a grandfather?" I was grasping for common ground.

"Oh, yes," he smiled. "Many times, many times."

"As a grandfather to a grandmother, do you promise to tell the truth, the whole truth, and nothing but the truth?"

Bowing from his waist several times over and over, he replied, "Yes, oh yes. As grandfather to grandmother, I promise."

"Thank you, sir," I said. "Please sit down; you have just taken the oath." So far my career in law has kept me from cutting up any chickens—in, or out, of the kitchen. I plan to get through both my career and my life without ever having to chop off a chicken's head.

However, I've failed to make it through my career without losing my own head. When it happened, everyone in the vicinity of my courtroom heard me screaming like a wild banshee—at least that is the sound I intended to make.

The defendant before me in a criminal case tore loose from the deputies in the courtroom. This man wasn't just a pickle shy of a whopper I believe he was missing the whole patty. In no time at all he had stripped down to nothing but his buns, which he ran from one end of the courtroom to the next. The deputies and bailiff were all trying to catch him. Everyone else in the courtroom was gasping and jumping up from their own seats, and backing towards the exits.

But before either of the deputies or bailiff could grab this fellow, he jumped up on the bench in front of me! Raising his hands high above his head, he let out his best Tarzan scream, then began pounding his chest.

I do not recall being frightened, but I must have been disoriented. Sticking out my tongue, crossing my eyes and cocking my head, I began screaming back at Tarzan. My mimic of the jungle man was apparently better than the defendant's. Pleading with the deputies, Tarzan cried out, "Take me away from this woman!" Within a week, this same defendant quietly entered a guilty plea before me.

However, it didn't take long for me to earn a reputation for being just as vocal out of court as I was in it. During a speech to Columbus Kwanis Club shortly after being elected to State Court, I made the following statements regarding the U.S. Supreme Court. As reported in the *Columbus Enquirer* on June 29, 1978:

"The courts have gone beyond their constitutional powers—they've filled vacancies on school boards; the courts have canceled school elections...they've told employers who they should hire; they've thrown out convictions on generalities....

The Supreme Court now tells this nation as a whole what it must do. The courts are not passing judgments anymore. They're passing public policy...As it is now, the people have no relief. If we don't like public policy passed by the Supreme Court there's nothing we can do about it.

The Constitution defines ten rights we're entitled to, and these are in the Bill of Rights. The courts have given us a whole new series of rights—the right to an abortion, the right to medical care, the right to decent employment, the right to a clean environment, gay liberation rights. These are not rights. As least I don't think that the Constitution says they are rights."

In my address I explained that part of the legislative trend of the 70's was the popularity of taking problems to the courts rather than to the lawmakers.

"'It used to be that people were told, 'Don't make a federal case out of it.' Now that is exactly what everyone does.'"

Apparently this legislative trend has become our national custom.

## Bowers' Case

Although he initially stated he would, Albert Thompson did not oppose me for Followill's State Court position. However, in 1980, Albert Thompson and I found ourselves seeking the same job once more when Superior Court Judge Oscar Smith retired.

Because Oscar Smith's retirement came mid-term, Governor Busbee would appoint someone to complete Smith's elected term through January of 1983. An election for that post would be held in late 1982. Both Thompson and I, as well as District Attorney Bill Smith, were being considered by Busbee for the initial appointment.

There was much speculation about why Judge Oscar Smith retired in mid-term. Part of the speculation revolved around a death penalty case that Georgia's Supreme Court had remanded back to Superior Court for a retrial of the penalty phase. Judge Smith was rumored to be upset about having to try the penalty phase of the case again.

The case involved a sixteen-year-old black youth who had shot and killed Officer James Bowers of the Columbus Police Department on April 4, 1979. Officer Bowers had responded to a call regarding attempted robbery at a convenience store. Entering the store alone, Bowers encountered the youth who then killed Bowers with just one shot to the head.

There was never any question about the youth's guilt in this case, but Georgia's Supreme Court wanted the penalty phase to be retried. In spite of the crime this fellow had committed, sending a sixteen year-old to the electric chair seemed inhumane. The Bowers' case would be retried in Superior Court.

Of course, this remanding of the penalty phase back to Superior Court upset more than just Judge Smith. Bowers was a father of young children and a very well-respected member of the Columbus Police Department. Bowers had attended law school at night, working towards becoming an attorney himself.

In the police department's eyes, the kid had executed Bowers. The police felt the youth had received a fair trial and the appropriate sentence—the death penalty. Many felt that by sending a convicted murderer back for a retrial, the Supreme Court was participating in a game of political volleying. Emotions ran deep among Columbus' Law Enforcement and among Columbus' racially polarized community.

## Thompson vs. McCombs

So I guess I should have been relieved when Governor Busbee appointed Albert Thompson to Judge Smith's Superior Court seat. But I wasn't. I was very disappointed.

I felt the doors of opportunity were being marked male and female, black and white. And I realized that all those doors, male and female, black and white, had one common lock—age. And at age 63, I knew that before long all those doors of opportunity would be shut completely. I wanted the position that Busbee had given to Thompson.

In many ways, Judge Thompson's career paralleled my own. We both had left Georgia for Washington, D.C.—Thompson to pursue his law degree at Howard University and I for a job with the U.S.D.A.. We both returned to Georgia, pursuing careers that were notable, in part, because we were both minorities in the legal field.

We both sought the appointment to Judge Davis' Superior Court seat in 1978 and we both lost that appointment. We both were going to seek Followill's State Court position after he was appointed to Judge Davis' seat, but Thompson decided to wait for another position. Unopposed, I won Followill's State Court job.

Many people have categorized me as a very ambitious female. I never thought of myself that way. I still don't. I just have been blessed, or maybe cursed, with an extreme interest in the law. That interest has motivated me like nothing else. This passion for the law still sparks fire in my mind and my soul.

Because of Thompson's abilities, it was no surprise that on December 23, 1980, Albert Thompson was sworn in by Governor Busbee as the first black man to serve the Chattohoochee Judicial

Circuit as Superior Court Judge. On that same day, I declared my
intentions to be Thompson's opponent in the 1982 election.

When I announced that I would run for the position in 1982, I
never suspected anyone would view my challenge as a possible
commentary on Thompson personally, or on his abilities. Thomspon
is a fine man and he was a fine judge. A worthy opponent, he made
the election of 1982 my most difficult race. In some ways, I wish
things could have been different. I wish we could have served alongside
each other. I think we would have come to see our similarities sooner.

Albert Thompson was not a man who would volley away his ethics
to maintain his political position. He knew when he was sworn in that
the Bowers case would come before his court and Thompson may
have wished, like Smith did before him, for this case to be decided by
someone else.

Thompson had few choices—he could retry the penalty phase of
the case, or he could commute the young man's sentence to life
imprisonment. I didn't really understand Thompson's position myself
until he granted my collaborator an interview during September, 1993,
in preparation of this book:

> "Judge Howard Hill, on the Supreme Court at the time,
> wrote an opinion at the time about how barbaric it was to
> execute people below a certain age. He went on to say that
> very seldom does this come up because before it gets to this
> particular stage, they usually have done something other than
> give the person the death penalty.
>
> I looked at all the circumstances of the case. I had actually
> seen some of the trial and felt the he (sic. the defendant) had
> got an exceptionally poor defense....
>
> I noticed when I was sitting in court that the judge
> permitted them to stack all the first three or four rows, sitting
> right there by the jury, with police officers in uniform. I
> thought to myself: this is intimidating.
>
> And then I looked at the thing 'cause I had another concept
> of what had happened. These two kids walked into this store
> carrying an old raggedy pistol with one bullet in it. And the
> officer walks in, doesn't draw his weapon, does not wait for
> back up. Nothing. He just walks in there. The boy turned
> around and saw him. Bam! No thought to it, you know. It's a
> wonder he hit him. Just one of those things.
>
> Anyways with all of that, I thought this was a good time to
> do just exactly what the court said should be done—either

retry the penalty phase or commute the sentence to life in prison. I commuted it. I made the District Attorney irate. I have never lost any sleep over it....I thought it was the right thing to do, so I did it.

Some members of my campaign team, when Rufe started emphasizing the death penalty, suggested, 'Well, Al, maybe you ought to moderate your position on the death penalty.' Nuh huh, win, lose or draw.

I'm not totally opposed to the death penalty. I'm ambivalent about it. I think that the manner in which we arrive at the death penalty is wrong. I think the procedures are bad. I don't think it's consistent.

We are talking about death, not imprisonment. Of course, I have seen crimes where I think I could pull the switch on people. It's a matter of individual judgment. I'm not so crazy that I figure everybody who commits a bad crime oughta walk. I don't feel that way.

But being black and having seen so many miscarriages of justice, particularly involving black people in the courts here, I don't trust the courts with the death penalty. I also saw some other things going on. For instance, the district attorney's office using the death penalty to coerce guilty pleas. 'If you don't plead guilty, they're going to ask for the death penalty.' A lot of people will plead guilty under those circumstances.

I knew commuting that sentence there were going to be some people who did not like it. Yes, I knew that.

...The thing about it is I didn't know this black kid from Adam's house cat. Still don't know him. Don't know his family. Know nothing at all about him as an individual. I didn't do it on the basis of personalities.

The only thing I do recollect is that sometime after I commuted the sentence his mother called me. She said, 'Judge, my son is not really a good person and I know that. He's done things he shouldn't ought to have done, but I just want to thank you for commuting his sentence.' She never said anything more than that...never heard from her. That was my only contact with anyone in that family."

Thompson's decision upset many. Columbus' District Attorney was incensed. Thompson's decision rankled much of the police force and much of white Columbus. Many people felt that Albert

Thompson commuted the sentence because of race. Those same
people felt that if Thompson were white, the youth's death sentence
would have stood. The Bowers case highlights the racial issues that
have forever divided our communities.

Let me say, I respect Thompson for doing what he felt was right.
Thompson proved in the Bowers case that he was motivated not by
political alignments, but by his own commitment to justice. As a black
man, Thompson understood that his commuting the death sentence
of a black youth would ignite the racial embers of our community.

I suspect that he also knew it might be political suicide. But
Thompson overlooked the threat to his own political fortunes and
focused on his commitment to justice.

Would I have done the same thing? Yes. I would have focused on
my commitment to justice being served. Would I have commuted the
sentence? No. I believe my choice would have been to retry the
penalty phase. In the same 1993 interview Thompson himself
revealed:

> "One of the judges afterwards said, 'Al, I sure wish you had
> not done it that way. One thing I want you to know is you did
> the right thing. But you could have gone on and retried the
> penalty phase where you might have gotten a different result.
> And then you still would have had an opportunity to change
> or commute the sentence.'"

I suppose some would maintain that I would choose to do this
because it would relieve me of the responsibility, and blame, of the
penalty. Very politically aware, some would say.

Perhaps that allegation is true. But I have always felt that I was
elected by the people to represent the people. And so if I was given a
choice to make the decision myself, or to give the people a chance to
decide, I would opt for giving the people a chance.

Maybe my motives are not pure. I know I do not like conflict,
never have liked it, and do seek to avoid it. But I do not believe I
have ever traded my convictions to pursue political popularity. If I
felt the young man did not receive a fair trial, as Thompson
concluded, I would have been distressed. I would have wanted to retry
the case. It took strength of character and conviction to do what
Thompson felt was right. Albert Thompson is an admirable man.

Which is why running against him in 1982 was difficult. I liked
him. Opposing a peer who is unworthy can actually make a person
feel good about herself. I have heard of judges who come to the job

late, unprepared, and sometimes even under the influence. To defeat one of these characters would be a favor to the community; to defeat a man of quality like Albert Thompson was a bittersweet victory.

I knew from the beginning of the 1982 election that this particular race would be significant. By running against Thompson, who had been appointed, I was challenging an incumbent—and incumbent judges are rarely defeated, especially judges the caliber of Albert Thompson. Albert had always been very popular with the voters. (I realize as I write this that a man would not feel this need I do to justify my decision to run against Thompson.)

The race was intense. Albert Thompson had the backing of Columbus' business community. According to 1982's campaign disclosure forms, Thompson had the backing of John Amos, founder and owner of American Family Life, one of the most influential votes in Columbus. Elena Amos, bless her, backed my campaign with a contribution of $150. However, John must have had Elena on a budget because his own contribution to Thompson was $1,000.

Actually, looking back over the disclosure forms two things become very apparent—many of my contributors were women, and many of Thompson's were black. Thompson's own analysis of the race alludes to this polarization, as he explained in 1993:

> "I think she (sic.Rufe) realized my race was going to be an impediment to me. The percentage of population was still 30-40% black...Rufe's biggest strength was being a woman.
>
> This was just at the beginning of the period when women were running for office and being very successful. Women had been denied public office and other things just like black people. When you get a good female candidate, I guess all the women got together. There are a lot of women's organizations here in town. They were all for her, the women were. That was the biggest thing going for her."

Besides financial heavyweight John Amos, Thompson received contributions from Columbus Bank and Trust's Political Action Committee, as well as a $10,000 loan from C.B.&T, and several congregational donations.

My dear friend, Larry Taylor, ran the financial end of the campaign for me.

I told Larry from the beginning that I never wanted to know who contributed to my campaign. I felt that if I won and I faced a contributor in court, there was no way I could be impartial. So until I retired, I never knew who contributed. Larry assured me that he never had any trouble raising the needed funding. Usually, just one phone call would result in a contribution.

But Thompson didn't appear to have any trouble either. All in all, Thompson disclosed a total figure of $24,216.99 to my $18,532.30 campaign total.

I knew the business community of Columbus backed Thompson long before I ever knew who was funding Thompson because those same business leaders approached me and asked me not to oppose Thompson.

*"You're going against Albert won't do nothing but stir up trouble, Rufe. Don't do it."*

*"If you defeat Thompson, Rufe, the race, and the racial issues will tear apart this city. Don't do it."*

*"Why don't you wait, Rufe? Wait until another seat opens up, then run for that one. Thompson's a good man; we need him on the bench."*

Why didn't I wait for another seat? It was as if these businessmen thought that Georgia ran blue light specials on Superior Court seats. The first person to get there would surely be able to get one. But in 1982 there were only four Superior Court seats in the Chattahoochee Circuit. Once a seat is filled in Superior Court, whether by election or appointment, it is usually occupied until that person retires or dies.

In 1982 those four seats were occupied by Judge John Land, Judge Kenneth Followill, Judge Mullins Whiznant and Judge Thompson. Judge John Land did retire later in 1982, but everyone knew that District Attorney Bill Smith, Columbus-born and bred, was going to run and that he would win. If I had waited for another available seat on the bench, as was suggested, the first opportunity available would not come about until eight years later, when in 1990 the Chattahoochee Circuit was granted approval for a fifth judgeship. At age 72, what chance would I have had then of being elected or appointed?

Did I want to run against Albert Thompson? No. But if I wanted the opportunity to move into a Superior Court position, then running against Thompson was my only choice. Of course, I suspect that if I had been a male, the businessmen of Columbus probably never would have approached me with their personal opinions on my campaign. Most men just are not very forward in their advice to each other— not the way they are with women.

And I was not the only one receiving pressure during the campaign. My friends, William and Cricket Crittenden, had the political police after them as well, monitoring their involvement in my campaign—these individuals had determined the Crittenden's support was a threat to the interest of Columbus' black population.

William and Cricket agreed to let the campaign pay for and place a neon *VOTE FOR RUFE MCCOMBS* sign in their front yard. The sign had been up a week when the Crittendens were paid a personal visit, which they later described for my collaborator in some detail:

"Mind if we visit with you a moment, William?" someone spoke up from a group of men gathered on the Crittendens' front porch.

"Okay," William said as he joined them. Cricket followed William, shutting the screen door behind her. "Something I can help y'all with?" William directed his question at a couple of the men he knew.

"We're here about the sign." One of the men nodded toward the luminous sign that apparently was attracting more bugs than votes.

"Y'all want to one for your yards?" Cricket knew better, but she cared less. "I'll arrange to have it delivered." William squeezed her waist a bit too tight—his signal for "Hush up, woman."

"We don't want no sign in our yards. We don't want no signs t'all." The spokesman didn't smile; his hands fumbled with the change and keys in his pants pockets. "William, I ain't gonna tell you how to vote, but Albert Thompson is a good man. What you got ag'nst hem?"

"I ain't got nothing 'gainst Albert," William replied. "I'm just for Rufe McCombs."

"Be for McCombs if yo' wants," came the suggestion of another, "but take the sign down. It don't look right to have you supportin' that white woman in our neighborhood."

"Are you telling me to take down the sign?" William asked.

"We's just askin'; that's all. Lots of people pass by this road see the sign."

"I want them to see the sign. That's why I put it there and that's where it's goin' to stay. Now if you all will 'cuse me, Cricket just put dinner on." William opened the door for Cricket and left those fellows mulling about the front porch. The *VOTE FOR RUFE MCCOMBS* lighted the path back to their cars.

The media did its part to stir up the racial waters as well. Just minutes after I officially announced my candidacy for Superior Court the *Columbus Enquirer* asked me to respond to Thompson's decision in the Bowers case. I told them: "I have no criticism of anyone. I am running on my record of what I have done, and I wish to be judged on my record." (*Columbus Enquirer*, Feb. 24, 1982.)

And when the NAACP sponsored a debate in May headlines announced me as a proponent of the death penalty, and Thompson as an opponent. Was this the shadow of the Bowers case? I suppose the media would have addressed these differences with any candidates, but the Bowers case seemed always to lurk in the shadow of any spotlight on the campaign. In the 1993 interview, Thompson confirmed that he felt the pressure:

> "I went up and spoke to the FOP (sic. Fraternal Order of Police) and they were sitting there waiting for me on that death penalty case I commuted. The hall was full of police officers. I was the last person on the program that evening. I got up, I told them in the beginning, 'Let me tell you before we start, I am not here to justify anything I've done while I was on the bench. I don't think that's proper for a Superior Court Judge to do that.
>
> I don't think it is even proper for me to discuss decisions I made while I was on the bench. I'll talk generally about anything you want to talk about, but when it comes to specific cases I'm not going to discuss them.' Almost half of 'em got up and left, because they came there just to hear what I had to say about this case. That was all they were interested in.
>
> I know they were against me."

Neither Thompson nor I ever talked about the Bowers case, but we both knew that the voters were talking about it.

## Superior Court ... Finally

On August 10, 1982, ignoring precedent, the majority of Columbus voters elected me to replace the incumbent Thompson. Actually, the election was just a primary and the voters had elected me as their Democratic nomination for Superior Court, but there was no Republican opposition for the post. Columbus voters ignored precedent, mostly because they were unaware of it, by ousting

Thompson, the incumbent. I don't know of any other case in the state where an incumbent Superior Court Judge has been unseated.

In 1991, Thompson said, "I think race had something to do with it. I think she choose to oppose me rather than someone else because I was black. She tried to find the person she could beat. She chose me because I was black. This is the South." (*Columbus Ledger*, September 2, 1991.)

There is no denying the shortage of blacks among Georgia jurists. Out of the 144 state-wide Superior Court seats in 1993, only nine judges were black, out of the State Court bench, 86 seats, only seven of those were black. (*The Daily Report*, Vol.104, No. 170, September 1, 1993) Obviously, justice in Georgia is dispensed by whites.

In reality, the election of 1982 polarized voters—whites voted for me, blacks for Thompson. The turnout for that race was 55.7 percent, the size of my winning percentage. Thompson carried the eight predominantly black precincts and two white precincts.

I carried every other white precinct by almost a two-one vote. People's biases were prevalent.

Thompson's assessment of my motives was wrong. I did not run against him because he was black. Frankly, I think that I probably could have beaten almost anyone—regardless of skin color or sex. Remember Harry Pettigrew's remarks about certain middle-age women in Columbus? That they could do no wrong in the eyes of the community? Well, Pettigrew's remarks proved true for me. The Columbus' voters believed in me—they proved that trust by electing me to every office I sought. Of course, there is no denying that it was the white vote that put me into office. Later, Thompson asserted that it was primarily women who put me in office:

> "My race played a part, I guess. But the main factor was that she was woman. To be honest with you, I think there were very few white lawyers in town who would've beat me. Male. I think it took a Rufe McCombs and her being female. She was a seated judge, who had a history, a record as a judge. She was well-thought of and well-liked, and she got the support of women's groups" (Thompson-Zacharias interview, September, 1993).

There can be no denying that the women of Muscogee County helped elect me. To this day, I remain humbled by their support and confidence in me. In my case, the voter's trust kept me honest. I never wanted to be unworthy of their confidence. So I felt that I needed to justify their faith in me, which is why I worked so hard every day. The harder I worked, the more convinced they were that I was the right person for the job.

Annamaria Barrentine was one such voter. When I ran for Municipal Court, Annamaria regarded me as nothing more than a liberal do-gooder.

"Trying to get people things for nothing," Annamaria charged.

Ms. Barrentine was a property-holder, a landlord. Occasionally my work at Legal Aid required me to represent her tenants. Annamaria definitely did not appreciate my representation on behalf of her tenants. When I ran for Municipal Court, Annamaria Barrentine actively campaigned against me. Fortunately for me, not every one in Columbus regarded me as the liberal Annamaria pegged me to be.

However, by the time I ran for State Court, Annamarie had become one of my most active campaigners.

"Why?" I asked Annamaria. "Why did you change your perception of me?"

"I didn't change my perception of you," Annamaria protested. "You did. You changed my perception by your commitment to your job. When I heard others speak of how hard you were working in Municipal Court, I realized you weren't just trying to get people something for nothing."

Today, Annamaria Barrentine remains one of my most devoted supporters and my friend.

The compulsion I felt to prove myself is probably why voters kept electing me. Local headlines followed me throughout Municipal and State Court covering the conviction of court clerk Rob Welch and the clearing up of the backlog in both courts. Voters could see that I was motivated by their trust to work hard.

I believe that the kind of trust that the voters displayed by electing me to every position I ever sought cannot be generated by race or gender alone. I never ran against Thompson. I declared from the moment Busbee appointed Thompson that I would run for the position. I was not *running against* Thompson; I was *running for* the position.

To this day, any assertion that I chose to run on the basis of racism grieves me deeply.

# 12

# JUSTICES & INJUSTICES

## Defining Moments

By its very nature, Superior Court challenged my skills as a jurist. Being elected to Superior Court in 1982 mollified my competitive spirit. The difference between being a jurist in Municipal Court versus being a jurist in Superior Court is similar to the difference between parenting a three-year old versus parenting a thirteen-year old—the bigger the kid, the bigger the problems.

Each of the different courts of records has its own jurisdiction. Municipal Court does not handle criminal cases except as a court of inquiry. In other words, if a defendant of a misdemeanor wishes to plead guilty, the Judge of Municipal Court can sentence him/her.

Other than that exception, the Judge of Municipal Court will remand all other criminal cases to State or Superior Court. When I served in Municipal Court, there was a $5,000 limit to civil cases. Anything more had to be remanded to State Court. Today that amount is higher, around $10,000, I believe.

State Court has no limitations regarding the civil cases within its jurisprudence. However, State Court has no jurisdiction over equity or divorce actions. Criminal misdemeanors are most often tried in State Court.

Superior Court is the last stop before moving on to the Court of Appeals or Supreme Court. Every county seat has a Superior Court. It is the highest court within the local system. Complicated civil cases, a continuous current of criminal cases, divorce and custody cases, as well as all felonies—which includes all Capital cases—fill the dockets of Superior Court.

I figured that aspiring to the Appellate Court or even the Supreme Court was unreasonable considering my age. In 1982, I was sixty-three-years old, an age when many are pursuing travel plans instead of promotions. But Superior Court would not have pacified my interest in the law if I had been young enough to seek a position in the Court of Appeals, Supreme or Federal Court. Perhaps the greatest regret of my life is that I ran out of time. I guess I should just be thankful that I'm still lucid after all these years.

Raymond and Irene, my faithful court recorder and secretary accompanied me to Superior Court. As did a host of other suspicious looking folks. Superior Court depositions are often more entertaining than a John Grisham novel; this may explain why Grisham's move from the courtroom to the screening room is more like a mental sidestep than a literary leap.

Divorce cases were always Raymond's favorites—good reading, he claims. But sometimes the divorce cases distressed me more than the nine capital cases I have tried. I have never enjoyed bickering and I do not like to see children treated as parental possessions. During one particularly messy divorce, a woman, obviously a descendant of the woman Jesus met at the well, yelled at me.

"There's no justice anywhere anymore!" The dark-haired, well-dressed woman shouted across the courtroom from where she sat next to her attorney.

Maybe I should have, but I just couldn't leave her accusation alone. "Why do you say that?" I inquired.

"Because you've just awarded my ex-husband custody of those four kids and NOT A ONE OF THEM IS HIS!" she screamed back at me.

I looked over at counsel's table where her ex-husband sat. His face was as white as plain yogurt. Was this the first time he'd heard this?

Of course, even that case was not as bad as the time I sat listening to an attorney, who was representing the husband in a divorce case, cross-examine the wife. The attorney was seeking to establish that this woman lacked fidelity in marriage and, therefore, was not entitled to any alimony.

"Were you faithful to your husband during the course of your eighteen years together?" The attorney stood directly in front of the woman. His eyes were penetrating, accusatory. In order to see her own attorney, this lovely blond had to shift in her seat and lean a little to her left.

"Why yes!" she declared.

"You claim never to have had relations with anyone else besides your husband for the duration of your marriage?" The attorney was pressing her.

"No, never," came her adamant reply. Then a pause. She leaned to her left. Perhaps, she recalled she was under oath to tell the truth. "Well, no one besides *my own attorney.*" She hurled the words at her cross-examiner like rocks. Too late, though. Her own attorney was sputtering and coughing worse than anything I had ever heard during my two years in the sanitarium. The rest of the courtroom was howling like a bunch of yard dogs.

## Victims

I have never been a very temperamental person. I suppose the ability to keep one's composure is due in part to genetic disposition and to one's cultural upbringing. Early on I was taught that exposing one's emotions was equivalent to public indecency; to do so humiliated everyone. It is my belief that a jurist who displays emotions outwardly like a sergeant's stripes should be relieved of duty.

Thus, I am sure that others have often assumed that I am emotionally retarded, repressed, detached, or mute. Anyone who has thought this of me is wrong. Just because a river runs quiet does not mean the current is not strong. Nothing stirred my emotions more than sexual cases.

Never did a rape victim sit before me, or a child testify, when I did not hear my own mother's hesitant voice as I heard it that day she told me how her drunken father had taken liberties with her. I always sought to give such offenders the maximum punishment allowed by law.

Never did I sentence a rapist without reflecting on the violence the victim endured. Not just because of the incident between my grandfather and my mother, but because I knew of such violence myself. Two women I cared for very much were raped. Date rape, we call it now. Both rapes occurred on college campuses. One back in the early forties, and one in the seventies. Neither women reported the rapes. Both rapes occurred before the Rape-Shield Act.

The Rape-Shield Act prevents the courts from prying into a woman's history as a measure of protection for the defendant. No longer can a rapist claim, "She wanted it."

I really had no say in the first rape, as to whether I thought the victim should report it or not, but I did in the second. I pleaded with the victim to report the rape.

"You know that he will do this again to someone else if you don't report it," I implored. "I know people. I will make sure he is prosecuted to the fullest extent of the law. Please," I begged.

But she refused to report it. For all the conventional reasons. The humiliation of a trial. The publicity. The judgment of her character. She was devastated. The rapist penetrated her sense of security, her self-esteem. I encouraged her to see a rape counselor in her community. She did.

Violence is no respecter of people or position. Allowing offenders to avoid consequences makes all of us co-conspirators to the crime. My loved one should have reported the rape. But like many victims, she believed the system would expose her wound, not seek her healing.

And frankly, I understand why she felt this way. Over the years I have noted a trend among jurors that troubles, and yes, terrifies me. The trend has me thinking that we should give serious consideration to establishing a professional jury system.

The trend started, of course, as so many of our legal problems did, in the 1970's. Possibly in an effort to overcompensate for previous inequities, juries began to overlook facts and base many of their judgments upon more nebulous elements. We have to look no further than the infamous O.J. Simpson case—we all know that the pursuit of truth and justice was irrelevant to the case.

Recently, I have begun to wonder if jury decisions are personal manifestations of anti-authority complexes. People are sick of government intervention in their lives. They are tired of the legislating of public policy, which I addressed as a State Court Judge in a *Columbus Enquirer* interview:

> "The Supreme Court now tells this nation as a whole what it must do. The courts are not passing judgments anymore. They're passing public policy...as it is now, the people have no relief. If we don't like public policy passed by the Supreme Court there's nothing we can do about it." (*Columbus Enquirer*, June 29, 1978)

Quite possibly the public has found a way of getting relief. Perhaps, the manner in which they restore balance to their world is to ignore the facts and go with whatever feels right. And at the moment, anything anti-government feels pretty darn good.

Of course, the justice system has only itself to blame. Attorneys seek jurors with biases, as long as those biases are favorable to their clients. Our justice system has become blinded by the sweat of competitiveness. And ultimately, green-eyed with greed. The truth has become a secondary issue for far too many of us.

Jurists are also responsible for losing sight of their responsibilities. In 1989, I wrote the following concerns in honor of the Bi-centennial of the U.S. Constitution:

> "É There is little doubt that today's judges legislate ... Reforms have been made in education, abortion, and school prayer. Supporters of reform often lobby in Congress and, failing there, go to the court. There is nothing in our Constitution which remotely suggests that judges should participate in the lawmaking process...We are a society which gives the powers of government to our elected represen-tatives. Thus, judicial lawmaking is against our form of government. Judges acting outside the Constitution make law for which no consent has been given. Judicial lawmaking takes away a power given Congress. In addition, often Congress will not legislate on unpopular issues and shifts its responsibility to the courts..." (*Columbus Enquirer*, September, 1989).

Sadly, I don't blame people for their basic distrust of our system. Two cases tried in my courtroom have underscored the failure of our system. The first was a drunk driving case. The second was a child molestation case. These cases had two common denominators—both inflicted great harm upon children, both involved men who were very prominent in our community. Apparently, although violence is no respecter of people, justice respects men of status.

In the drunk driver's case, a golf-pro employed by one of Columbus' private clubs, with a prior history of drunk driving, headed down Columbus' Manchester Expressway in the wrong lane, striking a sixteen-year old boy on a motorcycle.

The boy's mother, a single parent, had called him just moments before from the hospital where she worked. During trial, this mother recalled her last conversation with her son.

"Honey, my car won't start."

"Aw, Mom."

"Think you could meet me in the parking lot?"

"Give me a few minutes, okay, Mom? I'm on my way."

"I'm parked out back. Just look for the stranded lady in white. Bye, sweetie."

"G'bye, Mom."

The boy was killed upon impact.

Anguish could be heard all over the community. Outcries of grief...for...the golf pro. Letters poured into my chambers. There were three stacks of them, each a foot high. Every who's who in Columbus petitioned me on behalf of this man. The signatures of these town criers were embossed on corporate letterhead throughout the city. Each plea attested to the golf-pro's true character:

> *A fine individual.*
> *He contributes so much to our community.*
> *I've known him for years. He would never intentionally harm anyone.*
> *A productive man.*

My personal favorite:

> *It would be a waste to sentence this man to jail. Instead, why not give him a sentence of community service? Our community could benefit greatly if you would sentence him to teach golf skills to young men, rather than having him idle away his talents in prison.*

Not a one of these notable stockholders wrote a letter on behalf of the boy.

The golf-pro was found guilty of manslaughter and I handed him the maximum sentence—16 years—one year for each the boy lived. The man's attorney sent copies of all those letters stacked in my office to the Sentencing Review Board. They lowered his sentence to only five years, I believe. It was the only time I ever felt compelled to write the Sentence Review Board. I declared that they had been "taken" by all those petitions.

The golf-pro was released from prison in less than three years. He still teaches golf, socializes with his supporters, and continues to be cited for drunk driving.

The child molestation case involved a teacher, a very popular teacher, who directed our local Boy's Choir, and a boy from a single-parent family. And an ambitious District Attorney, who wanted to avoid the publicity that illuminates this kind of case.

Columbus residents raised over $2,000 for the teacher's defense. They sent letters of petition to the D.A. and members of the grand jury. Many of these supporters had contact with this teacher through his work as Director of the Boy's Choir. They insisted that the man was innocent.

Except for one, the D.A. successfully intercepted the letters to the grand jurors. One grand juror member asked the D.A. if it would be inappropriate to contribute to the teacher's defense fund prior to trial. This sort of community lobbying angered both the D.A. and myself. Efforts to influence a grand juror is a crime.

Anyone who has ever had to run for office is not immune to public pressure. When community members rally behind a defendant the way they did in this case, emotional turmoil ensues for both the prosecutor and the jurist.

But the distress we felt was not comparable to the grief felt by the thirteen-year old victim and his family. In the weeks following the youth's report of molestation, he was ridiculed and judged by his peers, community members, and yes, other teachers. His character came into question. His performance as a student. His home life. Judgment shadowed the victim.

This case, more than any other, brought to my mind the dilemma of Pontius Pilate. What's a jurist to do? As an elected official I had an obligation to the people and to the law. My gut-instinct was to send this teacher away for 25 years. In order to do that, I needed a jury who would discern the differences between the indiscretions of a thirteen-year old boy and those of a thirty-seven-year old man.

The D.A. asserted, and I agreed, that any jury was likely to respect the authority figure over the word of a teen, particularly a teen who had not endeared himself to other teachers. We reached a plea bargain.

In court, I summoned the teacher before the spectators, mostly his supporters, and the media. He admitted that he placed his hand in the youth's crotch. He admitted that he placed the youth's hand in his own crotch.

"Did you commit this crime?" I asked.

"Yes," he replied.

"Are you aware that you have a problem?" I inquired.

"Yes," he confessed.

The D.A. discovered that the teacher had lost a previous youth minister job after another teen accused him of molestation. I sentenced the teacher to ten years intensive probation. He lost his teaching certification. I ordered that he was not to associate with any children under the age of eighteen. I declared that he would receive medication and psychotherapy at his own expense, waive his right to confidentiality, and perform 350 hours of community service. It was the only child molestation case in which I failed to incarcerate the guilty.

The Board President of the Boy's Choir felt there were other reasons the teacher plea bargained:

> "'That was in his (sic. the defendant's) best interest at this point ... Personally, I have absolute faith in him and consider him to be innocent,' she declared. 'Even after being in court and hearing what I heard, I believe he's innocent ... There has never been in the eight-year history of our Boy's Choir a hint of impropriety'" (*Columbus Ledger–Enquirer*, September, 1993).

"It was not in the best interest of the child to testify," I pronounced.

The press found other defenders:

"In this case we had an unusual victim who had suffered an unusual amount more by the defendant's defenders," the D.A. explained. (*Columbus Ledger-Enquirer*, September, 1993)

The last I heard, the teacher was employed in an administrative position with the Columbus' Boy's Choir.

## Defendants

Prior to my retirement from Superior Court in 1993, I received the following letter from a former defendant:

Dear Judge McCombs:

> No one deserves to be in this place that you sent me to—I don't care what they've done. You sentenced me and I want a new trial. But I sure don't want to come before you again! Please write me and let me know when you are retiring. And remember it can't be too soon for me."

Throughout my career I have been considered a tough jurist, mostly by offenders. The public, I think, knows me to be committed to the law. During the sentencing phase of my first death penalty case, I read the sentence and then declared, "May God have mercy upon your soul."

Mac received a phone call the next morning from Dr. Haywood Turner, his personal physician.

"Mac, I want you to know I saw Rufe on t.v. tonight and I'm proud of the way she handled that case. But I sure didn't like what she said," Haywood proclaimed.

"What do you mean you didn't like what she said?" Mac asked, surprised by Haywood's commentary. "What did she say?"

"When Rufe stated, 'May God have mercy on your soul.' I don't want anybody to have mercy on his soul!"

Most people are unaware that I have not always been a proponent of capital punishment. Especially, considering I have sat on the bench for nine capital cases.

Capital cases are assigned to a jurist on a lottery basis. It is the court clerk's responsibility to make the assignments. Many have suspected that I have received more than a jurist's fair share of death penalty cases. In retrospect, I believe I did receive more than a servant's helping.

I think there are two reasons why I was given the assignments. Prosecutors want judges who are knowledgeable of the law specific to death penalty cases, since any error can be grounds for an appeal.

Secondly, I think I was singled out because death penalty cases are high profile cases. They make morning headlines. If one is hoping to advance themselves politically, there is no better advertising than a successful high profile case. And being the only woman jurist in Muscogee County's Superior Court, I received media attention anyway.

It is possible that certain politically ambitious people pursued working cases in my courtroom, since I had found favor with the media and with the public, attaching one's self to my robetails might propel a prosecutor to the limelight. I suspect prosecutors may have selected me instead of entrusting their cases to the randomness of a lottery.

But I doubt many knew when I was first elected Superior Court Judge, my position on the death penalty was a reluctant one. I really had no desire to send anyone to the electric chair. I was unconvinced that doing so would bring about any sort of benefit to society. Would doing so result in less crime? I doubted it. Would it restore healing to the offended? Not likely. Would killing one person rationalize the death of another? Hardly.

Initially the only reason I publicly supported the death penalty was because the citizens of Georgia had voted to enact it. As an elected jurist, I perceived my obligation was not to make laws but to enforce them. Many elected officials, who are personally opposed to the death penalty, have still carried out the will of the people. That is democracy in action.

One man convinced me of the need for the death penalty. It was my first capital case. Ronald Spivey was a violent man. If he wanted rob or rape and someone got in his way, Spivey didn't hesitate to kill them. He needed no provocation. And because of his violent nature and his size, few could stop him.

Spivey's killing spree began Monday, December 27, 1976, in Macon, Georgia and ended when police captured him in Roanoke, Alabama, on Tuesday, December 27, 1976. The *Columbus Ledger* offered this account:

> "A Macon man suspected of killing a Columbus policeman and a Macon man last night and early this morning was captured today near Roanoke, Ala.
>
> "A woman hostage, the arrested man—Ronald Spivey, 38—was holding was released unharmed.
>
> "The slain Columbus policeman was identified as Bill Watson, 41. He was a nine-year veteran of the Columbus police force, was married and the father of three children.
>
> "The suspect described by Macon police as 'extremely demented' shot and wounded two other men in a Peachtree Mall bar after killing Watson. He then escaped with a 34-year-old hostage.
>
> "The hostage, Mary Jane Davidson, a Columbus College history instructor, was freed early today unharmed but was frightened and upset...
>
> "...Columbus police Chief Curtis E. McClung said Watson was making a final check in the lounge when he was shot at point blank range twice with a .38 caliber pistol. He died instantly, McClung said.
>
> "An employee of the Brer Rabbit's Restaurant, who walked in the lounge with Waston was shot three times, police said. "Buddy" Allen was listed in satisfactory condition at St. Francis Hospital.
>
> "...Police said the night of bloodshed, for which Spivey faces charges, began about 10 p.m. in Macon when Charles McCook was shot to death over betting in a pool game.

"Tommey Chapman, 28, of Warner Robins was wounded in that shooting and is in satisfactory condition in Macon...Spivey then ran five blocks and held up a clerk and fired five shots into the wall of the building.

"Police Cmdr. Herman Boone in Columbus said a 'man calling himself Ronnie Spivey drank for about two hours in the Final Approach Lounge in Columbus and at times bragged about killing two men and told others in the bar they'd read about it in the morning headlines'...." (*Columbus Ledger* Tuesday, December 28, 1976)

Macon police noted that Spivey had been previously booked for aggravated assault charges and was free on bond for a rape charge out of Tampa, Florida. Columbus Police confirmed that Spivey had previously been confined to a cell at the State Mental Hospital in Milledgeville. (*Columbus Ledger,* Tuesday, December 28, 1976)

Spivey was tall, a man of tremendous size and intelligence. He possessed an impressive IQ, which gave him a demeanor of arrogance. He believed he was smarter than the average person. To my knowledge, he was not involved with drugs.

At the time of Spivey's first trial, I was still working in State Court, which does not handle capital cases. The only choices a jury may reach in a capital case are death, life imprisonment, or acquittal.

One day I went over to S & S Cafeteria for lunch. It was packed full, but I found a table off to myself and was there only a brief time before an elderly gentleman approached me.

"Could I share this table with you, Ma'am?" his voice seemed as hesitant as a kindergartner on the first day of school.

"Why, sure," I looked up from my salad.

"I'm visiting Columbus," he remarked before I could ask.

"You have family here?" I inquired. An observant waitress refilled my sweet tea.

"I don't have much family, most my kinfolk live over in Macon. I'm here for a trial," he stated as easily as if reading off his social security number. "My son is up on a murder charge. They say he killed a police officer. Raped a girl. I reckon he did it, but the D.A. is trying to send my boy to the electric chair."

"I'm sorry, sir," I said.

"Thank you, ma'am. My boy ain't to blame for his actions—I am. His momma died when he was young and I just didn't pay the boy any mind. He's smart, real smart. Maybe too smart. He's been in jail before. All that idle time in jail then he gets out and kills somebody.

Maybe he ain't such a quick study. But I sure hope that jury don't give him the chair. I'm the failure, not my boy. I should've made him mind when he was little. I just felt so sorry for the little fellow."

As I finished my lunch that day, I thought about how sorry I felt for this father.

While I was still serving in State Court, Spivey was found guilty and given the death penalty, in spite of his plea of insanity. I think the specific testimony provided by some of his victims probably convinced the jury that Spivey was mentally alert at the time. The community was said to be shocked by testimony from the hostages:

> "Bert Martin, a customer in the bar that night, said he and Mrs. Davidson and waitress Lucy Weaver were lined up against a wall by Spivey and when Martin saw a policeman coming in the bar with another man, Martin tried to signal him... But Spivey saw Watson before the officer realized a holdup was going on, and the huge man turned, paused a second or two, and fired into Watson's face, Martin testified.
>
> "Spivey then wheeled and fired at the other man, Martin said. Both Martin and Mrs. Davidson said that Spivey then ordered Mrs. Davidson to get Watson's gun and marched them out of the bar. As they filed out the narrow walkway, the second man shot, Welton "Buddy" Allen ... moaned and Spivey fired more shots at the two men on the floor ...
>
> "The witnesses said Spivey saw a door of Brer Rabbit's move and said, 'I left someone alive.'..." (*Columbus Ledger,* December 31, 1976)

But Spivey's case was overturned on appeal. It would have to be retried.

The second trial took place in November, 1983. It was my first Superior Court capital case. I am not sure that Spivey's father recognized me from our previous cafeteria visit. He never requested a visit in my chambers, which I believe he might have done if he had remembered our prior contact.

The second jury found Spivey guilty and gave him the death penalty again. This capital case was a very emotional one for me. My secretary, Irene Conner, recalled the case this way:

"Spivey was just mean. A big man — about seven feet tall and 350 lbs. His thighs were as big as my waist. When he was asked why he shot one of his victims a second time he replied, 'Because he wasn't dead yet.'

"When Judge McCombs tried the Spivey case, she was so tired and emotional that Tuesday when we got the guilty verdict at 1:00 a.m., she turned to me and asked, 'Irene, will you take me home? I just don't think I can drive.'

"Spivey's 77-year-old father had sold his home to pay Doug Peters to represent his son. It was terrible. Raymond cried. I cried. We all cried. Judge McCombs was visibly upset. It was her first capital punishment case." (Conner-Zacharias interview, January, 1996.)

Spivey was surprised. He had successfully gotten off before—I think he really believed the jury would accept his insanity plea. In my opinion, the jury made the only right decision.

In his short life, he had seemingly without remorse, killed two people, injured others with the intent to kill and subjected at least 2 women to the nightmare of rape. Ronald Spivey would likely go on to kill again.

I am familiar with all the arguments against the death penalty, particularly where my neighborhood is concerned. I know the foes of capital punishment would have the public believe the real issues are racial and economic—only poor blacks are sentenced to death row. But if the capital cases I sat through are any indication, seven out of the nine cases I tried involved white men. Ronald Spivey was white.

Ronald Spivey murdered for the sense of power and control it gave him. Unless stopped, I believe he would continue to murder to seek the elation that he obtained from exercising that kind of control over others.

But one is never elated about sending someone off to die in the electric chair, no matter how evil they may be. In fact, the only positive thing that I believe came out of the whole Spivey incident occurred only one week after his killing spree, when local policemen received the first step toward seeking a pay increase. (Billy Watson, the policeman killed by Spivey, was working a second job at Peachtree Mall to supplement his family's income.)

Wives of 25 Columbus policemen appealed to the city council for higher pay for their husbands and Mayor Jack Mickle provided the tie-breaking vote to grant the request of the Fraternal Order of the Police for a dues check-off. Many saw this as the first step toward a police union. What policemen were really seeking, however, was equitable pay.

According to the *Ledger*, Mrs. Florence Taft, speaking on behalf of the policemen's wives, said that it was impossible to support a family with the 1977 salary.

"'We want to see that police officers don't have to moonlight, to be a target,' said Mrs. Taft. She asked the council to grant the raise 'so policemen can spend more time with their families.' " (*Columbus Ledger,* Tuesday, January 4, 1977)

Representing several of the policemen seeking a pay hike was my former opponent for Municipal Court, attorney Norwood Pearce, who had his own moonlighting job—as a State Senator!

## The Jurist

Thankfully, not all my work as a Superior Court Judge was as demanding as capital cases. I believe that every capital case I tried took six months off my life. The intensity of each case robbed me of some of life's energy, but, gladly, not of my wit.

Speaking engagements were one of those public servant obligations that I did, and still do, thoroughly enjoy. Perhaps, Mother's investment into speech classes with Mrs. Justin Bates finally paid off. Mac and I have spent more evenings eating chicken and rice covered with canned mushroom soup than I care to recall. But it is always a pleasure to have an audience who actually wants to be seated before me and to hear my declarations.

Once a small college in southeastern Alabama asked me to speak to their student body. As anxious as ever for an audience, I accepted. Mac was always my shadow at these engagements. In fact, if Mac had not been willing to drive, I would not have accepted. To this day, I do not drive unless there is no other way to get there but to walk.

On the drive over, I read over the invitation again, to clarify when and where we were to meet.

"Mac," I exclaimed, "there's been an awful mistake."

"What's that, honey?" Mac's brown eyes flashed at me.

"It says here I should feel free to bring along 'my wife.' Mac, these people are expecting a male judge!" I realized.

"Aw, Rufe, don't fret," Mac counseled. "I've heard your speeches so many times, I'm sure I could recite one, word for word, if need be."

"Mac McCombs, if that is your way of insulting me, you've succeeded!"

When we arrived at the college, late, Mac was whisked off to the podium and I was given a seat in the audience. If Mac had not been so delighted with himself over his insult, I might have intervened on his behalf. As it stood, I wanted to make Mac prove just how well he listened to me.

Much to my own chagrin, Mac gave a great speech. Obviously, he had memorized my speeches and could recite at least one of them almost verbatim. Unfortunately, for Mac, the program allotted for an ensuing question and answer period. "Judge McCombs," one student stood and called out his question, "could you define *res ipsa loquitur* for me?"

I detected a certain icy whiteness outlining Mac's lips. Mac paused. The auditorium was hushed, waiting for his reply.

"Young man," Mac's face was drawn as taut as Jane Fonda's butt, "that is such a stupid question even my wife could answer it! Rufe?"

Mac always was a quick study. And he'd been studying me ever since he gave up on Homer. If loyalty came in the form of seedlings, Mac planted enough for us to grow our very own redwood forest.

Life with Mac has been enchanting. Life without him has been like living in the grasslands. There's no tree to rest my head against at night.

# EPILOGUE

# IN THE SHADOWS

## Appointed Retirement

Retirement was never part of my career plan. Tuberculosis, childrearing, and cancer had demanded the immediate attention of my youth. By the time I put these three characters to bed, there was not much daylight left. That meant I needed to work well into my twilight hours. But I found that the eighteen years between 1975, when I was elected to Municipal Court and 1993, when I retired from Superior Court, moved faster than a lunar eclipse.

I have always maintained that the only retiring I have ever been interested in is a nine o'clock bedtime. Of course, within the State of Georgia, I had no choice: the law requires judges to retire by the first of the month succeeding their seventy-fifth birthday.

For me that day came August 14, 1993. Normally, a judge would be able to complete his/her elected-term before retiring. For me that was never an option. A federal suit filed by Rep. Tyrone Brooks of Atlanta challenging the way Georgia elects its judiciaries complicated matters.

Elected to serve four-year terms in 1982 and 1986 as Superior Court Judge, I completed those terms and filed in 1990 for another term. No one filed to run against me in either 1986 or 1990, but in response to Brooks' suit, a federal court initiated a freeze upon some of Georgia's judgeships.

That freeze put my 1990 term into limbo. No one was sure if I was coming or going. Due to the freeze, I had never been technically elected to my last term. Thus, when I turned seventy-five I did not know if I was serving mid-term or just hanging on from the election of 1986. Apparently no one else could decide either. Never one to gamble, I decided that I did not have time to wait on a declaratory judgment from Georgia's Supreme Court—I knew first hand just how slowly an old woman like Lady Justice moves—I retired to avoid jeopardizing my pension.

Knowing me as well as he did, Mac did not book a cruise to celebrate. "I'm not ever going on a cruise," Mac decided even before my retirement forced us into a travel schedule appropriate for a gubernatorial candidate. "Not unless you loan me one of your wigs and a dress to match."

"Mac, do you have something you need to share with me?" I cajoled, raising my eyebrows in mock surprise.

"No, darling, but if I'm on one of those cruise ships, I want to be able to dress up so that when the ship is going down and the Captain calls 'Women and children first,' I'll be ready!" Mac never overcame his childhood fear of drowning. His brother Fletcher's death in the Oconee River haunted Mac throughout his life.

However, my daughter, Beth, was not going to let me just pull the covers up over my head and sleep in. Unbeknownst to me, Beth arranged a retirement party on my behalf. A stretch limousine big enough for four caskets carried Beth's family of five, and Mac and me to downtown Atlanta where Raymond, Irene, Larry Taylor, Doug Pullen, Chief Appellate Court Judge Dorothy Toth Beasley, and many of my longtime friends and associates joined in a night of revelry.

We boarded the New Georgia Railway Dinner Train for a trip to Stone Mountain. The train took us right past the College Avenue depot where Daddy used to board the train every morning for his ride into Atlanta, right past my girlhood home on Feld Avenue where I had been sitting the day Frannie hit me with the rock, past the street where Schley Howard's family lived, past the field where I played ball with Charles and threw down the nickel I stole from Mother's purse. Right past the porch where I used to watch for my Daddy return home from Atlanta every night. How I had longed to ride the train to Atlanta and work like one of the fellows! To be just like my Daddy.

Indeed, in a fashion I had become like him; but unlike Daddy, I never became one of the fellows. And that was never clearer to me than the night I took the New Georgia Railroad past the Decatur Depot. Not a one of Muscogee County's male jurists from any court, Municipal, State, or Superior, had boarded the train with me. If they had not been such an integral part of my city retirement party that the County Clerk's office had previously hosted and if I had not been enjoying my steak and wine so much, I might have been hurt by their absence.

What is that saying about a rolling stone gathers momentum? Within weeks of my retirement, I became a Senior Superior Court Judge for the State. I feel like all retirement did for me was to increase the degree of incline; my life moved into fifth gear.

Now a Senior Superior Court Judge, I travel throughout Georgia sitting for cases that other jurists either have no time to hear or do not want to hear. A Senior Superior Court Judge is appointed by the Governor to the position with the only stipulation that he/she must have served a minimum of ten years in Superior Court. As Senior Superior Court Judge I have the same unlimited jurisdiction allotted any Superior Court Judge. I can even hear cases in State Court by order of that court. My work as a Senior jurist has primarily been in Superior Court.

## Left behind

Because he was the driver, Mac was glad we were traveling in fifth gear. In spite of his work as an insurance claims manager, Mac liked to drive fast. In truth, Mac just plain liked to drive and did so long after he should have. In 1988 Mac suffered a stroke which had left him walking with a cane. I believe his right foot may have been nothing more than dead weight. Mac seemed unaware of the relationship that existed between the pressure of his foot and the acceleration of the car.

"Slow down!" Some days I thought Mac was going to kill us both. "Watch out Mac!" I'd yell as Mac would swerve into the shoulder of a corner he was taking much too fast.

"Save your hollering for the courtroom, darling. I know where I'm going," Mac defended, abruptly guiding the car back between the lines.

My work as Senior Superior Court Judge requires that I travel from Merriweather County to Cobb, Butts, Fulton, Henry and back to Muscogee County, and any other place that might schedule a court date for me. Mac was my constant companion. He drove me to each of the different courthouses, sat attentively through the cases, joined me and others from the courthouse for lunch. When I finished in the afternoons, Mac would drive me to a motel or home, round up dinner, and leave me to my work. Because he enjoyed his role as chauffeur and cook, I always told Mac he would make a great wife. As a husband, Mac was unprecedented and irreplaceable.

On December 23, 1994, Mac and I celebrated our 51st wedding anniversary with a quiet dinner at home. We called our daughter who was in the Pacific Northwest hunting for a white Christmas. Mac had been feeling sluggish for a few weeks, yet had insisted upon driving me wherever court was held. I was worried.

I scheduled a doctor's appointment for Mac on January 5, 1995, in Columbus with his personal physician. "It's not good ... ." I barely recall any words the doctor related besides those.

Mac had been a smoker for sixty years. When we first started dating, he rolled his own. Cheaper, he said. Mac continued his habit non-stop until his stroke. Then he quit. No patches. No hypnosis. Mac put down the pack of cigarettes and never picked it up again.

"One rotor-rooter job is enough," Mac reasoned after undergoing an artery cleansing.

The doctor's prognosis burned, searing me while branding Mac with the emblem of death.

Lung cancer.

"You have maybe six months," the doctor stated.

Six days later, January 11, 1995, Mac died. Fast. Just like he drove. Drowning, not in the Oconee like his brother Fletcher had, but in a bed at St. Francis Hospital in Columbus, Georgia, in his own body fluids. Mac never overcame his fear of drowning. I heard his voice calm me in my muted sorrow, "Sugar, I know where I'm going."

I barely cried. Beth cried enough over the loss of her father to flood the Chatahoochee. I miss Mac. More each day, really. When I arise to the hushed breath of morning, I miss him. When I hurry alongside raspy workers throughout the day, I miss him.

Mac's gentleness and hilarity combined to propel a romance that lasted fifty-one years. Our life together had been full of celebrations. I came across a newspaper clipping recently of some award I had earned. I cannot even recall what the award was, or what the clipping said, but in red pen across the top was a note from Mac: *"I'm so proud of you, darling."* Mac's constant support, faith and pride in my achievements made my life meaningful.

The hallway of our home is lined with plaques and awards noting my various civic contributions. Mac called it "Rufe's Gallery." But now I notice that the hallway of our home echoes the absence of Mac. I believe the only thing that gave meaning and a sense of purpose to my life was being loved by a man such as Mac. Since childhood I strived to make people take notice of me. Mac noticed. I am so glad he did.

## Senior Superior Court Judgeship

Unlike Mac, however, other men have sometimes overlooked my presence. Mac's attentiveness to me is one reason why I valued him so much. But with my gavel in hand commanding the attention of disinterested parties can be as easy as knocking on wood.

Recently, I had a divorce hearing in Sumpter County. I am sure the husband in this particular divorce hearing would have agreed with the juror of Merriweather County who stood up in the jury box, pointed an accusatory finger at me, and declared: *"You're a mean woman!"*

The juror did this in response to a plea bargain that had occurred just moments before. The defendant had decided to accept the plea, so the juror was suggesting that the defendant wanted to plea rather than face trial in my court.

*"Don't worry,"* the juror consoled, *"we like mean women around here!"*

This particular divorce case involved a woman from Jacksonville, Florida, and a local attorney, her ex-husband. The issue was that of child-support. The attorney was $20,000 in arrears. Since he was a local attorney, I was called in on the case. A local jurist wanted to avoid the case; especially considering he had previously held the respondent in contempt of court.

"Your Honor." The respondent was representing himself. While Mr. Levy began to defend his check book balance, I took note of his $350 suit, his $95 wing-tips, and his $35 haircut. I would have bet money that he had a 1996 car with all the trimmings parked right outside. His ex-wife had taken the bus from Jacksonville.

"I had to buy a one-way ticket, Judge," she testified. "I didn't have enough money for the return ticket." Did she risk everything for this trip to Bountiful, I wondered?

"If you could just give me thirty days to get the money up, Your Honor, I'm sure I could come up with half the $20,000 in that time," Mr. Levy pleaded.

"Sir," I replied, "I'm betting that you can come up with $10,000 by this evening. As a matter of proof, I order the deputy to place you in jail until a cashier's check for that amount is delivered to Mrs. Levy. Deputy?"

"But, Judge ... " Levy began his protest in earnest, " ... a week, give me a week, okay?"

"Take however long you need, Mr. Levy," I advised. "But you will be in jail until that check is delivered. Do you understand?" The deputy stepped up beside Mr. Levy.

"Yes ma'am," Levy replied as the deputy led him away.

Mrs. Levy had a check in the amount of $10,000 by two 'clock that same afternoon. Irene, who was my driver for the day, hooted all the way home.

"I wish I had a picture of Levy when that deputy came alongside him," Irene smirked. "He looked like he'd sucked a dozen eggs!"

Not that Dads are the only deadbeats around. I have received phone calls from many a father concerned about the environment that their kids are enduring. Mom is using the child-support payments to make monthly installments on her own personal wardrobe while the kids are wearing the same Ninja sweat suit everyday of the week. Or, Mom is so busy sporting around town in a new Jeep Cherokee that she does not have time to attend Jake's soccer game. Moms neglect kids too.

Whenever, I receive one of these calls, I encourage Dad to go back into court, document the neglect and fight for custody of the kids. In the meantime, I encourage him to be the best father he can be whenever he is around the kids.

Our society will pay the cost for child neglect, one way or another. I believe the increase in teen violence over the years is a direct result of the rage kids have because of the emotional, physical, and spiritual abuse they have suffered. But as a society we seem to be unaware of the relationship between our dead-weight parenting and the acceleration of our anger. Do we know where we are going? Can we steer back between the lines? Where are the lines that used to guide us to our destination?

In the courtroom I have witnessed how anger can lead normally rational, dignified people into behaving like drunk drivers. They become totally unaware of how their behavior may harm another. They act out of a total disregard for the law that was established to protect them in the first place. Such behavior rattles me more than a a tambourine toting pentecostal at a tent revival.

When I first received one such case I thought I was in for just another tedious trial. The GBI had conducted thorough investigations statewide into charges of theft and fraud. This particular case involved a local business owner out of a rural county of about 20,000 in population. I had already sat in on several of these cases in which the business owners were being charged with the theft of stolen property.

I have to admit that after doing several of these trials I considered that having a root canal might be more inviting. At least with the root canal, dentists administer anesthesia to deaden the senses. Jurist have no such medication available to halt the droning of dull attorneys.

Counsel for the State consisted of a much respected and very refined attorney who was waging his own legal battle. Two other attorneys were assisting him. The younger one of those attorneys, an Oregon transplant, was relatively green in Georgia's political grove. But whatever he lacked due to inexperience was easily grasped by his passionate nature.

The defendant and the local business were represented by a cracker-jack attorney and state legislator who is always looking to take up residence at the Governor's mansion; and a quiet-spirited attorney, with enough legal background to make him a fine Supreme Court Justice. They were assisted by two local attorneys — one who sat mute throughout the majority of the trial and one that made many wish I had a muzzle nearby, or at the very least some duct tape. Remember, the more money involved, the longer the trial? This one lasted seven weeks.

Jury selection had not even been completed before we made Atlanta's headlines:

### JUDGE: NO MORE COMPUTER CHECKS

"Prosecutors ... were ordered by a judge last week to stop using the GBI computer system to check the arrest records of potential jurors.

"Superior Court Judge Rufe McCombs said special prosecutors from the attorney general's office didn't break the law when they ran the names of all prospective jurors through the Georgia Crime Information Center computer.

"But she told prosecutors to stop using the GCIC in jury selection ... The GCIC is the clearinghouse for Georgian's criminal records. It lists arrests and court dispositions for all felonies and most misdemeanors ... By law, enforcement officials are only supposed to use the information for the apprehension and prosecution of criminals. The information is not public.

" ... Defense lawyers said they didn't realize the prosecution had GCIC data until the 27th potential juror was interviewed.

"'It became apparent by the question they were asking ... What did you do on such and such a day? Were you convicted of DUI on this day?' ... prosecutors gained an unfair advantage because the GCIC data wasn't shared with the defense.

"'Knowledge is power when you're picking a jury ... '

"Jack Martin, a past president of the Georgia Association of Criminal Defense Lawyers called it 'an abuse of that whole system. It's a little like a prosecutor running a GCIC on his next-door neighbor.'

"Mike Hobbs, special counsel to the attorney general, said prosecutors pulled the files to find out if jurors have something that could disqualify them from serving, like a felony conviction.

"'You can go to the courthouse and get the same information,' Hobbs said. 'What makes this different is that it's a compilation. It might require a little extra work by defense counsel.'

"..Paul Hepner, director of the GCIC, said there is no way to trace how often prosecutors check juror's backgrounds because they do it by computer from offices around the state.

"He said jurors should not complain about having their criminal records made public because jury lists are compiled from voter registration lists" (*The Atlanta Journal-Constitution,* Ralph Ellis, Sunday, May 5, 1995).

That revelation set the antagonistic tone for the rest of the trial. By June 6, 1996, tempers were hotter than Atlanta's midsummer asphalt. As best I recall the courtroom brawl began this way:

The youngest of the prosecuting attorneys asked to approach the bench. At the bench, he noted that when the primary defense attorney was doing his direct examination, he used a chart to write up some figures and then tossed the charts out.

"Those have now been removed from the courtroom," he said, stating that he believed they were shown to the jury as demonstrative evidence. "I'd like to have them to go back over in my cross-examination. I think it's improper to be removing demonstrative exhibits from the courtroom."

The primary defense attorney responded that it was his policy when he wrote on something to remove it after his examination.

"If they want to create theirs, they can create theirs. It's not in evidence and it is not used as demonstration. I'll re-create it for him if he desires," the defense attorney offered.

"Your Honor, I'd like it back," the prosecutor declared.

But the defense attorney had already tossed the items in question.

"I threw them away in the trash can," the defense admitted.

Like a kid who runs up to defend his wrongly accused brother, the local defense attorney bellowed out, proclaiming the defense had every right to discard the charts.

Taken aback by the heated nature of the banter, I pointed out that the chart had not even been declared evidence yet.

The prosecuting attorney challenged my remarks.

"It was demonstrative and was shown to the jury, Your Honor. Now it's been destroyed," he said.

Apparently the defense attorney felt the need to defend everyone in the courtroom.

"Let me tell you something, if you accuse me one more time ... ," he retorted while pointing his finger towards the prosecutor.

"Don't you point your finger at me," the prosecutor defended himself to no avail. The defense attorney was fired up now.

"Don't you, don't you—let me tell you something. Don't you dare accuse me again," he came back at the prosecutor, not only verbally, but by now physically pushing him.

At this point a shoving match ensued and I was frantically searching for a gavel, or a deputy, neither of which were to be found. A whistle would have been nice.

"Hold on, just a minute!" I implored.

A rather formidable attorney got between the two rascals who were creating a bar room brawl scene in my courtroom.

"Please, gentlemen," he pleaded.

Gentlemen? There had been no evidence introduced to support that conclusion, I thought.

Once physically separated, the two continued their pecking at each other.

"I'm tired of you accusing me of being a crook," the defense attorney pouted rather loudly.

"Can we send the jury out?" someone else asked.

Still searching for a gavel, a whistle, or a frying pan, I had completely forgotten the jury was present during the wrestling match that ensued until bystanders stepped between the two old bucks.

"You handle yours and I'll handle mine," the local defender instructed the gap-mouthed prosecutors drooling nearby.

Ever the politician, the defense attorney had to have the last rebuttal.

"I'm tired of him calling me a crook," he whined.

After the sparing attorneys were disengaged, I dismissed the jury, and an attorney for the Georgia Bureau of Investigation (GBI) handed me a note detailing the highlights of what I had thought was going to be just another tedious trial:

*World Championship Wrestling*
*Live*
*Upon Superior Court*
Patrick "The Weasel" Deering
versus
Sugar Ray "Baggy Pants" Barnes
3-3 minute Bench Conference/Falls
Announcer
"Ruthless Rufe" McCombs
Referee
"Bouncing Bob" Morton
Time Keeper
"Dandy Doug" Carter
Trainers
"Jousting Joe" Chambers
"Vicious Virgil" Brown
Promoters
"Gorgeous George T." Smith
"Mean Michael" Bowers
Come One, Come All! Jury seats still available!

I did not declare a mistrial the next day when I called the fisticuffs to the bench prior to summoning the jury:

In perhaps a display for my sake only, the defense attorney offered his apology, which was, in my opinion, more wordy than contrite.

"Your Honor," he began, "I am tired of being called a crook and all these snide remarks ... I apologize to the Court, but I am tired of being called a crook ...."

The apology was interrupted by the prosecutor, who now found himself on the defense.

"Your Honor, the word 'crook' never left my mouth. He keeps referring to himself as though I say he's a crook. I never said that, and I believe the Court would know that. It's theatrics on his part of in front of the jury," he said.

I wasn't about to let this kind of acerbic abuse continue.

"You've certainly got a right to argue your point, but neither of you has a right to hit each other and start a fight in this courtroom. And that really bothers me.

"Certainly you're going to disagree on a lot of things. But to come right out and start fighting in the courtroom in front of the jury, even though I was sitting right here. I don't believe I could swear who hit the other first, because it confused me, but let's just say if one started it the other one should have walked away. Nevertheless, both of you engaged in it." (I felt like a mother mediating a fight between siblings.)

"I can't tell you how disappointed I am in both of you," I added. "I think you've hurt your case and I think you've hurt your clients in carrying on like this. I have never been so near giving a mistrial than I am right now, but I'd like to go ahead and finish this case. Nothing I could do would hurt you as bad as what you've already done to yourselves. But the first sign of any trouble and I'm going to hold you in contempt. If anymore fighting takes place in this courtroom, somebody is going to spend the night in jail," I declared my judgment, which they seemed to realize was not a trifling threat.

The local defense attorney piped up:

"Anybody hits me I'm going to run!"

If law schools awarded graduates "Most Likely to Be Hit" titles this fellow would have been everybody's first choice.

At my instruction both attorneys made their apologies to the jury. The main reason I was reluctant to declare a mistrial is the amount of money the county had spent to conduct the trial. They had paid each juror for seven weeks of service; expenses had been incurred for a trial that held up the court and the city employees. There was concern that these types of trials could bankrupt small rural counties. Just like Daddy, I was aware that "time is getting short and money shorter." My sense of frugality outweighed my disgust with the attorneys.

I continue to grow tired of being disgusted with some attorneys. Our legal system has changed much since I first arrived on the scene in 1942. Some of those changes have been good—more minorities have the freedom to practice law; there is better representation in the courtroom for defendants, in and out of the jury box; and technology makes it possible for me carry my laptop to work everyday. In a matter of moments, I can refer to the law itself, without having to rely on the word or interpretation of another.

But not all changes have been beneficial. And in my opinion, advertising amputated the foothold of ethics from our legal system. I do not believe that attorneys who advertise are working out of a love and respect for the law. They are fleecing carcasses. Their main interest is not in justice, but in theatrics and just reward for services rendered. Media-conscious moguls, these attorneys seek the high-profile case, the cheapest kind of advertising.

Someone asked me, "What is the answer? How do we stop the violence? Where is justice to be found today? Where is our hope?"

"Well," I replied, "the only hope we have is that Jesus might return soon."

The sooner the better, I say. But, of course, I realize this is just avoidance on my behalf. If Jesus returned and established a new heaven and new earth, justice would be served with a quick and mighty hand. Until then, all we have to rely upon are frail human hands to balance the scales of justice.

It is not an easy task. Balance is hard to achieve. While watching the USA 1996 Olympic Gymnastics Team I held my breath as those young girls flipped hand over feet on the balance beams. Where do they get the confidence to do that, I wondered? Aren't they afraid?

Sometimes they do fall. Sometimes they miss their mark. Sometimes they lose their balance. But most of the time they move swiftly, confidently, unwaveringly through their routines, sure of that which has steadied them in the past will steady them again. And, crippled or not, they stretch every inch of their bodies to the most upright position to secure a solid landing. It is a glorious thing to watch.

I believe the same is true for our legal system. We need to stretch ourselves individually, and collectively, to our most upright position in order to land on our feet. We do this, not by government mandate, but as individuals who decide to discipline ourselves. Not just for our own benefit, but for society as a whole. It is our obligation.

How is this done? By individually choosing to be ethical people. People who respect the law for the protection it provides. Government can mandate all the changes it wants, prisons can fill to the brim, but until change comes from within each of us, in our homes, in our hearts, we will needlessly empty our piggy banks. Our society is in danger of bankrupting itself—financially, morally, ethically and yes, legally.

When I was a young girl, I would walk alongside my mother in her shadow. I would try to emulate her steps, her movements, her shape. Often I was frustrated with my efforts. My own shadow, puddled about my feet, looked puny in comparison with Mother's upright figure. But on family walks, I always sought out Mother's shadow. She was the standard by which I compared myself.

I believe Justice seeks out Truths—the shadow of God. Too often though, Justice fails to see anything but its own silhouette. In order to find Truths, Justice must arch its back and walk uprightly. Human justice is a puny reflection of absolute Truths, but until God reveals to us more than just His shadow, it is our best hope.

I am thankful for the opportunity to have spent time in the shadow of people like Schley Howard, Mr. B.B. Williams, Mrs. Justine Case, Mac and my parents. Some of these people kept me from entertaining any further thoughts of killing Frannie.

A lack of vision can render us so blind that no amount of focusing will correct our perspective. Perhaps having just one good eye to rely upon forced me to look at the shadows of others. With the clarity of hindsight, I see how watching others helped me focus, encouraged me to work hard, and ultimately, enabled me to be the visionary I needed to be in order to have my own dreams.

I have not walked in the shadow of another since Mother died. Standing tall, striving to walk uprightly, working hard and staying focused has helped me cast a shadow I am able to finally claim as my own.

Is there, I wonder, a girl hiding in the shadows, seeking justice as I did?

If so, I pray I have left her an image worthy of emulation.

*Benched: The Memoirs of Judge Rufe McCombs*
    by Rufe McCombs with Karen Spears Zacharias
Published by Mercer University Press
November 1997

Book design by Marc A. Jolley
Camera-ready pages composed on a MacIntosh
    Performa 636CD, via Microsoft Word 6.0.1.
Text font: Times New Roman 11/12
Printed and bound in the United States.
Cased and covered with cloth, smyth-sewn, and
    printed on acid-free paper.